"While the world of psychotherapy has historically been divided into separate spheres of isolated schools, modalities, and orientations, we increasingly witness dialogue, borrowing, recognition of commonality, and even efforts toward integration. Jason Stewart has gathered a first-rate lineup of contributors who are known for their serious scholarship on, and leadership in, psychotherapy integration from a broadly relational psychodynamic perspective. The book will advance this important academic and professional trend."

> —**Lewis Aron, PhD**, director at the New York University
> postdoctoral program in psychotherapy and psychoanalysis
> and author of A Meeting of Minds: Mutuality in Psychoanalysis

"In this creative and scholarly volume, Stewart brings the integration of mindfulness, acceptance, and relational psychodynamic therapy to a new level. [The contributors'] combined vision is balanced, flexible, and mature. Clinicians new to either psychoanalytic inquiry or mindfulness will quickly find themselves drawn into this exciting conversation through compelling case studies, historical background material, and practical discussion about clinical decision-making. Lynchpin issues, such as non-duality, compassion, mentalization, and the pursuit of a valued life, receive special attention. This book will invite readers to grow their work for years to come."

> —**Christopher Germer, PhD**, clinical instructor at Harvard
> Medical School, coeditor of Mindfulness and Psychotherapy,
> and author of The Mindful Path to Self-Compassion

"Acceptance and mindfulness have always been integral to therapeutic change, but their roles and applications have only been recently recognized. Editor Jason Stewart's new book offers a penetrating and insightful look at the natural overlap and differences between newly emerged mindfulness-based therapies and psychodynamic work. This exploration reveals a rich potential for clinicians who want to support and strengthen their psychodynamic work through the integration of mindfulness-based approaches."

> —**Tara Brach, PhD**, author of Radical Acceptance and
> True Refuge

"Psychoanalysis, mindfulness-based psychotherapies, and traditional Buddhist meditation practices have evolved from existing in non-communicating, conceptually dissociated spheres through a stage of over-eager merger and identification, in which each was reduced to a variation of 'evenly hovering attention' in the service of a presumed common goal of engaging the totality of the mind. At last, we are moving into a more sophisticated and challenging stage where genuine differences and conflicts are allowed to emerge and be meaningfully engaged. This volume is a welcome addition to that process of genuine engagement and mutual influence."

> —**Barry Magid, MD**, faculty at The Stephen Mitchell Center
> for Relational Studies and author of Nothing Is Hidden:
> The Psychology of Zen Koans and Ordinary Mind: Exploring
> the Common Ground of Zen and Psychoanalysis

"As the evidence in support of Freud's, Bowlby's, and Winnicott's (among many others') works accumulates through mindfulness research, the neuroscience of psychotherapy, and interpersonal neurobiology, Jason Stewart's book comes along as a practical and engrossing guide to an ongoing synthesis of ancient and modern wisdom aimed at addressing human suffering. He has assembled an impressive group of authors who remind us that when we are doing psychoanalysis, engaging clients in the process of systematic desensitization, or teaching mindfulness meditation, we are all involved in deeply interpersonal encounters with the intention of helping people 'pay attention' and, eventually, change their brains in salubrious ways. The highest praise I can give this book is that it will become required reading for my current and future psychotherapy students and supervisees."

> —**Mark B. Andersen, PhD**, professor and coordinator of the
> doctoral program in applied psychology at Victoria University,
> Melbourne, Australia

THE
MINDFULNESS & ACCEPTANCE
PRACTICA SERIES

As mindfulness and acceptance-based therapies gain momentum in the field of mental health, it is increasingly important for professionals to understand the full range of their applications. To keep up with the growing demand for authoritative resources on these treatments, *The Mindfulness and Acceptance Practica Series* was created. These edited books cover a range of evidence-based treatments, such as acceptance and commitment therapy (ACT), cognitive behavioral therapy (CBT), compassion-focused therapy (CFT), dialectical behavioral therapy (DBT), and mindfulness-based stress reduction (MBSR) therapy. Incorporating new research in the field of psychology, these books are powerful tools for mental health clinicians, researchers, advanced students, and anyone interested in the growth of mindfulness and acceptance strategies.

Visit www.newharbinger.com for
more books in this series.

MINDFULNESS, ACCEPTANCE,
——— AND THE ———
PSYCHODYNAMIC EVOLUTION

Bringing Values into Treatment Planning
and Enhancing Psychodynamic Work with
Buddhist Psychology

Edited by
JASON M. STEWART, PsyD

CONTEXT PRESS
An Imprint of New Harbinger Publications, Inc.

"To Know the Dark" copyright © 2012 by Wendell Berry from NEW COLLECTED POEMS. Reprinted by permission of Counterpoint.

"Wordlessly" from HSIN-HSIN MING: VERSES ON THE FAITH-MIND by Seng T'San, translated by Richard B. Clarke. Copyright © 2001 White Pine Press, Inc. Reprinted by permission of White Pine Press.

Poems 16 and 19 from COLD MOUNTAIN: 100 POEMS BY THE T'ANG POET HAN-SHAN by Han Shan, translated by Burton Watson. Copyright © 1970 Columbia University Press. Reprinted with permission of the publisher.

Chapter 4 of this text reprinted from Safran, J.D. (2006). Before the ass has gone the horse has already arrived. Contemporary Psychoanalysis, 42(2), 197–211. Copyright © 2006 William Alanson White Institute of Psychiatry, Psychoanalysis, and Psychology. Reprinted by permission of the publisher.

Copyright © 2014 by Jason M. Stewart

Context Press, An Imprint of New Harbinger Publications, Inc.

5674 Shattuck Avenue, Oakland, CA 94609, www.newharbinger.com

Distributed in Canada by Raincoast Books

All Rights Reserved.

Acquired by Catharine Meyers; Cover design by Amy Shoup; Edited by Jennifer Eastman; Text design by Tracy Carlson;

Library of Congress Cataloging-in-Publication Data

Stewart, Jason M., author.
  Mindfulness, acceptance, and the psychodynamic evolution : bringing values into treatment planning and enhancing psychodynamic work with Buddhist psychology / edited by Jason M. Stewart ; foreword by Steven C. Hayes.
    p. ; cm. -- (The Context Press Mindfulness and Acceptance Practica Series)
  Includes bibliographical references and index.
  ISBN 978-1-60882-887-6 (paperback : alk. paper) -- ISBN 978-1-60882-888-3 (pdf e-book) -- ISBN 978-1-60882-889-0 (epub)
  I. Title. II. Series: Context Press Mindfulness and Acceptance Practica Series.
  [DNLM: 1. Acceptance and Commitment Therapy--methods. 2. Buddhism--psychology. 3. Mindfulness--methods. 4. Psychotherapy, Psychodynamic--methods. WM 425.5.C6]
  RC489.C63
  616.89'1425--dc23
                                    2014017236

Printed in the United States of America

16 15 14   10 9 8 7 6 5 4 3 2 1   First printing

To Theresa—my wife, my friend, my life companion

To my parents—whose love and support has allowed me to develop the values that make my life sweet.

I prefer to retain the label of my forefathers as long as it does not cramp my growth and does not debar me from all that is good anywhere else.

—Mohandas Gandhi

Our appointment with life is in the present moment.

—Thich Nhat Hanh

Contents

PART 1: Roots and Foundations:
Key Concepts and Processes for Integrating
Psychodynamic and Acceptance- and Mindfulness-Based
Approaches to Psychotherapy

PART 2: The Evolution Continues:
Psychodynamic Psychotherapy in Action

Alphabetical List of Contributors

Michael Fayne, PhD, is a clinical psychologist teaching with the Contemplative Studies Society at New York University's Postdoctoral Program in Psychotherapy and Psychoanalysis. Dr. Fayne is the clinical supervisor for chemical dependency services at the Freedom Institute in New York City, and he also maintains a private practice of both clinical psychology and mindfulness training in Manhattan.

Jerry Gold, PhD, ABPP, is professor of psychology at the Derner Institute for Advanced Psychological Studies, Adelphi University. He was the editor of the *Journal of Psychotherapy Integration* and is the author of *Key Concepts in Psychotherapy Integration* (Plenum Press, 1996).

Geoff Goodman, PhD, ABPP, is associate professor of psychology at Long Island University and a fellow of the International Psychoanalytical Association (FIPA). He has published five books, including *The Internal World and Attachment* (Analytic Press, 2002) and *Transforming the Internal World and Attachment* (Vols. 1 and 2, Jason Aronson, 2010). In 2013, Dr. Goodman was awarded the J. William Fulbright Foreign Scholarship by the US Department of State.

Steven C. Hayes, PhD, is a founder of acceptance and commitment therapy (ACT, pronounced "act") and is Nevada Foundation Professor and director of clinical training at the Department of Psychology at the University of Nevada. He is the author of thirty-seven books and over 525 scientific articles, and his career has focused on an analysis of the nature of human language and cognition and the application of this to the understanding and alleviation of human suffering. Dr. Hayes has been president of Division 25 of the APA, of the American Association of Applied and Preventive Psychology, of the Association for Contextual Behavioral Science, and of the Association for Behavioral and Cognitive Therapies, from which he received the Lifetime Achievement Award.

Debra Kissen, PhD, MHSA, is clinical director of the Light on Anxiety Treatment Center in Chicago, IL. Dr. Kissen has a special interest in mindfulness and its application for anxiety disorders.

Morton Kissen, PhD, is professor emeritus at the Derner Institute for Advanced Psychological Studies, Adelphi University, in Garden City, NY. He is the author of *Affect, Object, and Character Structure* (International Universities Press, 1995) and editor of *Gender and Psychoanalytic Treatment* (Routledge, 1992). He works in private practice in both Huntington and Forest Hills, NY.

Barbara Kohlenberg, PhD, is associate professor at the University of Nevada School of Medicine. She has done both conceptual and empirical work in the areas of functional analytic psychotherapy (FAP) and acceptance and commitment therapy (ACT), and has long been interested in the overlap and integration of FAP, ACT, and psychoanalysis.

Robert J. Kohlenberg, PhD, ABPP, is professor of psychology at the University of Washington, past director of clinical training, and received the Washington State Psychological Association's Distinguished Psychologist Award. He is a cocreator of functional analytic psychotherapy (FAP) and has coauthored books, articles, and research publications including *The Practice of FAP* (Springer, 2010), *Functional Analytic Psychotherapy* (Springer, 1991), *Functional Analytic Psychotherapy: Distinctive Features* (Routledge, 2012), and *A Guide to FAP* (Springer, 2008).

Delia Kostner, PhD, is a clinical psychologist and psychoanalyst in private practice in Amherst, NH. She is on the faculty of the Pine Psychoanalytic Center in Needham, MA. She has studied Buddhism in the Theravada tradition and more recently has turned to an examination of early Buddhism as depicted in the Pali Canon. She has lectured and taught on the confluence of psychoanalysis and Buddhism and, as a child and adolescent therapist, leads groups for young people incorporating mindfulness and meditation.

Lisa Lyons, PhD, is a psychoanalyst and psychologist. She was the founder of—and for six years director of—the adult dialectical behavior therapy program at Montefiore Medical Center in New York City. Dr. Lyons is on the faculties of the Stephen Mitchell Center for

Relational Studies and the National Institute for the Psychotherapies and is in private practice in New York City and Teaneck, NJ.

Jeremy D. Safran, PhD, is chair and professor of the psychology department at the New School for Social Research and former director of clinical training. He is also cofounder and cochair of the New School Ferenczi Center, along with Lewis Aron and Adrienne Harris. In addition, Dr. Safran is on faculty at the New York University Postdoctoral Program in Psychotherapy and Psychoanalysis, and former president of the International Association for Relational Psychoanalysis and Psychotherapy. He has authored and coauthored more than 150 articles and chapters, as well as several books, including *Psychoanalysis and Psychoanalytic Therapies* (APA, 2012), *Psychoanalysis and Buddhism: An Unfolding Dialogue* (Wisdom, 2003), and *Negotiating the Therapeutic Alliance: A Relational Treatment Guide* (Guilford, 2000).

Mark Sisti, PhD, is the founder and director of Suffolk Cognitive-Behavioral (SCB), a group treatment and training center committed to "third-generation" cognitive behavioral therapies. He is an adjunct clinical supervisor at Ferkauf Graduate School of Psychology at Yeshiva University, a founding fellow within the Academy of Cognitive Therapy, and president of the Greater New York chapter of the Association of Contextual Behavioral Science (ACBS). Dr. Sisti also has postdoctoral training in relational psychotherapy.

Alan J. Stern, PhD, is a psychoanalyst and psychotherapist in Chapel Hill, NC. He is a training and supervising analyst and faculty member of the Psychoanalytic Education Center of the Carolinas (PECC). He has studied mindfulness at the Duke University Center for Integrative Medicine and the Insight Meditation Society in Barre, MA.

Jason M. Stewart, PsyD (editor, see back cover).

George Stricker, PhD, is professor of psychology at the American School of Professional Psychology at Argosy University in Washington, DC. Prior to that, he was distinguished research professor of psychology and former dean of the Derner Institute of Advanced Psychological Studies, Adelphi University, in Garden City, NY. His principal interests are psychotherapy integration, clinical training, and ethics. His most recent book is *Psychotherapy Integration* (APA, 2010).

Mavis Tsai, PhD, is cocreator of functional analytic psychotherapy (FAP) and director of the FAP Specialty Clinic at the University of Washington, where she is involved in teaching and research. She maintains an independent practice in Seattle, WA.

Foreword

Steven C. Hayes, PhD

Building a Powerful and Productive Relationship

The relationship between psychodynamic perspectives and behavior therapy used to be difficult. I'm old enough to have seen it—at least the tail end of it.

Behavior therapy began with both a positive and negative vision. Positively, it embraced a vision of clinical approaches that were well specified, subjected to rigorous tests of their efficacy, and based on well-established scientific principles of psychological change (Franks & Wilson, 1974). But, negatively, early behavior therapists thundered against what they viewed as the unrestricted theorizing of the deeper clinical traditions. They ridiculed what they took to be Freud's theoretical excesses (Bandura, 1969, pp. 11–13; Wolpe & Rachman, 1960), such as his explaining little Hans's fear of horses with the idea that "the falling horse was not only his dying father but also his mother in childbirth" (Freud, 1928, p. 128).

I sat in on my first behavior-therapy session in 1967 (a systematic desensitization session conducted by Irving Kessler, my undergraduate mentor, in his private practice). Irv had done classical conditioning work for his dissertation at the University of Southern California. He was a very skillful clinician and was thoroughly knowledgeable in learning theory. In class he railed against psychodynamic thinking, calling it "fanciful" and "untestable." Still, even as an undergraduate student, I could see that much of what Irv was doing was not well described in behavior-therapy texts. He reflected back statements that seemed meaningful, he asked probing questions, he showed compassion, and he asked about what the client really wanted. Yes, this was recognizably behavior therapy. But it was a lot more. It was a relationship between two human beings that modeled something the client currently lacked: a deep sense of acceptance, wholeness, and curiosity about human experience, even the parts of it that were difficult.

For their part, psychodynamic theorists of the day were not very impressed with behavior therapy. They thought behavior therapy was superficial, and predicted that a direct focus on behavior change would lead to symptom substitution that would far outstrip the gains obtained from behavior therapy (e.g., Bookbinder, 1962; Schraml & Selg, 1966). But to be honest, I doubt if many well-trained psychodynamic psychotherapists were sitting in on behavior-therapy sessions. If they were, they weren't watching people like Irv Kessler.

That was then. This is now.

Both psychodynamic and behavioral approaches have evolved considerably in the last forty to fifty years. Throughout the 1970s, behavior therapy largely transitioned to cognitive behavior therapy (CBT) as first-order change efforts grew from their original base in behavior and emotion to cognition. Then, in the last fifteen years or so, a third wave of methods has entered CBT. These are focused on second-order and contextual-change methods, such as acceptance, mindfulness, values, and relationship (Hayes, 2004). Some of these ideas are drawn from spiritual and religious ideas, especially Eastern or mystical traditions, but others come from the deeper clinical traditions, including psychodynamic approaches. This new wave of work *"reformulates and synthesizes previous generations of behavioral and cognitive therapy and carries them forward into questions, issues, and domains previously addressed primarily by other traditions, in hopes of improving both understanding and outcomes"* (Hayes, 2004, p. 658, italics in original).

A consensus has gradually emerged (Hayes, Villatte, Levin, & Hildebrandt, 2011) that change in therapy generally involves learning to be more psychologically open, more aware, and more actively engaged in life, and that the therapeutic relationship provides a key context to instigate, model, and support these processes. As this consensus has emerged, a notable flow of research has come to the fore on such processes from the CBT tradition (Hayes et al., 2011).

At the same time, psychodynamic methods, particularly from the relational wing, have grounded theory in the therapeutic relationship and in the issues of self and experiencing that the therapeutic relationship can contain (Wachtel, 2008). Psychodynamic approaches have explored some of the same processes of the spiritual traditions that are being explored in contextual CBT, such as acceptance and mindfulness. The result is a remarkable moment in which psychodynamic and behavioral traditions seem prepared finally to build a productive relationship—one that goes beyond the cartoons each tradition historically made of the other and explores their theoretical and practical overlaps. The book you are reading does that, using the touchstone of Eastern ideas that have penetrated both traditions.

There are several models of integration that are explored in this volume: technical eclecticism, common factors, assimilative integration, and theoretical integration. Of the four, the last is the most ambitious and the most difficult if one demands that a new theory emerge as a result. The third-wave approaches put additional avenues of interconnection into the mix, including a more limited form of theoretical integration. It seems possible that the measures and models of change processes drawn from contextual CBT can help psychodynamic methods be better understood. This is theoretical integration at a micro-level. Instead of a wholesale application of behavioral or cognitive theory to psychodynamic work, more narrowly cast questions can be asked. For example, is it the case that psychodynamic therapy alters patient mindfulness, acceptance, self-compassion, values clarity, or psychological flexibility? If so, are these change processes key to outcomes in relational psychodynamic approaches?

In addition, we can ask whether these processes apply to the therapist as well. This is common-factor work, focused on the therapist. Is a therapist who is more mindful, self-accepting, or connected to personal values also one who is more able to build powerful and sustaining therapeutic relationships?

I suspect that the answer to all of these questions is yes. If that is true, it makes it a lot easier to draw from contextual CBT methods that are known to modify these processes in patients and therapists alike, and it makes it easier to use these measures and concepts to help understand and advance psychodynamic work itself. Integration can advance across multiple levels at once.

If you read the present volume with such a mindset, you will see that the authors gradually fill in how this might be done and why it might matter. Jason Stewart, the editor, has done an excellent job in selecting authors with the experience and vision needed to find what is useful in the overlap between these areas of clinical work. The processes of exploration these chapters reflect in turn establish a basis for a fundamentally different kind of relationship between these two traditions—a powerful and productive one grounded in mutual respect and in a sense of common purpose. Such a relationship is worth the deeper exploration this book embodies.

References

Bandura, A. (1969). *Principles of behavior modification*. New York, NY: Holt, Rinehart, & Winston.

Bookbinder, L. J. (1962). Simple conditioning vs. the dynamic approach to symptoms and symptom substitution: A reply to Yates. *Psychological Reports, 10*, 71–77.

Franks, C. M. & Wilson, G. T. (1974). *Annual review of behavior therapy: Theory and practice*. New York, NY: Brunner/Mazel.

Freud, S. (1928). Analysis of a phobia in a five-year-old boy (little Hans)/ [Analyse d'une phobie chez un petit garcon de cinq ans (Le petit Hans)]. *Revue Francaise de Psychanalyse, 2*, No. 3. Reprinted in J. Strachey (Ed. & Trans.). (1955), *The standard edition of the complete psychological works of Sigmund Freud* (Vol. 10). London, England: Hogarth.

Hayes, S. C. (2004). Acceptance and commitment therapy, relational frame theory, and the third wave of cognitive and behavioral therapies. *Behavior Therapy, 35*, 639–665.

Hayes, S. C., Villatte, M., Levin, M., & Hildebrandt, M. (2011). Open, aware, and active: Contextual approaches as an emerging trend in the behavioral and cognitive therapies. *Annual Review of Clinical Psychology, 7*, 141–168.

Schraml, W., & Selg, H. (1966). Behavior therapy and psychoanalysis. *Psyche, 29*, 529–546.

Wachtel, P. L. (2008). *Relational theory and the practice of psychotherapy*. New York, NY: Guilford Press.

Wolpe, J., & Rachman, S. (1960). Psychoanalytic "evidence": A critique based on Freud's case of little Hans. *Journal of Nervous and Mental Disease, 131*, 135–148.

Acknowledgments

I would like to thank the following people for helping this book come together: Steven Hayes; Matthew McKay; Catharine Meyers, Melissa Valentine, Jess Beebe, and Jennifer Eastman at New Harbinger; Lew Aron; Jeremy Safran; Chris Germer; Marjorie Maltin; Bruce Hammer; my incredible wife, Theresa; my wonderfully supportive and loving family; and my writing companion, Otis.

Introduction

Jason M. Stewart, PsyD

The unfaced and unfelt parts of our psyche are the source of all neurosis and suffering.

—Carl Jung

The more artful and courageous analytic work entails knowing when other ways of interacting should be considered.

—Judith Brisman

Relational psychodynamic psychotherapy emphasizes interpersonal relationships as central to the development of personality, psychopathology, and therapeutic growth. The approach is holistic in that it also considers biological drives and intrapsychic conflicts (Aron, 1996). Recently, there has been emphasis on the role of compassion as mutative in psychodynamic psychotherapy (e.g., Young-Eisendrath, 2003). Acceptance- and mindfulness-based approaches to psychotherapy emphasize acceptance, compassion, and overt behavioral change as means for developing well-being and life satisfaction. This volume presents perspectives on psychotherapy that balance these approaches. It emphasizes how these approaches function cohesively, and how acceptance- and mindfulness-based psychotherapies can increase the effectiveness of psychodynamic work. The ultimate goal of this volume is to help psychodynamically oriented clinicians enhance their treatment conceptualizations and technique by integrating acceptance- and mindfulness-based approaches into their practices. This volume also develops an explicit dialogue between psychodynamic and functional contextual psychotherapies, and it continues an ongoing dialogue between psychodynamic and Buddhist psychotherapies (e.g., Epstein, 1995, 2007; Safran, 2003). Functional contextual psychotherapies (e.g., acceptance and commitment therapy, ACT, Hayes, Strosahl, & Wilson, 1999; dialectical behavior therapy, DBT, Linehan, 1993; functional analytic psychotherapy, FAP, Kohlenberg & Tsai, 1991) are a recently developed family of approaches that emphasize acceptance, mindfulness, values, and the therapeutic relationship as important therapeutic variables. Functional contextualism conceptualizes events, or "acts," as meaningful only in relation to their contexts; the basic "unit of study" is the "act in context." This perspective also holds that therapeutic variables function based not on objective evaluation of therapy outcomes (e.g., symptom reduction) but on "workability" (i.e., pragmatism) as the gauge for the effectiveness of psychotherapy. The workability of psychotherapy is the extent to which the interaction between patient and therapist cultivates an ongoing developmental process, and the effectiveness of this process is based on the patient's personally developed constructs of meaning and vitality (i.e., values). This means that there is no objective truth, rather, that truth is subjectively determined (i.e., constructivism); what is "true" is what works best at achieving a specific goal (Hayes, Strosahl, & Wilson, 2012). Thus, the approaches are expansive, not eliminative, like some more traditional approaches to psychotherapy. The workability-truth criterion connects philosophically to relational psychodynamic perspectives, which emphasize the personal construction of meaning and the development of vitality as general treatment goals (e.g., Mitchell, 1993). For example, Safran (2012) emphasizes the importance of basing transference interpretations on workability rather than objectivity. He writes that "an interpretation can be accurate without being useful" (Safran, 2012, p. 80). Similarly, Hayes et al. (2012) state that, from a functional contextual perspective, "a 'true' case conceptualization … is a useful one" (p. 31). Maroda (2010) writes that the patient is the "ultimate authority" on the effectiveness of an intervention and that "correctness of content is irrelevant if the client cannot hear what the therapist is saying, understand its meaning, and use it productively" (p. 83).

From a relational psychodynamic perspective, psychological development is conceptualized as occurring within a "relational matrix" (see Mitchell, 1988), and the psychotherapy relationship is considered a layer in the matrix. The concept of the "relational matrix" reflects the idea that "neither the self nor the object are meaningful dynamic concepts without presupposing some sense of psychic space in which they interact, in which they do things with or to each other" (Mitchell, 1988, p. 33). In other words, self and object are only meaningful in relation to their contexts. The basic "unit of study" is the "interactional field" (Mitchell, 1988).

Recently, psychodynamic theory and technique have become increasingly action oriented. For example, Aron (1996) notes that the predominance of the terms "interaction," "enactment," and "actualization"—each of which includes the word "act"—in the contemporary psychodynamic lexicon "points to a major shift in theory that moves psychoanalysis from a treatment that relies on associations and interpretations, words and understanding alone, to the recognition that the psychoanalytic process involves verbal and nonverbal action and interaction" (p. 190). Recent relational psychodynamic theories have focused on self-states (e.g., Bromberg, 1998), dissociation (e.g., Bromberg, 1998; Stern, 1997), unformulated experience, and enactment (e.g., Stern, 1997) as significant factors in both psychological development and psychopathology. A brief description of these constructs follows.

Self-States

Bromberg (2010) defines a "self-state" as a "highly individualized module of being, each configured by its own organization of cognitions, beliefs, dominant affect and mood, access to memory, skills, behaviors, values, actions, and regulatory physiology" (p. 73). From Bromberg's (1998) perspective, character consists of multiple self-states that, in favorable circumstances, are experienced in an integrated way, with a central "I" as the experiencer. He states that psychological health is the capacity to embody one's self-states authentically while maintaining contact among them—not "integration" but the healthy "illusion" of integration. This occurs when "each self-state is compatible enough with the modes of being that are held by other self-states to allow overarching coherence across self-states, which in turn creates the capacity for sustaining the experience of internal conflict" (Bromberg, 2010, p. 73). Acceptance of internal conflict and ambivalence allows for self-acceptance, acceptance of deprivation (e.g., impulse control), and acceptance of others. This process does not refer to acceptance of conflict between drive and defense; unconscious and conscious; or id, ego, and superego—it refers to acceptance of the conflict between "purposes, interests, and desires" (Stern, 2010, p. 101). Such conflict is important in the development of choice; without conflict, choice is relegated to compulsion. Additionally, without conflict, perspective taking cannot occur; conflicting perspectives are necessary to provide context for others (Stern, 2010). From this perspective, psychological functioning is essentially a dialectic of conflict and dissociation (Bromberg, 2010). Pizer (1998) adds that psychological health includes the capacity to accept paradox, which he differentiates from conflict. He suggests that conflict occurs between dichotomized entities and can be resolved; whereas paradox occurs as "multiplicity" that "yields not resolution but a straddling, or bridging, of contradictory perspectives" (p. 65).

Wachtel (2011a) emphasizes that different self-states emerge as a function of different contexts. From this perspective, "context" is not limited to external circumstances but includes internal circumstances, such as affective states and unconscious thoughts. Wachtel (2011a) also emphasizes the cyclical nature of self-states: the conditions under which a particular self-state emerges "must be understood very centrally in terms of the overall relational and personal context—the product of the continual back-and-forth between the individual's actions and subjective experience and the responses those actions and the accompanying affect evoke in others" (p. 58). This cyclical process accounts for complex interpersonal phenomenon such as projective identification and enactment (Wachtel, 2008).

Dissociation

Stern (1997) writes that dissociation is "the refusal to allow pre-reflective experience to attain the full-bodied meaning it might have if we left it alone and simply observed the results of our own capacity to create it. Dissociation is an intervention designed, in advance of the fact, to avoid the possibility that full-bodied meaning will occur. Dissociated meaning is style without substance, the story that accounts for what it addresses but tells us nothing we don't already know, the conversation we can fill in without having to listen. Dissociation is the deletion of imagination" (p. 98). Relational psychodynamic psychotherapy is influenced by Sullivan's (1953, 1954, 1956) interpersonal psychodynamic theory, which identifies domains of dissociated experience in the development of personality in all people. In other words, dissociation is a normative function that we all "do"; it is when dissociation prevents adaptive functioning that it becomes problematic. This occurs when the patient in a particular self-state cannot make contact with his or her other self-states (for Bromberg, this is essentially the definition of "resistance"). Sullivan's theory posits that dissociation, as a means to avoid anxiety, is the basis for the development of the "self." Bromberg (2006) writes "dissociation is what the mind does. The relationship between self-states and dissociation is what the mind is. It is the stability of that relationship that enables a person to experience continuity as 'I.' A flexible relationship among self-states through the ordinary use of dissociation is what allows a human being to engage the ever-shifting requirements of life's complexity with creativity and spontaneity…to stay the same while changing" (p. 2). He differentiates between the "creative use of dissociation" and dissociation as a defense; defensive dissociation is "enlisted in a post-traumatic rigidification of self-state boundaries that transforms normal process into pathological *structure*" (2010, p. 47, italics in original).

Safran (2012) writes that consciousness is a "coalition" of different self-states that forms "a self-organizing system that is influenced in an ongoing fashion by current interpersonal context" (p. 55). He emphasizes that there is "no hypothetical psychic agency" (p. 56) keeping potential experience unconscious, but that selective inattention and the resulting lack of experiential construction results in dissociation. Selective inattention is the act of *not* paying attention to particular events, because doing so would arouse too much anxiety; it is "*controlling awareness* of the events that impinge upon us" (Sullivan, 1956, p. 38, italics in original).

Bromberg (1998) conceptualizes selective inattention and subsequent "defensive dissociation" as facilitating different "islands" of experience—"a rigid Balkanization of the various aspects of self" (2006, p. 5). This occurs due to traumas, which can range from endemic nonrecognition by caregivers early in life (i.e., developmental or relational trauma) to extreme cases of abuse or other acute trauma. Regarding defensive dissociation, Bromberg (2006) writes "each island vigilantly protects itself from potentially disjunctive input of the others by the dissociative 'gap' surrounding it. Self-continuity is now preserved within each state, but the overarching coherence among states is sacrificed" (p. 5).

Unformulated Experience

The dissociated domains of experience comprise what Stern (1983) refers to as *unformulated experience*. The word "domain" aptly describes what is dissociated, because it is not mental processes or content but the *potential* for authentic meaning to be developed with "imagination" instead of defensive avoidance that is dissociated. The development of unformulated experience into imagination occurs through the construction of "creative speech" (Stern, 1997). From Stern's (1997) perspective, it is not preexisting experience but the capacity to let fluid experience develop that is dissociated. The construction of narrative is not the discovery of preestablished structures but the openness for the range of stories that can potentially emerge. In discussing Stern's work, Wachtel (2008) writes "the unconscious is not so much a *hidden* realm, fully formed and lying unseen below, but rather an *unarticulated* set of potentials for fuller experience, a set of proclivities and inclinations that guide and shape experience without the patient's fully elaborating, acknowledging, or endorsing them" (p. 149, italics in original). Highlighting the underlying social-constructivist philosophy of these ideas, Hoffman (1998) writes that patient and therapist "are contributing to *shaping* the relationship in a particular way among many ways that are possible. Both the processes of explication and the moment of interpersonal influences entail creation of meaning, not merely its discovery, and whatever is explicated by the patient and the analyst about themselves or about each other, out loud or in private thoughts, affects what happens next within and between the two people in ways that were not known before that moment" (p. 150, italics in original).

By suggesting that a person allows "pre-reflective experience to attain the full-bodied meaning it might have if we [leave] it alone and simply [observe] the results of our own capacity to create it," Stern (1997) means that narratives are articulated in language. The unformulated experience is not "translated" into language; instead, the development of language to symbolize the experience is part of the experience itself. Stern (1997) emphasizes that this process is not a matter of finding something that exists and labeling it with language. Rather, it is the acceptance of "previously rejected uncertainty" (Stern, 1997, p. 75) that significantly impacts the actual formulation of experience into language and thus has an inextricable impact on the phenomenology of the subsequent experience that develops and is cocreated with others. This is similar to the Buddhist notion that consciousness "is simultaneously the agent, instrument, and activity of awareness" (Bodhi, 2000, p. 245, as cited in Olendzki, 2005). Thus, the mind "does not *exist* as much as it *occurs*" (Olendzki, 2005, p. 246, italics in original). Hayes et al. (2012) note that the use of the noun "mind" is misleading, because "the mind is a behavioral repertoire rather than a specific organ" (p. 68), and thus the verb "minding" more accurately captures this process.

Enactment

Maroda (1998) identifies two elements that comprise an enactment: powerful unconscious affect and ensuing behavior. Stern (2010) defines "enactment" as the "interpersonalization of dissociation" (p. 86). He writes that enactments occur when "conflict that cannot be experienced within one mind is experienced *between* or *across* two minds. The state dissociated by the patient is explicitly experienced by the analyst, and the state explicitly experienced by the patient is dissociated in the analyst's mind" (Stern, 2010, p. 86, italics in original). Enactments occur when the patient and therapist are unwittingly stuck in the "grip of the field" (Stern, 1997), referring to the interactional field discussed above.

Bromberg (1998) states that "*enactment is the primary perceptual medium that allows narrative change to take place*" (p. 391, italics in original). He follows that an effective therapist response to an enactment is acceptance. He states that a goal of relational psychodynamic psychotherapy is the patient's expansion of his or her current reality based on consensual validation between patient and therapist of a new narrative, which "*depends on the ability of the analyst to avoid imposing meaning so that the patient can feel free to enact new ways of being without fear of traumatically losing the continuity of 'who he is'"* (Bromberg, 1998, p. 386, italics in original).

Safran (2012) states that enactments occur because "people are inevitably influenced by complex nonverbal communications from others that are difficult to decode" and that "therapists, like other human beings, are never fully transparent to themselves" (p. 65). He conceptualizes the resolution of an enactment as occurring when the current relational schemas being acted out are modified. The relational schemas are modified not by conscious, control-oriented, mechanistic means, but as an evolutionary process of growth and development, through gradual "negotiation" of "shared reality" (Pizer, 1998). As Aron (1996) puts it, patient and therapist "weave the complex tapestry of the transference-countertransference; through negotiation they reach a meeting of minds" (p. 69). He states that "interpretations are negotiated between patient and analyst, that we negotiate the location of the resistances, that we negotiate the quality of our relationships with patients, and that we negotiate the construction of psychoanalytic narrative" (p. 139).

Acceptance and Mindfulness in Psychotherapy

There has been a surge of empirical and clinical support for the use of acceptance- and mindfulness-based approaches for the alleviation of human suffering in psychotherapy (see Hayes & Strosahl, 2004; Germer, Siegel, & Fulton, 2005). The movement toward these approaches within the behavioral theoretical tradition has been labeled the "third wave" of behaviorism and, more recently, "contextual cognitive behavioral therapy." These are approaches based on functional contextual philosophy (discussed above). There has not been much professional literature written on the points of contact between psychodynamic and functional contextual–based psychotherapies. This volume is an attempt to help fill that void.

Acceptance

From a functional contextual perspective, acceptance is "active nonjudgmental embracing of experience in the here and now" (Hayes,

2004, p. 21). It is not "toleration" or "resignation," but an "active" process of *changing one's relationship to—not the content of—one's internal world* (Hayes et al., 2012). Acceptance, from this perspective, is similar to Ghent's (1990) conceptualization of surrender: "rather than carrying a connotation of defeat, the term will convey a quality of liberation and expansion of the self as a corollary to the letting down of defensive barriers" (p. 213). Epstein (1995) notes that Freud's initial concept of working through is essentially a form of acceptance. From a relational psychodynamic perspective, acceptance includes the process of approaching the patient in such a way that different aspects of his or her personality are considered authentic and worthy of understanding, in contrast to the more classical psychodynamic view that certain parts of the patient's experience are underdeveloped and must be "renounced" (Wachtel, 2008, p. 136).

Mindfulness

Mindfulness is "the awareness that emerges through paying attention on purpose, in the present moment, and nonjudgmentally to things as they are" (Williams, Teasdale, Segal, & Kabat-Zinn, 2007). Hayes, Villatte, Levin, and Hildebrandt (2011) write that "awareness of the present moment is thought to increase one's sensitivity to important features of the environment and one's own reactions, and thus enhance self-management and successful coping…and can also serve as an alternate behavior to ruminating about the past and worrying about the future" (p. 146). They further write that "the capacity to notice difficult thoughts, feelings, and sensations in a nonjudgmental and open manner without avoiding, suppressing, or otherwise trying to change their occurrence is argued to reduce distress and reactivity as well as reduce problematic avoidance/escape behaviors and increase engagement in important actions" (p. 146). Barney and Andersen (in press) suggest that mindfulness is a means to be "attuned" to self and others and "progress beyond the stage of telling cognitive, linear, and rational stories to deeper, more meaningful self-reflections on who we are and what we do" (in press).

Brach (2003) suggests that in order to be mindful, we also have to be compassionate, because "we cannot be accepting of our experience if our heart has hardened in fear and blame" (p. 199). Frederickson (2012) suggests that compassion toward oneself and others can generate positive emotions and that these emotions broaden one's awareness and facilitate a more objective, less negative perspective on stressful life conditions.

Germer (2005) compares psychodynamic psychotherapy and mindfulness, saying they are "both introspective ventures, they assume that awareness and acceptance precede change, and they both recognize the importance of unconscious processes" (p. 21). Germer (2009) further describes mindfulness as a means for assessing and increasing the efficacy of one's psychological functioning. He suggests that mindfulness decreases psychological defensiveness, increases flexibility, facilitates the "holding" of emotions, and deactivates both the brain's stress response and "default system" of operating mindlessly. He also states that attention, a key component of mindfulness, is the first step in the process of regulating emotions.

Olendzki (2005) states that mindfulness "leads to insight into the subjective construction of experience" (p. 289). Epstein (1995) conceptualizes mindfulness as a means to develop insight into unconscious processes. He writes, "in mindfulness practice, self is experienced as a flow, a process, a rushing and teeming patterning that changes over time" (Epstein, 1995, p. 151). He suggests that mindfulness is a means of releasing the grasp of our "false self" personifications. This process. facilitates more creativity and freedom of authentic self-expression, which is conducive to developing a holistic sense of values and commitment to embody those values (see chapter 9).

Mindfulness and Concentration Meditations

In order to further conceptualize mindfulness, a brief description is in order of what mindfulness is not. The concepts of mindfulness and concentration meditations need to be differentiated. Epstein (1990) notes that "concentration meditation" is what Freud was referring to in his book *Civilization and Its Discontents* when he described the "oceanic feeling" of immature ego development that is associated with certain types of meditation. Concentration meditation is single-point attention (Brach, 2012). It is often oriented toward altering consciousness into a relaxed and trance-like state (e.g., Benson, 1975). From a classical psychodynamic perspective, what occurs is a "merger" of ego boundaries (Epstein, 1990). Epstein (1990) further states that Freud equated concentration meditation with a return to "primary narcissism," in which libido is directed toward one's own ego and relations with the external world are foreclosed. In contrast, Epstein (1990) notes that mindfulness strengthens the ego from within. This occurs by facilitating the development of the "synthetic capacity of the ego" (p. 130). Epstein (1988) writes that "mindfulness allows each moment to be experienced in its entirety; it is synthetic because it binds awareness to the object, neither holding on to or rejecting, whatever projects itself into the mind" (p. 50).

The difference between concentration meditation and mindfulness has significant implications for increasing psychological health. Specifically, concentration meditation is an attempt to change internal experience, whereas mindfulness is an invitation for all psychic phenomena to occur as events to be observed compassionately, *as they are*. This provides room for playful and spontaneous interaction to occur intrapsychically and within the therapeutic dyad.

Mindfulness as a Technique

The difference in technique between mindfulness and concentration forms of meditation is at times vague. This is because there is an element of concentration used in mindfulness in order to develop the necessary "stability of mind" (Epstein, 1990, p. 126) to engage in mindfulness. For example, some mindfulness meditations focus on bringing attention to the breath, but this is done specifically to create a point of reference from which to observe free-floating experience— not to engender trance or relaxation. The purpose of the single-point attention of mindfulness is to provide a "sensory anchor" or "home base" from which experience can be observed mindfully (Brach, 2012, p. 32). Germer (2005) considers this aspect of mindfulness as helping one "to *find*" (p. 117, italics in original) one's attention. Germer (2005) compares the return to the sensory anchor in mindfulness as a process of waking up and says that the concentration aspect of mindfulness acts as a "refuge" when the mind is overwhelmed with difficult memories. He states that "mindfulness meditation is a dance between mindfulness and concentration" (p. 18). Brach (2012) conceptualizes the dynamic between concentration and mindfulness as a dialectic of "coming back" and "being here."

The purpose of mindfulness meditation is to increase awareness. Thus, the "concentration" aspect of the practice prepares the mind for "open field awareness" (Germer, 2009) by providing context for mental processes to emerge spontaneously. This has potential to facilitate articulation into language, which then can be applied to developing an authentic set of values with which to regulate behavior (see chapter 9). Recently, mindfulness-oriented clinicians (e.g., Brach, 2003; Germer, 2009; Gilbert, 2009) have been integrating concentration meditations based on compassion for self and others into their practices (see chapter 5).

Mindfulness and Psychodynamics: Technical Perspectives

Freud's (1912) technical stance of evenly hovering attention and the corresponding patient stance of free association have been connected to mindfulness from both theoretical and technical perspectives (e.g., Epstein, 1988; Lanagan, 2003). From a relational psychodynamic perspective, Stern (2010) suggests that a favorable therapeutic stance is one that facilitates an "open kind of curiosity, a freedom of thought and feeling, an unconstrained imagination" (p. 65), which are all attributes of a mindfulness-based approach. He writes of the transformation of potential experience into conscious experience as a matter of developing "creative speech" (Stern, 1997), or consensually validated experience, that helps facilitate the conscious emergence of previously dissociated self-states. Stern's (1997) concepts of dissociation as the "refusal to *allow*" (italics added) experience and "observation" of experience as its corollary connect theoretically and technically to acceptance and mindfulness, as observing internal experience and allowing it to occur spontaneously are key elements of mindfulness. Walsh (2008) writes, "the repeated return to the present moment invites both the therapist and the client to remain open to surprise and spontaneity, and thereby experience themselves (individually and collectively) in novel ways" (p. 78). Stern (1997) refers to a similar therapeutic process, "courting surprise," in which the therapist "questions what he thinks he already knows about the patient, and about his reactions to the patient....These conditions constitute the climate in which unbidden perceptions flourish" (p. 250). Thus, the concept of mindfulness, in terms of the therapist's "attitude" (see chapter 4), conceptualizations, and technique, can be used to enhance treatment focused on facilitating imaginative, creative experience over dissociated experience. This more complete experience of self-in-relation-to-others facilitates a more reflective, less emotionally reactive behavioral repertoire that has the capacity to increase patients' life satisfaction.

Summary

Due to the similar philosophical grounding of relational psychodynamic and acceptance- and mindfulness-based approaches to psychotherapy, there are significant areas of connection between them in terms of how to understand and work with patients. There are also significant points of departure between the approaches. This volume considers different perspectives on theory and technique within a broad-based integration of psychodynamic and acceptance- and mindfulness-based interventions, with particular emphasis on relational psychodynamic, functional contextual, and Buddhist psychological approaches. It is ultimately an attempt to utilize these points of contact to increase the effectiveness of our work as psychotherapists.

References

Aron, L. (1996). *A meeting of the minds: Mutuality in psychoanalysis.* New York, NY: Routledge-Taylor & Francis Group.

Barney, S. T., & Andersen, M. B. (in press). Mindful supervision in sport and performance psychology: Building the quality of the supervisor-supervisee relationship. In Z. Knowles, D. Gilbourne, B. Copley, & L. Dugdill (Eds.), *Reflective practice in sport and exercise sciences: Contemporary issues.* London, England: Routledge.

Benson, H. (1975). *The relaxation response.* New York, NY: Harper.

Bodhi, B. (2000). *A comprehensive manual of Abhidhamma.* Seattle, WA: BPS Pariyatti Editions.

Brach, T. (2003). *Radical acceptance: Embracing your life with the heart of a Buddha.* New York, NY: Bantam Books.

Brach, T. (2012). *True refuge: Finding peace and freedom in your own awakened heart.* New York, NY: Bantam Books.

Brisman, J. (2001). The instigation of dare: Broadening therapeutic horizons. In J. Petrucelli & C. Stuart (Eds.), *Hungers and compulsions: The psychodynamic treatment of eating disorders and addictions* (pp. 53–64). New York, NY: Aronson.

Bromberg, P. M. (1993). Shadow and substance: A relational perspective on clinical process. In S. A. Mitchell, & L. Aron (Eds.). (1999), *Relational psychoanalysis: The emergence of a tradition* (pp. 379–406). New York, NY: Routledge-Taylor & Francis Group.

Bromberg, P. M. (1998). *Standing in the spaces. Essays on clinical process, trauma, and dissociation*. Hillsdale, NJ: Analytic Press.

Bromberg, P. M. (2006). *Awakening the dreamer: Clinical journeys*. New York, NY: Routledge- Taylor & Francis Group.

Bromberg, P. M. (2010). *The shadow of the tsunami and the growth of the relational mind*. New York, NY: Routledge-Taylor & Francis Group.

Epstein, M. (1988). Attention in analysis. In M. Epstein (Ed.). (2007), *Psychotherapy without the self: A Buddhist perspective* (pp. 101–122). New Haven, CT: Yale University Press.

Epstein, M. (1990). Beyond the oceanic feeling: Psychoanalytic study of Buddhist meditation. In M. Epstein (Ed.). (2007), *Psychotherapy without the self: A Buddhist perspective* (pp. 123–139). New Haven, CT: Yale University Press.

Epstein, M. (1995). *Thoughts without a thinker. Psychotherapy from a Buddhist perspective*. New York, NY: Basic Books.

Epstein, M. (2007). *Psychotherapy without the self: A Buddhist perspective*. New Haven, CT: Yale University Press.

Frederickson, B. L. (2012). Building lives of compassion and wisdom. In C. K. Germer & R. D. Siegel (Eds.), *Wisdom and compassion in psychotherapy: Deepening mindfulness in clinical practice* (pp. 48–58). New York, NY: Guilford Press.

Freud, S. (1912). Recommendations to physicians practicing psycho-analysis. In J. Strachey (Ed. & Trans.), *The standard edition of the complete psychological works of Sigmund Freud* (Vol. 12, pp. 109–120). London, England: Hogarth Press.

Germer, C. K. (2005). Teaching mindfulness in therapy. In C. K. Germer, R. D. Siegel, & P. R. Fulton (Eds.), *Mindfulness and psychotherapy* (pp. 113–129). New York, NY: Guilford Press.

Germer, C. K. (2009). *The mindful path to self-compassion: Freeing yourself from destructive thoughts and emotions*. New York, NY: Guilford Press.

Germer, C. K., & Siegel, R. D. (2012). *Wisdom and compassion in psychotherapy: Deepening mindfulness in clinical practice*. New York, NY: Guilford Press.

Germer, C. K., Siegel, R. D., & Fulton, P. R. (2005). *Mindfulness and psychotherapy*. New York, NY: Guilford Press.

Ghent, E. (1990). Masochism, submission, surrender: Masochism as a perversion of surrender. In S. A. Mitchell & L. Aron (Eds.). (1999), *Relational psychoanalysis: The emergence of a tradition*. New York, NY: Routledge-Taylor & Francis Group.

Gilbert, P. (2009). *The compassionate mind: A new approach to life's challenges*. Oakland, CA: New Harbinger.

Hayes, S. C. (2004). Acceptance and commitment therapy and the new behavior therapies: Mindfulness, acceptance, and relationship. In S. C. Hayes, V. M. Follette, & M. M. Linehan (Eds.), *Mindfulness and acceptance: Expanding the cognitive-behavioral tradition* (pp. 1–29). New York, NY: Guilford Press.

Hayes, S. C., & Smith, S. (2005). *Get out of your mind and into your life: The new acceptance and commitment therapy*. Oakland, CA: New Harbinger.

Hayes, S. C., & Strosahl, K. D. (2004). *A practical guide to acceptance and commitment therapy*. New York, NY: Springer.

Hayes, S. C., Strosahl, K. D., & Wilson, K. G. (1999). *Acceptance and commitment therapy: An experiential approach to behavior change*. New York, NY: Guilford Press.

Hayes, S. C., Strosahl, K. D., & Wilson, K. G. (2012). *Acceptance and commitment therapy: The process and practice of mindful change.* New York, NY: Guilford Press.

Hayes, S. C., Villatte, M., Levin, M., & Hildebrandt, M. (2011). Open, aware, and active: Contextual approaches as the emerging trend in behavioral and cognitive therapies. *Annual Review of Clinical Psychology, 7,* 141–168.

Hoffman, I. Z. (1998). *Ritual and spontaneity in the psychoanalytic process: A dialectical-constructivist view.* New York, NY: Routledge-Taylor & Francis Group.

Kohlenberg, R. J. & Tsai, M. (1991). *Functional analytic psychotherapy: Creating intense and curative therapeutic relationships.* New York, NY: Springer.

Lanagan, R. (2003). The dissolving of dissolving itself. In J. D. Safran (Ed.), *Psychoanalysis and Buddhism: An unfolding dialogue* (pp. 131–145). Somerville, MA: Wisdom.

Linehan, M. M. (1993). *Cognitive-behavioral treatment of borderline personality disorder.* New York, NY: Guilford Press.

Maroda, K. J. (1998) *Seduction, surrender, and transformation: Emotional engagement in the analytic process.* Hillsdale, NJ: Analytic Press.

Maroda, K. J. (2010). *Psychodynamic techniques. Working with emotion in the therapeutic relationship.* New York, NY: Guilford Press.

Mitchell, S. A. (1988). *Relational concepts in psychoanalysis: An integration.* Cambridge, MA: Harvard University Press.

Mitchell, S. A. (1993). *Hope and dread in psychoanalysis.* New York, NY: Basic Books.

Mitchell, S. A., & Aron, L. (1999). *Relational psychoanalysis: The emergence of a tradition.* New York, NY: Routledge-Taylor & Francis Group.

Olendzki, A. (2005). The roots of mindfulness. In C. K. Germer, R. D. Siegel, & P. R. Fulton (Eds.), *Mindfulness and psychotherapy* (pp. 241–261). New York, NY: Guilford Press.

Pizer, S. A. (1998). *Building bridges: The negotiation of paradox in psychoanalysis.* New York, NY: Routledge-Taylor & Francis Group.

Safran, J. D. (1998). *Widening the scope of cognitive therapy: The therapeutic relationship, emotion, and the process of change.* Northvale, NJ: Aronson.

Safran, J. D. (2003). *Psychoanalysis and Buddhism: An unfolding dialogue.* Somerville, MA: Wisdom.

Safran, J. D. (2012). *Psychoanalysis and psychoanalytic therapies.* Washington, DC: American Psychological Association.

Safran, J. D., & Muran, J. C. (2000). *Negotiating the therapeutic alliance: A relational treatment guide.* New York, NY: Guilford Press.

Stern, D. B. (1983). Unformulated experience: From familiar chaos to creative disorder. In S. A. Mitchell & L. Aron (Eds.). (1999), *Relational psychoanalysis: The emergence of a tradition* (pp. 77–108). New York, NY: Routledge-Taylor & Francis Group.

Stern, D. B. (1997). *Unformulated experience: From dissociation to imagination in psychoanalysis.* New York, NY: Psychology Press-Taylor & Francis Group.

Stern, D. B. (2010). *Partners in thought: Working with unformulated experience, dissociation, and enactment.* New York, NY: Routledge-Taylor & Francis Group.

Sullivan, H. S. (1953). *The interpersonal theory of psychiatry.* New York, NY: W. W. Norton.

Sullivan, H. S. (1954). *The psychiatric interview.* New York, NY: W. W. Norton.

Sullivan, H. S. (1956). *Clinical studies in psychiatry*. New York, NY: W. W. Norton.

Wachtel, P. L. (2008). *Relational theory and the practice of psychotherapy*. New York, NY: Guilford Press.

Wachtel, P. L. (2011a). *Inside the session: What really happens in psychotherapy*. Washington, DC: American Psychological Association.

Wachtel, P. L. (2011b). *Therapeutic communication: Knowing what to say when*. New York, NY: Guilford Press.

Walsh, R. A. (2008). Mindfulness and empathy: A hermeneutic circle. In S. F. Hick & T. Bien (Eds.), *Mindfulness and the therapeutic relationship* (pp. 72–86). New York, NY: Guilford Press.

Williams, M., Teasdale, J., Segal, Z., & Kabat-Zinn, J. (2007). *The mindful way through depression*. New York, NY: Guilford Press.

Young-Eisendrath, P. (2003). Transference and transformation in Buddhism and psychoanalysis. In J. D. Safran (Ed.), *Psychoanalysis and Buddhism: An unfolding dialogue* (pp. 301–318). Somerville, MA: Wisdom.

PART 1

Roots and Foundations:
Key Concepts and Processes for
Integrating Psychodynamic and
Acceptance- and Mindfulness-Based
Approaches to Psychotherapy

CHAPTER 1

Implications of Psychotherapy Integration for Psychodynamic and Acceptance- and Mindfulness-Based Approaches

Jerry Gold, PhD, ABPP

The term "psychotherapy integration" refers to the theoretical or conceptual enterprise of synthesizing two or more discrete systems of psychotherapy into a more complete and expanded system. The corresponding term "integrative psychotherapy" refers to the clinical application of this type of conceptual synthesis. An integrative psychotherapy is one that utilizes strategies, tactics, and techniques that are drawn from two or more types of therapy.

There exists a great deal of consensus within the field of psychotherapy integration that four general modes of integration can be identified. These modes are differentiated by the degree to which they rely on the complete integration of separate theories, as well as methods—some modes focus more simply on the selection of techniques (Gold & Stricker, 2013).

Modes of Psychotherapy Integration

The first mode is *technical eclecticism*. This does not involve the integration of the basic theories on which the separate schools of psychotherapy are based. Integration is achieved either in an atheoretical framework or by retaining a reliance on a single theory of personality, psychopathology, and treatment, while using an expanded palette of interventions. Integration occurs solely at the point of the selection of interventions and techniques, which are drawn from a wider range of choices than a single theory would permit. A therapist working in this mode does not rely on theory to select techniques. Instead, he or she is guided by empirical literature and by clinical experience, which are used to find those methods that have been demonstrated to be the best match to the patient's characteristics and need. Two examples of technical eclecticism that are widely discussed and applied are systemic treatment selection (Beutler & Hodgson, 1993) and multimodal therapy (Lazarus, 2002).

The second integrative mode is the *common factors approach*. First described by Rosenzweig (1936), this approach is based on the assumption that there exists a relatively small set of change factors that are shared to some degree by all effective psychotherapies. Integration thus proceeds by identifying those factors and the techniques most closely connected to them and then constructing a therapy that is most likely to deliver those factors as accurately and powerfully as possible. Assessment in this type of integration is focused first on identifying the specific common factors that will be of greatest use in any particular case. A number of lists of these common factors have been proposed. One such list that is cited frequently is that by Weinberger (1993), which he developed through an extensive review of the common factors literature. His list includes the therapeutic relationship, exposure through the confrontation of problems, patient expectations or hope of change, the experience of mastery, and attribution of outcome to the self. Several common factors models of integration have been proposed. The classic example of this is Frank's (1961) discussion of the centrality of hope in psychotherapy, while Garfield (2000), and Beitman, Soth, and Good (2006) have offered more contemporary common factors models. In a section to follow I will discuss the emerging view of mindfulness as a central common factor and as a foundation for psychotherapy integration.

Assimilative integration is a third mode of psychotherapy integration. This approach involves the consistent use of a single home theory and method—for example, psychodynamic psychotherapy—into which techniques from other psychotherapies are periodically incorporated. These latter interventions are utilized for two simultaneous purposes: first, the intention for which they were originally developed, and second, to promote work in the home theory's approach. In the assimilative model discussed by Stricker and Gold (Stricker & Gold, 1996; Gold & Stricker, 2013), behavioral, cognitive, and other techniques are used both in their typical ways and, at the same time, to promote psychodynamic exploration and change.

The fourth mode of integration is *Theoretical Integration*. This is the most complete and ambitious approach to psychotherapy integration. It involves the construction of a novel theory, as well as an associated integrative treatment, from the raw materials of two or more approaches to psychotherapy. The most prominent example of theoretical integration is Wachtel's (1977, 1997) integration of psychodynamic, behavioral, systems, and experiential approaches known as cyclical psychodynamics. Cognitive-analytic therapy (Ryle, 1995) is another important example of a theoretically integrated, psychodynamically based therapy that has received considerable attention.

Psychotherapy Integration of Psychodynamic and Behavioral Approaches

The history of psychotherapy integration—and specifically of the integration of psychodynamic and behavioral approaches—is almost as long as the history of psychoanalysis. In one of his few papers on the clinical practice of psychoanalysis, Freud (1909) himself argued that the analysis of phobic and of compulsive patients often required active intervention in the patient's symptoms and behaviors. Freud suggested that the analyst require the phobic patient to face the object of his or her fears and that the compulsive patient be made to give up his or her rituals. In both cases, Freud suggested that failure to do so would lead to sterile and intellectualized analysis.

While most of Freud's words have been taken as gospel, the psychoanalytic community did not seize on this advice, for reasons that are probably obvious: these symptomatically focused, exposure-based approaches became more and more contradictory to the exclusively insight-oriented emphasis that dominated psychoanalysis through the latter part of the last century. However, there exist certain early, integrative exceptions to this trend. French (1933) was perhaps the first to argue that psychoanalytic theory and method needed to account for the phenomena of learning as documented in the work of Ivan Pavlov.

Kubie (1934) quickly followed up on this work with an exploration of the relationship of conditioned reflexes to psychoanalytic technique. Sears (1944) and Shoben (1949) discussed the role of learning and the utilization of learning theory and principles in the context of psychodynamic treatment, as did Dollard and Miller (1950), whose book *Personality and Psychotherapy* offered the first comprehensive synthesis of learning theory and psychoanalytic theory and proposed a set of theoretically based integrative interventions.

The 1960s and 1970s saw an acceleration of interest in integrating behavioral and psychodynamic approaches. Beier (1966) described an integration of psychoanalytic therapy with operant theories and methods that, in today's terms, might be described as a reformulation psychodynamics as occurring within a functional contextual framework. He demonstrated how unconscious processes are shaped and reinforced by their external consequences, and how the therapist could use his or her verbal contributions as positive and negative reinforcers. Alexander (1963) described a perspective on the therapeutic relationship and on change processes in psychotherapy that synthesized psychodynamic and learning concepts. Authors such as Marks and Gelder (1966), Brady (1968), and Birk (1970) argued that trends in psychoanalysis and behavior therapy pointed to a convergence of the two approaches, and they began to outline tentative models for combining the two technical approaches. Of particular interest in this regard was the work of Feather and Rhodes (1973), in which they introduced an approach they called psychodynamic behavior therapy. This integrative model was based on a psychodynamic formulation of the patient's difficulties, which then became the foundation that directed the use of behavioral interventions such as systematic desensitization.

The watershed event in the history of psychotherapy integration occurred with the publication of Wachtel's (1977) extraordinarily influential and well-received text, *Psychoanalysis and Behavior Therapy: Toward an Integration*. This book introduced what has come to be accepted as the most complete theoretical integration of learning theory and psychoanalysis, in the form of the theory of cyclical psychodynamics, and it demonstrated how this theory could be used as the basis for an integrative psychotherapy. In it, Wachtel (1977) described the ways in which learning and reinforcement principles, along with behavioral interventions, could be used to promote and expand psychodynamic exploration, and the ways that dynamic work could lead to effective behavioral change. Wachtel's (1977) seminal contribution not only became the first model of a complete integrative system of psychotherapy, it also legitimized the field of psychotherapy integration and promoted an explosion of study and writing about integration. Of particular note in the history of attempts to unite behavioral and dynamic models are cognitive analytic therapy (Ryle, 1995), accelerated experiential dynamic psychotherapy (Fosha & Yeung, 2006), and assimilative psychodynamic psychotherapy (Stricker & Gold, 1996; Gold & Stricker, 2013). All of these therapies owe a debt to Wachtel's work but exemplify singular ways of combining psychodynamic theories and methods with concepts and techniques that allow for active intervention.

In reviewing the literature just cited, it is possible to isolate certain shared ideas and assumptions that guide most psychodynamically informed, integrative therapies. In these models, unconscious mental processes are assumed to be shaped by learning and experience and therefore to be governed by the rules of learning that regulate conscious psychological processes and overt behavior. So the integrative therapist would embrace the notion that behavioral and cognitive methods can be employed to influence and change unconscious motives, conflicts, defenses, and structure, just as they can be used to change thinking and action. Integrative therapists see change as circular and multidirectional, and understand that change in one sphere of psychological life can have important effects on other spheres.

Mindfulness as a Common Factor in Psychotherapy

Among several important developments in psychotherapy integration that have emerged in its recent history is a growing emphasis on the role of mindfulness as a common factor that cuts across the various sectarian schools of psychotherapy. Mindfulness is purposeful and nonjudgmental attention (Kabat-Zinn, 1990). This literature suggests that we add mindfulness to the list of generally accepted common factors mentioned above, and that mindfulness be considered as a meeting point or foundation upon which integrative models of therapy can be built. Even before workers in this area specifically addressed the role of mindfulness as a common factor, there existed significant interest in the relationship between dynamic psychotherapy and Buddhist thought. This convergence makes a great deal of sense when we examine anew the processes that are crucial to at least three major systems of psychotherapy: psychoanalysis, cognitive behavior therapy, and person-centered therapy. In its own way, each relies on process related to mindfulness in prescribing the participation of the patient. Free association in psychoanalysis asks the patient to attend to all aspects of his or her psychic world as they flow by the window of his or her observing mind. Cognitive behavior therapists instruct patients to look for and stay with those thoughts and images upon which they might ordinarily be less inclined to dwell. Person-centered and other experiential therapies are based on unguided, honest examination of the patient's moment-to-moment experience. It is no wonder that as various forms of psychotherapy have converged and as integration has become a prominent goal, mindfulness has come to be seen as a meeting point common to many, if not all, therapies. A recent study exemplifies this trend. Carey, Kelly, Mansell, and Tsai (2012) suggested that the therapeutic value of the client-therapist relationship can be found in its ability to promote a state strongly resembling mindfulness.

> *Furthermore, we propose that when the therapeutic relationship is therapeutic, clients feel comfortable to consider whatever comes into their mind; with any filtering or evaluating happening after the ideas have been expressed, and not before. Psychological processes identified as maintaining psychological distress (e.g., thought suppression, avoidance, rumination) block this capacity. Our suggestion is that as internal experiences are being examined, the client has an opportunity to become aware of facets of the problem that were previously unattended to; and to continue this process outside therapy. Through this awareness-raising process the client's problem can be reorganized via intrinsic learning processes to achieve a more contented state of mind. (p. 47)*

Perhaps the classic example of these efforts was Fromm's exploration of the relationship between psychoanalysis and Zen Buddhism, written in collaboration with Zen master D. T. Suzuki (Fromm, Suzuki, & DeMartino, 1970). Other works of this type followed, most notably the work of Epstein (1995). Parallel to these developments was the growth of interest in the place of mindfulness within the maturing field of psychotherapy integration. Bohart (1983) described the process of *detachment* as a factor common to most forms of psychotherapy. He described this variable in ways that resemble greatly the concept of mindfulness: detachment is described as the process of stepping back from one's problems and preoccupations to achieve a state of *phenomenological attention* to one's immediate experience. Safran and Segal (1990), in their integration of interpersonal and cognitive therapies, utilize the concepts of *deautomatization* and *decentering*, which refer to the process of disengaging from the content of one's thinking, with the goal of increasing awareness of—and contact with—one's immediate experience.

Martin (1997) postulated that mindfulness is a common factor that plays an important role in both psychodynamic and cognitive behavior therapies. He further detailed the variant forms and uses of mindfulness in these two approaches and presented an approach to psychotherapy integration in which mindfulness, especially as experienced and used by the integrative therapist in his or her own work, plays even more important a role than that of a common factor. In Martin's (1997) view, integration will not proceed optimally from a static model or theory. Instead, he suggests that the activity of integration in psychotherapy might best be thought of as a way of thinking or a mindful process of decision making in which decisions about the choice of interventions are weighed and considered without theoretical bias, and the best are decided upon when the therapist has the most complete access to all of his or her knowledge about the patient and the literatures that are available. Successful integration can occur when the therapist has equal access to—and appreciation of—all of the relevant possibilities for intervention.

The importance of mindfulness as a common factor across therapies, as well as its role in the process of psychotherapy integration, has been explored in a number of other important contributions. Germer (2005) explored the role and utility of mindfulness in psychotherapy and concluded that it is a common factor that is an essential ingredient of both psychodynamic and cognitive behavioral therapies. Each system, he argued, encourages greater self-awareness in the immediate moment, especially with regard to the ongoing examination of one's thought processes, emotions, and bodily experiences. Both systems also take acceptance as a crucial goal, which they define as the increased ability to notice and to stay with painful experiences until they can be integrated and then let go. Germer (2005) further suggested that mindfulness techniques can and should be incorporated into both of these therapeutic approaches.

Kohlenberg, Kanter, Tsai, and Weeks (2010) identified mindfulness as a critical common factor in functional analytic therapy (FAP), an integrative model that combines elements of psychodynamic and behavioral models. They further identified mindfulness as a common factor in cognitive behavioral therapy and as a point of contact between that system and theirs.

Finally, in a recent review, Davis and Hayes (2011) described in detail the positive effects that accrue from the use of mindfulness within the context of psychotherapy and reemphasized its status as a common technique and change factor that operates across therapies.

Wachtel (2011) recently pointed out that the goals of psychoanalytic psychotherapy have moved away from insight and expression of unconscious fantasy to the attainment of enhanced awareness of, comfort with, and acceptance of one's complete range of thoughts, emotions, and memories. In this statement, we may find the reason why mindfulness has emerged as an area of such interest for psychotherapists. Since the aims of mindfulness are, in fact, identical with those goals just mentioned, it has become a concept and set of methods whose utility cuts across the boundaries of the various therapy systems.

The Use of an Assimilative Model to Integrate Psychodynamic and Functional Contextual Therapies

In reviewing the history of psychotherapy integration that was presented above, it is clear that during the past few decades this approach to psychotherapy was transformed from an obscure subfield with a dubious reputation to one that is highly influential and legitimate. How and why has this happened, and what are the advantages to this approach compared to the various traditional forms of psychotherapy?

Reviews of the psychotherapy outcome research repeatedly come to two conclusions: first, there is little difference between the various schools of psychotherapy in terms of overall effectiveness; second, most therapies "work" or are helpful about 50 to 70 percent of the time (Summers & Barber, 2010). If this is indeed the case, then integration of two or more therapies may yield a combined therapy that is more powerful than its components. As discussed above, one way to accomplish this is through common factors integration. Identification of the specific common factors that would be most effective with each patient might allow an individually tailored therapy to be offered. Similar advantages might be gained through the process of assimilative integration.

As described above, assimilative integration involves relying on a single home theory, such as psychoanalysis or cognitive-behavioral therapy, while periodically and selectively incorporating techniques from other schools of psychotherapy. These integrative shifts (Gold & Stricker, 2013) typically occur when standard work within the guidelines of the home theory reaches a limit to its effectiveness. In a psychodynamically based approach, this might occur when behavioral problems, repetitive patterns of relating to others, or conscious patterns of thinking and dealing with emotion cannot be changed through typical psychodynamic exploration. This is not, in fact, a novel idea within the psychoanalytic world. For example, Alexander and French (1946), in their controversial work, suggested that change frequently followed from those reparative interpersonal experiences within the therapeutic relationship that they labeled "corrective emotional experiences." They further suggested that insight is often a by-product of such experiences rather than their cause. An assimilative psychodynamic therapy therefore incorporates active interventions from other therapies in order to accomplish two simultaneous purposes. They are employed both for their standard impact and for the potential impact on the patient's psychodynamic processes as well. Changes in behavior—especially social behavior, thinking, emotional regulation and processing, and imagery—are important in and of themselves, and changes in these spheres of psychological life often make psychodynamic change more likely or even produce changes in unconscious functioning and structure. For example, a patient who learns to express tender and warm emotions more directly in important relationships typically experiences more success, closeness, and acceptance than he did previously. At the same time, new experiences with intimacy allow the patient to contact, explore, and revise previously unconscious images and representations of attachment figures and significant others that reflect the old hurts and disappointments that gave rise to those emotional difficulties. Also, new and positive experiences in relating to others can give rise to more positive and stable images and experiences of the self. In sum, an important premise of an assimilative psychodynamic therapy is the assumption that overt changes in behavior and conscious experience, valuable in themselves, are also invaluable because they can produce changes in unconscious conflict, self and object representations, and the structure of the self.

Since we have already established that mindfulness and acceptance are central change processes, it would seem obvious that in the search for an improved psychotherapy, an essential component would be the incorporation of such methods, drawn from mindfulness-based and functional contextual models. When might this be the case? To answer this question we must compare and contrast psychodynamic and acceptance- and mindfulness-based approaches with regard to their aims, advantages, and limitations.

Psychodynamic methods excel in their ability to put the patient's current life and problems in a historical-developmental context and to identify the near and distant internal causes of behavior. Traditionally, they have not aimed at or been particularly useful in finding or changing the behavioral, experiential, or environmental consequences that inhibit progress in therapy and that maintain the patient's problems. In fact, psychodynamic theory has failed to account for the fact that unconscious processes, structures, conflicts, defenses, resistances, and transference reactions can and should be seen as behaviors that have operant consequences that maintain and reinforce them, often to the point that psychoanalytic exploration becomes ineffective. Therefore, at these times, an integrative shift to mindfulness and acceptance techniques can offer the patients the usual gains associated with those methods and, at the same time, be extremely valuable in promoting psychodynamic exploration and intrapsychic change. Defenses and resistances are activated by the wish to avoid unpleasant emotion, and are reinforced by the reduction of those emotions. Unconscious images of self and of others are expressed through repetitive patterns of relating to others—both in and out of therapy—and the inability to give up old struggles in new contexts keeps those issues alive. Coming to terms with the need for—and the eventual advantages of—experiencing and accepting emotional pain and interpersonally derived sadness or disappointment leads to intrapsychic and contextual changes. The provision of such experiences seems to meet the criteria for the aforementioned "corrective emotional experience."

Using Assimilative Integration of Psychodynamic Psychotherapy with Functional Contextual Psychotherapies as a Means of Helping Clients Build "Psychic Structure"

Early versions of psychoanalytic theory portrayed the mind as taking in early childhood under the pressure of unconscious drives and conflicts. By the time the person had reached adulthood, his or her mental life was fixed and essentially unchangeable by life experiences. This overemphasis in classical versions of psychoanalysis on the conceptualization of the mind as immutable—a prematurely closed system—was described by Mitchell (1988) as the "developmental tilt," and he, with other modern psychoanalytic voices, suggested that an alternative perspective was necessary.

Contemporary psychoanalytic theories are more likely to describe the mind as a longitudinally developing, open system, wherein psychological conflicts and structures can change or develop in response to interactions with the outside world. That such structures seem to be immutable is more a reflection of the limited, repetitive patterns of relatedness in which the patient is stuck than of the essential characteristic of intrapsychic variables. These fixed patterns of relatedness invariably lead to fixed interpersonal results, with the consequence that there is no reason or way to examine or change the related internal structures. If the patient is able to encounter and relate to others in new ways, not only will her or his relationships change, but these new outcomes will give rise to new perspectives on past and present interactions, which may lead to changes in her or his unconscious world of self and object representations (Gold & Wachtel, 2006). To this end, a psychodynamic therapist may usefully incorporate aspects of functional contextual therapies toward the achievement of increased mindfulness and acceptance on the part of the patient. A central cause of those repetitive relationships that stabilize old intrapsychic structures is the pain and fear associated with relational change. Perhaps the pain of accepting loss, rejection, or the limits of relationships has been found to be intolerable and, therefore, the patient keeps trying to succeed where success is unlikely or impossible. The therapist works with that person to help him or her accept those relational experiences that cannot or will not change and to tolerate and integrate loss, hoping to give the patient new raw material out of which to build a more effective sense of self. Then, if a newly expanded ability to handle this pain emerges, the patient will have a greater chance of finding what is good in current relationships or moving on to new and better relationships. When this occurs, these new experiences can be enjoyed in their own right, and they also serve as the source of new, corrective internal structures that repair, revise, and replace old and faulty ways of representing the self and others.

Behavior Change Can Lead to Greater Access to Unconscious Processes and Contents

Anyone who is passingly familiar with psychoanalytically oriented psychotherapy would immediately recognize the task of "making the unconscious conscious" as a central goal of that form of treatment, typically, if not exclusively, through interpretation of latent verbal material. Integrative, psychodynamically informed therapies certainly make extensive use of interpretation but often also use cognitive, behavioral, and experiential techniques to expand the patient's access to previously disavowed issues.

In traditional psychoanalytic models, the defense mechanisms that the person uses to repress or dissociate troublesome ideas, wishes, fantasies, and images are considered to be purely intrapsychic. Modern integrative students recognize that some defensive processes are, in fact, purely mental operations or acts but that these actions can be addressed actively, directly, and through behavioral methods (Fensterheim, 1993). Defenses are seen as intrapsychic ways of avoiding anxiety or other dysphoria and are therefore subject to change through exposure-based techniques and modification of consequences. Mindfulness and acceptance techniques also directly lower the patient's fear of his or her own inner life and therefore allow new mental contents to emerge into awareness.

Most integrative models also recognize that defensive processes have a behavioral and interpersonal component and that when the patient learns to engage the world differently, particularly but not exclusively when avoidance is lessened, he or she often makes new contact with previously disavowed psychic processes.

Using Integrative Methods to Work with Transference

Repeated instances when transference analysis fails to deliver results as expected serve as an important reason to move from standard psychodynamic thinking and practice toward an assimilative model. Dynamic therapists often find that their expectations of the impact of transference analysis on the patient's significant ongoing relationships were not met. This occurs for at least three reasons. First, quite often the issues and problems that manifest in the patient's interactions outside of therapy fail to manifest themselves in the therapeutic relationship, leaving no opportunity for working on them in sessions. Second, patients fail to generalize or make use of what they experienced and learned in their sessions with others in their outside lives. Finally, even when patients attempt to make use of gains from transference exploration outside of their sessions, their efforts often are unable to lead to change, since things do not progress in the same ways with significant others as they did with the therapist, especially as those individuals often have different motivations than did the therapist. These impasses or failures often lead to worsening of symptoms, increased resistance, negative transference reactions, and alliance strains or ruptures as the patient becomes frustrated, angry, disappointed, and hopeless with regard to the possibility of the therapy leading to real-life interpersonal change and improvement.

In these instances, it is crucial to find ways to work with patients to directly change their interactions, especially if the others involved are reluctant to change or are, in fact, hostile to it. Therefore, a psychodynamic therapist might begin to use methods such as assertiveness and social skills training, empathy training, and others that impact directly on the patient's interpersonal skills and patterns of relating to others. When these are used successfully, this shift will lead to change at two levels, as would be expected in an assimilative, integrative approach. As the patient becomes more successful in negotiating the world of interpersonal relationships, he or she also acquires or regains a sense of hope and trust and confidence in the psychodynamic process, with a correlated strengthening of the therapeutic alliance, a reduction in resistance, and more productive exploratory work. Often, new insights and memories connected to the development of important interpersonal difficulties occur spontaneously after those difficulties are corrected through the assimilative use of active techniques.

The Use of Active Interventions as a Means to Transference Enactment Resolution

The need to intervene actively in the patient's transference reactions becomes most prominent when those reactions move toward the creation of a transference enactment. As described by Binder (2000) and many other contemporary psychodynamic thinkers, enactment refers to an interactional transformation of the therapeutic relationship, in which the therapist becomes an actual but unwitting partner in the re-creation of the patient's past, usually hurtful, interactions. Enactments seem always to lead to heightened distress on the patient's part and to strains and ruptures of the therapeutic alliance, since the therapist has now actually behaved in ways that are difficult for or dangerous to the patient.

Some enactments can be anticipated by tracking the patient's descriptions of past and current relationships and by looking for ways these interactions might be duplicated in session. At other times, enactments cannot be foreseen or prevented, and so they must then become the central issue to be explored until the impact of the interaction can be resolved and a trusting therapeutic alliance can be reestablished. The integrative shift into the use of active interventions sometimes can ward off or repair an enactment by meeting the patient's legitimate needs and thus proving experientially to the patient that the therapist is, in fact, different and separate from the person from the past. As one negative example, Gold and Stricker (2013) described how a therapist's deliberate decision to eschew such interventions, when those techniques might be a good fit to alleviate the patient's suffering or adaptive difficulties, may be an unwitting enactment of a parent's failure to teach the patient how to better function in the world or how to manage his or her hurt, disappointment, and other types of emotional pain. Should such an enactment occur, psychodynamic exploration of the enactment certainly is a necessity for successful resolution, but it may not be sufficient for the task.

Repair of the damage to the alliance may only occur when the therapist has, in fact, acted differently from the figure from the past by teaching the patient new skills. Weiss (1994), in his reconceptualization of psychodynamic theory that is known as control-mastery theory, hypothesized that patients come to therapy with grim, unconscious beliefs about other people, and that these beliefs are the source of unconscious tests for the therapist, to see if the therapist is different from past attachment figures. The decision to use active interventions may often be a conscious or unwitting answer to the tests and therefore meet the criteria for assimilative interventions: the techniques bring both their usual benefit and the benefit of passing the patient's tests, which allows the unconscious beliefs to be examined, modified, and perhaps given up.

Summary

I have described some history of psychotherapy integration, the rationale for mindfulness as a common factor of effective therapy, and some ways in which an assimilative integration of psychodynamic and acceptance- and mindfulness-based approaches to psychotherapy can potentially increase the effectiveness of the therapy process. In chapter 8, I explore the integrative assimilative dynamic approach in more detail and with examples of clinical application.

References

Alexander, F. (1963). Psychotherapy in the light of learning theory. *American Journal of Psychiatry, 120,* 440–448.

Alexander, F., & French, T. (1946). *Psychoanalytic therapy: Principles and application.* New York, NY: Ronald Press.

Beier, E. G. (1966). *The silent language of psychotherapy.* Chicago, IL: Aldine.

Beitman, B. D., Soth, A. M., & Good, G. E. (2006). Integrating the psychotherapies through their emphases on the future. In G. Stricker & J. Gold (Eds.), *A casebook of psychotherapy integration* (pp. 43–52). Washington, DC: American Psychological Association.

Beutler, L. E., & Hodgson, A. B. (1993). Prescriptive psychotherapy. In G. Stricker & J. R. Gold (Eds.), *Comprehensive handbook of psychotherapy integration* (pp. 151–163). New York, NY: Plenum Press.

Binder, J. (2000). *Key competencies in brief dynamic psychotherapy.* New York, NY: Guilford Press.

Birk, L. (1970). Behavior therapy: Integration with dynamic therapy. *Behavior Therapy, 1,* 522–526.

Bohart, A. (1983). *Detachment: A variable common to many psychotherapies?* Paper presented at the 63rd annual convention of the Western Psychological Association, San Francisco, CA.

Brady, J. P. (1968). Psychotherapy by combined behavioral and dynamic approaches. *Comprehensive Psychiatry, 9,* 536–543.

Carey, T., Kelly, R., Mansell, W., & Tsai, M. (2012). What's therapeutic about the therapeutic relationship? A hypothesis for practice informed by Perceptual Control theory. *The Cognitive Behavior Therapist, 5,* 47–69.

Davis, D. M., & Hayes, J. A. (2011). What are the benefits of mindfulness? A practice review of psychotherapy-related research. *Psychotherapy, 48,* 198–208.

Dollard, J., & Miller, N. E. (1950). *Personality and psychotherapy.* New York, NY: McGraw-Hill.

Epstein, M. (1995). *Thoughts without a thinker: Psychotherapy from a Buddhist perspective.* New York, NY: Basic Books.

Feather, B. W., & Rhodes, J. W. (1973). Psychodynamic behavior therapy I: Theory and rationale. *Archives of General Psychiatry, 26,* 496–502.

Fensterheim, H. (1993). Behavioral psychotherapy. In G. Stricker & J. R. Gold (Eds.), *Comprehensive handbook of psychotherapy integration* (pp. 73–86). New York, NY: Plenum Press.

Fosha, D., & Yeung, D. (2006). Accelerated experiential-dynamic psychotherapy: The seamless integration of emotional transformation and dyadic relatedness at work. In G. Stricker & J. Gold (Eds.), *A casebook of psychotherapy integration* (pp. 165–184). Washington, DC: American Psychological Association.

Frank, J. (1961). *Persuasion and healing.* Baltimore, MD: Johns Hopkins University Press.

French, T. M. (1933). Interrelations between psychoanalysis and the experimental work of Pavlov. *American Journal of Psychiatry, 89,* 1165–1203.

Freud, S. (1909). Notes upon a case of obsessional neurosis. In J. Strachey (Ed. & Trans.), *The standard edition of the complete psychological works of Sigmund Freud* (Vol. 10, pp. 153–318). London, England: Hogarth Press.

Fromm, E., Suzuki, D. T., & DeMartino, R. (1970). *Zen Buddhism and Psychoanalysis.* New York, NY: Harpers.

Garfield, S. (2000). Eclecticism and integration: A personal retrospective view. *Journal of Psychotherapy Integration, 10,* 341–356.

Germer, C. K. (2005). Mindfulness: What is it? What does it matter? In C. K. Germer, R. D. Siegel, & P. R. Fulton (Eds.), *Mindfulness and psychotherapy* (pp. 3–27). New York, NY: Guilford Press.

Gold, J., & Stricker, G. (2001). Relational psychoanalysis as a foundation for assimilative integration. *Journal of Psychotherapy Integration, 11,* 47–63.

Gold, J., & Stricker, G. (2013). Psychotherapy integration and integrative psychotherapies. In G. Stricker & T. Widiger (Eds.), *Handbook of psychology* (Vol. 8, pp. 345–366). Hoboken, NJ: Wiley.

Gold, J., & Wachtel, P. L. (2006). Cyclical psychodynamics. In G. Stricker & J. Gold (Eds.), *A casebook of psychotherapy integration* (pp. 79–88). Washington, DC: American Psychological Association.

Kabat-Zinn, J. (1991). *Full catastrophe living: Using the wisdom of your body and mind to face stress, pain, and illness.* New York, NY: Delta Trade Paperbacks.

Kohlenberg, R. J., Kanter, J. W., Tsai, M., & Weeks, C. E. (2010). FAP and cognitive-behavior therapy. In J. W. Kanter, M. Tsai, & R. J. Kohlenberg (Eds.), *The practice of functional analytic psychotherapy* (pp. 11–30). New York, NY: Springer.

Kubie, L. S. (1934). Relation of the conditioned reflex to psychoanalytic technique. *Archives of Neurology and Psychiatry, 32,* 1137–1142.

Lazarus, A. A. (2002). The multimodal assessment treatment method. In J. Lebow (Ed.), *Comprehensive handbook of psychotherapy* (Vol. 4, pp. 241–254). New York, NY: Wiley.

Marks, I., & Gelder, M. G. (1966). Common ground between behavior therapy and psychotherapy. *British Journal of Medical Psychology, 39,* 11–23.

Marmor, J. (1971). Dynamic psychotherapy and behavior therapy: Are they reconcilable? *Archives of General Psychiatry, 24,* 22–28.

Martin, J. R. (1997). Mindfulness: A proposed common factor. *Journal of Psychotherapy Integration, 7,* 291–312.

Mitchell, S. (1988). *Relational concepts in psychoanalysis: An integration.* Cambridge, MA: Harvard University Press.

Rosenzweig, S. (1936). Some implicit common factors in diverse methods of psychotherapy. *American Journal of Orthopsychiatry, 6,* 412–415.

Ryle, A. (1995). *Cognitive analytic therapy: Developments in theory and practice.* Chichester, England: Wiley.

Safran, J. D., & Segal, Z. (1990). *Interpersonal processes in cognitive therapy.* New York, NY: Basic Books.

Sears, R. R. (1944). Experimental analysis of psychoanalytic phenomena. In J. Hunt (Ed.), *Personality and the behavior disorders* (pp. 191–206). New York, NY: Ronald Press.

Shoben, E. J. (1949). Psychotherapy as a problem in learning theory. *Psychological Bulletin, 46,* 366–396.

Stricker, G., & Gold, J. R. (1996). An assimilative model for psychodynamically oriented integrative psychotherapy. *Clinical Psychology: Science and Practice, 3,* 47–58.

Summers, F., & Barber, J. (2010). *Psychodynamic therapy.* New York, NY: Guilford Press.

Wachtel. P. L. (1977). *Psychoanalysis and behavior therapy: Toward an integration.* New York, NY: Basic Books.

Wachtel, P. L. (1997). *Psychoanalysis, behavior therapy, and the representational world.* Washington, DC: American Psychological Association.

Wachtel, P. L. (2011). *Inside the session.* Washington, DC: American Psychological Association.

Weinberger, J. (1993). Common factors in psychotherapy. In G. Stricker & J. R. Gold (Eds.), *Comprehensive handbook of psychotherapy integration* (pp. 43–58). New York, NY: Plenum Press.

Weiss, J. (1994). *How therapy works.* New York, NY: Basic Books.

CHAPTER 2

The Arrival of What's Always Been: Mindfulness Meets Psychoanalytic Psychotherapy

Michael Fayne, PhD

In his story "The Three Hermits," Tolstoy tells of an archbishop, sailing among remote islands to spread the Gospel, who comes upon an island inhabited solely by a trio of hermits who have never known other society, much less the word of God. He teaches these men to recite the Lord's Prayer and sets sail, quite pleased with himself at the great gift he has just bestowed. Soon after, he observes a glow on the horizon in the direction from whence he'd come, drawing steadily nearer to his ship. It is the three hermits, walking on water. They call out to him, innocently and apologetically, "We have forgotten your teaching, O servant of God....We cannot remember any of it. Please teach us again!" (Tolstoy, 2005, p. 213).

While engaged in bringing mindfulness to clinical work, let us not be like this self-satisfied archbishop. The fundamental aspects of mindfulness—present-moment awareness; a spirit of openness, curiosity, and acceptance toward what emerges from moment to moment; and a sense of kindness and compassion for self and others—have not been invented for psychoanalysis by newly minted "mindful" analysts. They are and always have been inherent in psychoanalytic work, albeit expressed in different ways by the giants of the field: from Freud's (1912) famous dictum on "evenly hovering attention" to Fromm's interest in Zen and his collaborations with pioneering Zen teacher D. T. Suzuki (Fromm, Suzuki, & DeMartino, 1960) to Horney's (1987) emphasis, in her later years, on the central role of "wholehearted attention" to Bion's (1970) iconic advice that an analyst abandon memory and desire when entering a session.

Buddhist teachers seek to disabuse their students of the sense that the "enlightenment" they pursue is some esoteric experience. Harada Sogaku, a Zen master in the nineteenth and twentieth centuries, is said to have remarked, as his death drew near, "For forty years I have been selling water by the river. Ho, ho! My labors have been wholly without merit!" (Kapleau, 2000, pp. 303–304)—a typically wry Zen expression of the fact that what he has to teach has been there in all of us all along, and is never not there. In a similar sense, it is important to emphasize that those attributes and attentional choices we call "mindfulness" are, for any experienced and devoted clinician, already present somehow in the self he or she brings to the work.

Nevertheless, at the entrance of many Zen monasteries one finds the Evening Gatha, a prayer making it clear that something far more important than water by the river is being offered, something not gratuitous at all: "Let me respectfully remind you that life and death are of supreme importance. Time passes swiftly by and opportunity is lost. Take heed. Each of us should strive to awaken. This night your days are diminished by one. Do not squander your life." And so, while the qualities we call "mindfulness" are to be found innately in psychoanalytic work, still there is particular value in considering them more closely.

Definitions

Jon Kabat-Zinn is one of the most influential figures of our time in promoting mindfulness-based approaches in health care, and he is the developer of the now universally taught meditation curriculum mindfulness-based stress reduction (MBSR). He has defined "mindfulness" as "moment-to-moment awareness" (1990), and later elaborated on that: "paying attention in a particular way: on purpose, in the present moment, and nonjudgmentally" (1994, p. 4). In my work, whether as meditation instructor or as analytic therapist engaged in helping a patient become more mindful, I have defined mindfulness for myself as the practice of attending closely to present-moment experience, in a spirit of openness and acceptance toward whatever that experience may be, and with an intention of kindness and compassion toward self and others.

Distinctions

Recalling the hermits, let us distinguish between being mindful, which is a way of living, and mindfulness practice, which refers to a set of methods employed to attain that way of living. A colleague describes a patient who, unfamiliar with any form of meditation, begins each session by sitting in silence for a few minutes, breathing, collecting himself, so that he can truly speak from where he is at the moment. One can be mindful without ever pursuing or even knowing about mindfulness practice.

There is also the distinction between introducing mindfulness practice to one's patients in the sense of guiding them toward a helpful, complementary adjunctive process and actually combining it with the in-session work of analytic psychotherapy. To have the same person be your psychoanalyst and meditation teacher might risk complicating and even undermining the pure experience of the meditation teaching, not to mention whatever complications develop within the analytic work because of such dual-role behavior. So the "mindful" analyst might bring mindfulness to her patients most seamlessly and deeply in ways other than teaching it herself. We generally find with our patients that the truly formative factors in their relationships, be they parental or therapeutic, are the nonverbalized, nonconceptualized internalizations of the other's deepest qualities. This is what shapes them the most. And so with mindfulness, it's probably not so much what the analyst says, it's who he is, how he lives, that is most influential. And one can bring mindfulness to bear very powerfully in a session—in ways to be discussed below—without the words "mindfulness" or "meditation" ever being uttered.

In other words, there are multiple levels on which the practice of mindfulness can arrive in the analytic field, beyond overt and directed introduction. The analyst can hold key aspects of mindfulness in conscious focus and, without formally introducing or discussing them, be inclined to put more focus on themes of present-moment awareness, acceptance, detachment, impermanence, and compassion as these present themselves in the session's material. But arguably, the most natural and common way of arrival is that the analyst's personal practice of meditation will be present in the sessions as it influences her own life, without her necessarily holding any conscious plan to bring this part of her personal quest into the work.

Mindfulness and Psychoanalytic Psychotherapy: A Kinship

It is by now solidly established (e.g., Safran, 2003; Rubin, 2013) that a profound common purpose is shared between the psychoanalytic exploration of the self and the sort of self-discovery that occurs in mindfulness practice, which Rubin (1999) has described as "experience-near self-investigation." Both are pursuits of aliveness, though "aliveness" may be conceived of differently. Both pursuits address the pain that comes from clinging too tightly to either outmoded or false ideas about the self. Both are, or can be, fearless and relentless in their examination of what it actually means to be "oneself." And neither is an intellectual pastime—on the contrary, both are to be pursued with the conviction and faith that they will lead to real, tangible self-transformation. Let us now consider this kinship as it manifests in the qualities of attention most often associated with mindfulness.

Attention to Present-Moment Experience

For decades, numerous major trends in psychoanalysis have been pointing toward the vital importance of the present moment in the session. These include the rise of the interpersonal and relational schools and the shift toward greater focus on in-session interaction, as opposed to a primary emphasis on genetic reconstruction; the shift in emphasis from the historical truth of childhood to the narrative truth that is meaningful now (Spence, 1984); and, of course, the vast and growing body of mother-infant research that has yielded much about the power of a moment in interaction (Stern et al., 1998; Stern, 2004). In these ways and others, our field has been evolving to emphasize the present moment, the aliveness of the here and now, as being at the heart of analytic work. The practitioner of mindfulness meditation immediately becomes aware of the astonishing extent to which his awareness is nearly always in a fantasized past or future or some other kind of nonexistent space. As James Joyce (1993) wrote of one of his characters, "Mr. Duffy...lived at a little distance from his body" (p. 104), so most of us live at a little distance from our lives. This nearly universal way of living "somewhere other" than the present is a mental habit so deeply entrenched that most people have no idea they are doing it or that their lives could be lived differently.

With many patients, one sees the tendency to rush from one thought to the next in a session, not pausing to really sit with any in-session experience, from the more obvious experience, such as an upsetting topic, to the more subtle and fleeting experience that might be reflected in a momentary facial expression or an inflection of the voice. With all, if they can be helped to slow down, be more present—even once—something new can take place. Let us first look at the situation of Ellen, in which the cultivation of present-moment awareness has played a small but significant role in an overwhelming life problem. A fifty-two-year-old single mother, Ellen lives with her twenty-four-year-old daughter, her only child, who is afflicted with severe borderline personality disorder. The young woman refuses any psychotherapy or the help a program could offer and lives in a state of edgy, rageful dependency upon her mother. Her daughter's inability to create an independent life for herself, along with Ellen's own scared, guilty paralysis toward taking any substantive actions, breaks this mother's heart on a daily basis.

I introduced Ellen to meditation, explaining it might help her feel more grounded in the face of her daughter's verbal attacks. In her desperation, she was immediately receptive, and I referred her to a meditation instructor with whom I work collaboratively. Ellen began a meditation practice and gradually increased her capacity to take each difficult interaction with her daughter more on its own terms—that is, she developed a greater ability to not load onto the moment the accumulated feelings of all the prior crises with her daughter or the crushing fantasies of what life might hold for her daughter in the future. She was more able simply to be with her daughter in that given moment. In so doing, Ellen grew less agitated, more compassionate, and more skillful in responding to her child. She also has become able to notice the calm or even pleasant moments she and her daughter occasionally share in between the outbursts and crises. I advise her, in these pleasant moments as well, to endeavor to remain simply in the present—to notice the sweet lilts in her daughter's voice and her poignant smile when the young woman is calm, to notice the welcome absence of tension throughout her own body at such times. Thus, through her growing capacity to simply be present, there comes a lifeline in what had once seemed unlivable.

A different introduction of mindfulness occurred with Kim, a thirty-six-year-old businesswoman who sought treatment because of a vague sense of frustration with her life. She kept herself very busy with work, online dating, and compulsive exercising. Her in-session manner mirrored this: poised on the edge of the seat, rattling off strings of rapid-fire dyspeptic anecdotes of her day, details flying by. Kim had studied anthropology in college but only occasionally mentioned her studies, in what seemed a vaguely dismissive way, as if to say it was time wasted. During a moment in which she was recounting a dinner with an old college friend, Kim laughed self-deprecatingly about one day "changing the world through anthropology." From this, she moved on to talk in her usual quick, weary manner about a date.

I believe my meditation practice helps me, sometimes, to sit in greater inner stillness with a patient than I otherwise would. In that stillness, I sensed something in the way she'd made the remark, and said, "I don't think you were joking about changing the world." Kim looked at me, surprised, in mid-anecdote, and then nodded. We sat. After a moment, she resumed rehashing the date, and I said, "Wait. Let's not rush away from that. What about the wish to change the world?" After a pause, she began to tell me that her desire after college had been to go to Africa with the Peace Corps and, beyond that, to create a program to reunite families of war refugees there. She remarked without particular feeling that this dream had "slipped away." I thought I could relate this lack of following her desires to the chronic parental ambivalence she had internalized growing up. That would make sense, but would be a familiar, non-alive exchange. I said instead, "Can we just sit with that, with that sense that it slipped away?" And we sat in silence—new ground for us. After a few moments, she said, in a more deliberate and reflective manner than usual, "It slipped away because I always try to be what I think other people want me to be." I present this vignette as an example of movement toward present-moment awareness in a session, of trying to slow down the stream of content and just sit, just be. Something new and unexpected can emerge in such a moment of just-sitting, without the word "mindfulness" being said or thought by either party.

A Spirit of Acceptance, Openness, Curiosity

As stated above, Freud prioritized his method of "evenly-suspended attention" (1912, p. 111), advising his followers to give "*impartial* attention to everything there is to observe" (1909, p. 23, italics added). Freud here sounds much like he is prescribing the fundamental Buddhist method of bringing "bare attention" to experience, a way of being in life that "simply *sees* what is right there and does not add any comment, any interpretation, any judgment, any conclusion. It just *sees*" (Merton, 1968, p. 53, italics in original). Freud cautioned that if the analyst listens without this "evenly-suspended" quality, "there is the danger of never finding anything but what is already known" (1912, pp. 111–112). From Wendell Berry (1987), whose poetry is often cited in mindfulness training, comes "To Know the Dark," echoing both those words and Bion's (1970) emptiness of memory and desire:

> To go into the dark with a light is to know the light.
> To know the dark, go dark. Go without sight,
> and find that the dark, too, blooms and sings,
> and is traveled by dark feet and dark wings.

From many perspectives comes the idea that true insight and self-understanding can grow only if one begins by accepting experience unconditionally and unflinchingly. In this same way, analytic work will be truly alive to the extent that both parties are accepting, curious, open to whatever comes up. It is perhaps a desire for a lost sense in the work of truly bare and evenly hovering attention, and a desire for the spontaneity and aliveness that would be found in "going without sight" and entering "without memory or desire," that now fuels many analysts' interest in mindfulness practice.

More than other modalities, analytic work has an innately welcoming stance toward symptoms and other expressions of the patient's conflicts. They are often regarded not as problems to be eradicated but as essential information that might be pointing toward a deeper truth. Two core analytic developments—the emergence of negative transference and regression in service of the ego—can be painful, even frightening, for both parties, but are to be met with acceptance, openness, and curiosity on the analyst's part so that deeper understanding can be pursued. Relatedly, the analyst is called upon to tolerate, really to embrace with curiosity, the often profoundly disturbing experience of being "the bad object" in this intimate and vulnerable relationship. This includes sitting with the ambiguity surrounding the degree to which the patient's bitter complaints are simply a function of psychopathology or might actually be based in truth. At one point or another, every analyst has been in a clinical mess in which the only choice is to sit with confusion and doubt and to simply look more deeply into the nature of the thing. In such moments, the powerful and nonconceptual focus of mindfulness practice offers a way to do that which is outside of any theoretical cul-de-sac, beyond even any verbal construction of the problem, and therefore can sometimes yield a genuine solution. The analytic relationship, more than any other type of treatment, fosters and encourages the patient's exploration of the *totality* of himself. A basic working definition of healing, from an analytic perspective, has to do with healing of splits in the self, with the patient's growing ability to acknowledge disowned feelings and aspects of himself. Sara Weber (personal communication, 2013) states that the most powerful aspect of analysis is "to accept, but *really* accept, and feel compassion for, the patient's—and your own—darkest, ugliest qualities." She believes that through the practice of meditation, an analyst can achieve "a deeper acceptance, a neutrality that is somehow bigger and can embrace more. Meditation expands *what* you can be neutral about."

Weber (2003), applying Ghent's concept of surrender (1990), has also written of the analyst's "surrender" to the process, a word that connotes an experience of greater vulnerability than simply acceptance. You can accept many things, including a slice of pie handed to you, but you only *surrender* to something larger than you, stronger than you, perhaps frightening and irresistible. You truly surrender when nothing else works. There are many ways by which you can arrive at that juncture —where nothing works and all you have is your failure to fix "it"—with a patient. To focus on just one of these, sooner or later, we all have someone in our practice about whom we cannot escape a feeling of hopelessness—that they will ever find employment, love, any semblance of peace of mind. One such person for me has been David, a painter, whose earliest years were characterized by severe neglect, leaving him with a crippling, angry rigidity toward life. David is, in fact, gifted with pen and brush but has not been able to eke out a living with his art, I believe, because of its shocking, off-putting darkness and because of his furious refusal to consider any tailoring of his work to make it more accessible. As a result, he lives on the edge of homelessness. But every approach I make regarding less nihilistic artwork, other types of jobs, and so on is met with a cold, seething glare and the shutdown of dialogue. I often have the sickening sense that nothing good will happen for David, that the discrepancies between his psychological resources, his rigid and outsized expectations, and what the world requires are all simply too great to be reconciled. So how to be of help to David, how even to face him, feeling this hopelessness? Sometimes no answer presents itself. But William Auerbach (personal communication, 2013) has commented that his meditation practice has helped him be more aware that, even with the most disturbed patients, "there is always, if you're open to seeing it, some wisdom, intelligence, adaptiveness"—that if one loosens one's grip on the tendency to reflexively create dichotomies of everything, including the dichotomy of healthy/sick, one sees even the most challenged lives "in a more hopeful light, one sees better the human dignity of those lives."

In Buddhist terms, we all—"healthy" therapist and "ill" patient alike—have the same "Buddha Nature," the same potential for a profoundly alive existence. Of course, versions of this transcendent insight can be found in many places. In the 1950s, a Catholic priest, Father Daniel Egan, known as "the Junkie Priest" for his devotion to working with then-shunned heroin addicts, explained himself thusly: "If we had the vision of faith we would see beneath every behavior, no matter how repulsive, and beneath every bodily appearance, no matter how dirty or deformed, a priceless dignity and value that makes all material facts and scientific technologies fade into insignificance" (as quoted in Pace, 2000). And so with David, at times I feel all I can offer is to sit with him and contemplate his presence in those terms, accept him and his innate goodness, and also accept my bafflement at how to help him. To do so I need to be grounded, as Father Egan indicates, in a kind of "faith"—for me not a religious idea, but a broader sense that, beyond David and me, it is somehow all right. Weber (2003) writes that her meditation practice gives her a sense of a "holding that exists beyond the person, the self, and especially the ego of both analyst and patient." Just sitting faithfully in this frame of mind with a tormented person might sound like doing nothing useful at all, but it can, at moments, lead to a softening, a sense of possibility, when it seems no other therapeutic strategy could.

In speaking of acceptance, a sense of detachment and letting go is implied. The other side of allowing a thought, feeling, or self-representation to simply exist within you is that you will not cling to it. So in meditation, in mindfulness-oriented psychotherapy, in life, we are always letting the moment go and embracing the next one. Recently, a patient, describing a well-worn tendency to think *Doesn't anybody in this world want me?* observed, "If I just let that thought really *be*, not fight with it at all, I immediately see the other side of the coin—that I have this friend, that friend, friends all over the place. And the whole thing seems different." As this man demonstrates, we can aspire to a flow where each thought, feeling, and self-state that arises is allowed to be, is even cherished, and therefore, each moment frees us for the next.

The Intention of Kindness and Compassion for Self and Others

The centrality of compassion and kindness in Buddhism is made clear in the Metta Sutra, in which the Buddha advises his followers to wish, "may all beings be at ease. Whatever living beings there may be, whether they are weak or strong, omitting none…the seen and the unseen, those living near and far away, those born and to-be-born, may all beings be at ease! Even as a mother protects with her life her child, her only child, so with a boundless heart should one cherish all living beings" (in Salzberg, 1995, pp. vii–viii).

Mindfulness practice is like a kind of soup, with several ingredients: present-moment awareness, acceptance, letting go or surrender to impermanence, inhabiting of the physical self, perhaps other ingredients as well. In this soup, compassion (or *metta*, in Buddhist terms) is the sweetening ingredient. Without it, mindfulness or Buddhism might seem an austere discipline, a self-absorbed quest for solitary enlightenment, an aloof detachment from the day-to-day world, or just, to bring back a dismissive term from an earlier generation, navel-gazing. But compassion elevates it into a practice of love and connectedness with others, a powerful and necessary antidote to what could otherwise be isolationism and escapism.

An analogous statement could be made about the role of compassion in psychoanalysis. Young-Eisendrath (2001) has observed, "Bald insight can increase a patient's self-condemnation.…Bland empathy can seem weak and useless in the face of strong self-conscious emotions, especially shame. *Only compassion for oneself* seems to me to allow the effects of the analysis to ripen into a transcendent function or dialogical space that can be used fairly reliably in everyday life" (italics added). In contrast to some analyses, in which people come to see clearly all their quirks and foibles but never truly stop devaluing themselves because of them, a core aspect of analytic work informed by mindfulness practice is to be kind to oneself, kind to each moment-of-self as it occurs. As with the inability to simply be in the present moment and the refusal to accept one's experience, the tendency to regard oneself harshly and unkindly functions unnoticed within the self as a compulsive, repetitive, habitual way of being.

James, an insurance broker, forty-two years old, has sought therapy for a general sense of failure in relationships. He is verbally gifted, with many incisive observations about his depressed mother; his father, who lives in grim, joyless recovery from alcoholism; and his dysfunctional siblings. He articulates how these circumstances have left him an angry and insecure adult, the most successful member of his family but single and with a trail of failed intimate relationships. James has occasional one-night stands but finds something in each woman to make her undesirable for anything beyond that; he is very attracted to a coworker but cannot approach her, because he feels too ashamed and would certainly "screw it up somehow." In the early weeks of treatment, James was friendly, even jovial, but his critical opinions about himself and others were often implicit in the session material. One morning, I arrived fifteen minutes late for our session, and found myself the object of his previously muted capacity for harsh judgment—I was irresponsible, arrogant, and uncaring—but almost simultaneously he called himself a whiner, an "asshole" for making a fuss about my lateness, and wondered who would want to arrive on time to see him anyway. This led us into a direct study of the scolding, dismissive nature of his unspoken perceptions of self and others. He chuckled ruefully and commented, "When it comes to my mind, I live by the sword and I die by the sword." Did he want to change that? Approaching the possibility of compassion was not simple with James. He was so steeped in self-criticism that he experienced the notion of being compassionate as a discouraging, infuriating impossibility. It felt like another form of criticism, this one disguised as a therapeutic suggestion. It seemed to help when I said he could just have the intention to someday be kinder and more compassionate with himself and others and let it be the case that right now he simply could not feel those things. Not surprisingly, he then felt free to have some experience of it. James has rejected my suggestion that he explore meditation, and I have chosen not to belabor it. But he has become more watchful of the dimension of compassion or its absence in his inner life, noticing the myriad choice points he has throughout the day to regard himself or another either kindly or critically, and there seems to be a slightly gentler quality in his assessment of it all.

The cultivation of compassion can be relevant to addressing disorders of self-esteem regulation. Falkenstrom (2003), seeking an integration of Buddhist and psychoanalytic thinking around the phenomenon of narcissism, casts it as "the clinging to (seeking or avoiding) images of the self that arise in the mind" (p. 1551). A person naturally experiences an endlessly fluctuating stream of self-images that can run the gamut from idealized to devalued, which would, to varying degrees, generate an endless flux of pleasurable and painful feelings. In Buddhist terms, narcissistic pathology is related to the extent to which one tries to cling to these images and thoughts, holding rigidly to the positive and trying to drive away the negative. Since this amounts to snatching and shoving impossibly at the flowing water of a river, it leads unavoidably to suffering and to a personality that becomes in some way distorted. Here again, happiness is related to how much one can accept the river's entire flow, surrender to it, and allow all self-images to freely come and go. As Falkenstrom (2003) writes, "The more tightly the individual holds on to images of the self, the more conflictual it gets if something 'not belonging' to the self-concept is experienced....The degree of narcissistic vulnerability is thus directly related to the degree of clinging to images and concepts of self" (p. 1559).

An analyst, regarding narcissistic phenomena in this way, might find ways to increase the patient's awareness of the ceaseless flow of these value-laden fantasies of the self and how he clings to them or turns away from them. Of course, it would be essential that the analyst be aware of his own moment-to-moment shifts in this regard, from seeing himself as effective clinician to hapless hack to just...himself. It would also be essential, especially given the vulnerable self-esteem of such patients, to approach this type of material with compassion and closely attuned attention. Falkenstrom (2003) expresses the heart of it: "Mindful attention to momentary experience needs to be a kind attention" (p. 1563). From this perspective, emotional health is closely related to a sense of the self's fluidity. A meditation practitioner watches up close the transience of all mental activity and gradually gains a lighter hold on the experience of self: an increased sense of it as not fixed, not separate from the ever-changing stream of all his other perceptions. As Mitchell (1988) observes, "The determination of emotional health as opposed to psychopathology...is not so much what you do and think as your attitude toward what you do and think, how seriously you take yourself" (p. 194). (Or, your self.) Nichol (2006) says of the benefits of meditation practice that someone who has an insight into the self's fluidity "is able to discover new things, to create, to enchant the world, and to live with more of a sense of awe" (p. 170). There is the thrilling possibility that mindfulness and psychotherapy together will help our patients, and ourselves, achieve this kind of life.

The Introductions of Mindfulness: Directly, Analytically, Wordlessly

Directly

In conversing with colleagues, it becomes clear that most analysts, the theory they espouse notwithstanding, do occasionally depart from a "blank screen," noninterventional position in practice, in one way or another. A colleague recounted to me that, after years of making little headway with a patient's relentless self-loathing, having exhausted every mainstream analytic approach, and realizing the patient lacked the wherewithal to undertake meditation herself, she (the analyst) finally guided the woman through a breathing meditation in a session. The result was that the patient immediately felt the benefit and (aided, perhaps, by her obsessive personality) went on to become a regular practitioner. Meditation helped the patient identify her hypercritical voice as a problem; it also allowed her to create some space between herself and these thoughts and feel a sense of compassion for herself. Her softening was marked by an outflowing of tears—the first she had shed in many years. When asked how she had decided to step outside a more traditional role, the analyst shrugged and said, "Because nothing else had worked."

A less charged way of directly introducing mindfulness is to refer the patient to some other way of learning it—books, videos, a center, a colleague who provides the instruction. Despite the classical analytic reluctance to intervene in the form of advice-giving, suggestions about other services and resources are frequently made. What the patient makes of this should be explored, however, no matter how simple and benign the interaction seems. What meanings has the patient given to this business, your suggestions about meditation? Does she experience it as something simply helpful? Or as a special gift, an exciting and gratifying participation in something personal to you? Or a disturbing sign that you lack confidence in your work and are calling in reinforcements? Or something else entirely?

Analytically

Most patients enter treatment unaware of how "unmindfully" they live. As Biancoli (2006) puts it, "At least in Western society the defense mechanisms against the here and now are unconscious and highly powerful" (p. 496). We are not talking about the Freudian unconscious here, but rather processes that exist alongside but outside of consciousness, mental habits so deeply ingrained that one engages in them compulsively and ceaselessly, without any awareness of doing so. But the analyst experienced in mindfulness practice will notice the patient's tendency to not be in the present moment, to not respond directly to experience but to react to it from within the distortion of one preconception or another, to be oblivious to bodily experience, to relentlessly judge himself and others, to refuse to accept unavoidable adversity, and to struggle against the reality of impermanence. Noticing these things, the analyst can look for opportunities to bring them more fully into the patient's line of vision. Therefore, an essential contribution of mindfulness to psychoanalytic therapy is the expansion of the patient's conscious understanding of these matters of non-mindfulness, which could be overlooked even in the close attention of more traditional work.

As one might approach the patient's defenses in a traditional analytic context, looking to first simply direct the patient's attention to their existence, so too can the analyst, when the moment is ripe, approach these non-mindful habits. Does the patient observe how he avoids what he is feeling right now? Does she notice how harsh and self-critical her thoughts tend to be? How does he feel when having a particular thought about himself, and does he want to hold on to it or push it away? As with any other kind of investigative or uncovering work in psychoanalytic treatment, there are considerations of timing, attunement, and a compassionate approach. Also essential is that the study of these patterns be as free as possible of any desire on the analyst's part to "make" the patient more mindful: just as any defense or symptom must be respected, the patient must feel free to not change in these ways.

Wordlessly

Words, words,

the Way is beyond language,

for in it there is no yesterday,

no today,

no tomorrow.

—Seng-T'san, Third Zen Patriarch, "Verses on the Faith Mind"

Let us now consider the psychoanalytic version of Zen's "wordless transmission." Much as the nutrients a mother consumes are transmitted through her to her nursing infant, we can expect the patient will somehow be affected by the analyst's meditation practice. What are the subtle changes one might find in an analyst's work by virtue of her practice? One would expect a natural way of being more entirely present, of not being slightly removed from experience by attaching to an intellectual construction or theoretical idea, what Rubin (2013) calls, "perceiving with an innocent mind, holding your favorite theory—wheher psychoanalytic or Buddhist—lightly as opposed to tightly" (Loc. 314–331). Not holding on to a theory so tightly would go hand in hand with not holding on to a self so tightly, whether it be one's clinical persona or one's self in a deeper sense. The analyst might be more cognizant of her physical body, more able to tune in to the somatic and embodied nature of the patient's experience. The analyst might be less gripped by various other motives—to reassure himself of his worth, to be valued by the patient, to retain the patient, and so on.

There is an openness, an ease toward life one hopes would be internalized by the patient over time. But the most important matter is the analyst's acceptance of self, of being able to sit—with ambiguity, with the patient's often-unsolvable pain, with a sense of inadequacy and anxiety, but with an acceptance of human shortcomings, too;

51

having a greater capacity to wait and not know. To just sit with what is painful is a profound, if wordless, communication to the patient.

Another unspoken transmission can occur with respect to one's basic attentiveness to life. William Auerbach (personal communication, 2013) describes the analyst's function of modeling for the patient a different way of receiving experience, of attending to the nuances of the present moment, whether it be sensory, affective, or communicative. In almost any moment, he says, one can select from the multiplicity of communications one bit—an inflection, a physical shift, an expression—and say, in effect, "Slow down; let's look more closely at that." Over a great deal of time, these "slow down; let's really look at that" moments can, we hope, effect a change in a patient's awareness—awareness not only of the contents of his experience, but of the very nature of how he lives that experience, that it is possible to linger and look more closely.

Finally, there is the transmission of fundamental compassion and respect for all. Auerbach (personal communication, 2013) says his practice has helped him be "more appreciative of human nature, less cynical—seeing not the basic pathology but the basic goodness in people." A corollary of this insight is a loosened attachment to the therapist-patient dichotomy and an understanding that, unlike some problems patients bring to us, when it comes to falling victim to mindless living, everyone's afflicted, whether on the couch or behind it.

Conclusion

I believe becoming more mindful would help anyone. There may be reasons to limit or adapt what we call "mindfulness" based on individuals' needs and capacities—shorter or more structured meditations, movement-based work, individualized instruction, or other modifications—but almost anyone will live better if she is more present in her life. How, though, to convey it? How to *effectively* facilitate it?

The variability with regard to patients' receptivity to mindfulness, however presented, is striking. This greater-lesser receptivity to coming into the here and now is a dimension of human functioning that might be of enormous significance, one for which we as yet have no language or concepts. I recently began working with Nicholas, a young man plagued by anxiety and not at all grounded in his body. In an early session, it arose naturally to tell him of mindfulness and suggest a book (which he immediately bought and read), and subsequently to refer him to an MBSR teacher. He is enthusiastic about it and feels helped, and it does not appear to be complicating the deepening of our work in therapy.

But there are many like Corinne, working a seventy-hour week in finance, supporting an alcoholic husband, declaring the situation "manageable," but not paying attention to the proliferation of symptoms and illnesses her body displays. She fills each session with a narrative about the travails of her exhausting job and seems unreachable with respect to anything about present-moment living. I have proffered mindfulness in numerous ways, and she nods her head while her eyes go elsewhere, and then she resumes the narrative. She seems so deeply submerged in an unquestioned world of constant external activity that raising mindfulness with her has the quality of an attempt at proselytizing. With Corinne and some, I often feel they will only come to an interest in mindfulness as a result of their own quests, however long that may take, and that it does represent a deep turning toward an approach to life, a profound choice of priority that cannot be unilaterally created by anything I do. But who knows? Most patients fall between those extremes. With all, I do my work, watch the flow of my own desires and thoughts about what is or what should be taking place between me and this person in front of me, and wait for the opportunities that come in the fullness of time.

References

Berry, W. (1987). *The collected poems, 1957–1982*. San Francisco, CA: North Point.

Biancoli, R. (2006). Questions of technique following the psychoanalytic perspective of Erich Fromm. *Journal of the American Academy of Psychoanalysis and Dynamic Psychiatry, 34*(3), 489–504.

Bion, W. (1970). *Attention and interpretation*. Northvale, NJ: Aronson.

Cooper, P. C. (1999). Buddhist meditation and countertransference: A case study. *American Journal of Psychoanalysis, 59*, 71–85.

Falkenstrom, F. (2003). A Buddhist contribution to the psychoanalytic psychology of self. *International Journal of Psychoanalysis, 84*, 1551–1568.

Freud, S. (1909). Analysis of a phobia in a five-year-old boy. In J. Strachey (Ed. & Trans.), *The standard edition of the complete psychological works of Sigmund Freud* (Vol. 10, pp. 3–149). London, England: Hogarth Press.

Freud, S. (1912). Recommendations to physicians practicing psychoanalysis. In J. Strachey (Ed. & Trans.), *The standard edition of the complete psychological works of Sigmund Freud* (Vol. 12, pp. 109–120). London, England: Hogarth.

Fromm, E., Suzuki, D. T., & DeMartino, R. (1960). *Zen Buddhism and psychoanalysis.* New York, NY: Grove.

Ghent, E. (1990). Masochism, submission, surrender: Masochism as a perversion of surrender. *Contemporary Psychoanalysis, 26,* 108–136.

Horney, K. (1987). *Final lectures.* New York, NY: W. W. Norton.

Joyce, J. (1993). A painful case. In *Dubliners.* New York, NY: Penguin Books.

Kabat-Zinn, J. (1990). *Full catastrophe living: Using the wisdom of your body and mind to face stress, pain, and illness.* New York, NY: Bantam Doubleday Dell.

Kabat-Zinn, J. (1994). *Wherever you go, there you are: Mindfulness meditation in everyday life.* New York, NY: Hyperion.

Kapleau, P. (2000). *The Three pillars of zen: Teaching, practice, and enlightenment.* New York, NY: Anchor Books.

Merton, T. (1968). *Zen and the birds of appetite.* New York, NY: New Directions.

Mitchell, S. A. (1988). *Relational concepts in psychoanalysis: An integration.* Cambridge, MA: Harvard University Press.

Nichol, D. (2006). Buddhism and psychoanalysis: A personal reflection. *American Journal of Psychoanalysis, 66,* 157–172.

Pace, E. (2000, February 13). Daniel Egan, 84, drug fighter known as 'Junkie Priest,' dies. *The New York Times.* Retrieved from http://www.nytimes.com

Rubin, J. B. (1999). Close encounters of a new kind: Toward an integration of psychoanalysis and Buddhism. *American Journal of Psychoanalysis, 59,* 5–24.

Rubin, J. B. (2013). *Meditative psychotherapy: The marriage of east and west.* [Kindle Edition]: Abiding Change Press.

Safran, J. D. (2003). *Psychoanalysis and Buddhism: An unfolding dialogue.* Somerville, MA: Wisdom.

Salzberg, S. (1995). *Lovingkindness: The revolutionary art of happiness.* Boston, MA: Shambhala.

Spence, D. P. (1984). *Narrative truth and historical truth: Meaning and interpretation in psychoanalysis.* New York, NY: W. W. Norton.

Stern, D. N. (2004). *The present moment in psychotherapy and everyday life.* New York, NY: W. W. Norton.

Stern, D. N., Sander, L. W., Nahum, J. P., Harrison, A. M., Lyons-Ruth, K., Morgan, A. C., & Tronick, E. Z. (1998). Non-interpretive mechanisms in psychoanalytic therapy: The "something more" than interpretation. *International Journal of Psychoanalysis, 79,* 903–921.

Tolstoy, L. (2005). The three hermits. In *Master and man and other stories.* London, England: Penguin Books.

Weber, S. L. (2003). An analyst's surrender. In J. D. Safran (Ed.), *Psychoanalysis and Buddhism: An unfolding dialogue* (pp. 169–197). Somerville, MA: Wisdom.

Young-Eisendrath, P. (2001). When the fruit ripens: Alleviating suffering and increasing compassion as goals of clinical psychoanalysis. *Psychoanalytic Quarterly, 70,* 265–285.

CHAPTER 3

Suffering and the End of Suffering: Conundrum and Cure in Psychoanalysis and Buddhism

Delia Kostner, PhD

There are many ways and means of practicing psychotherapy. All that lead to recovery are good.

—Sigmund Freud, "On Psychotherapy," 1904, p. 259

Both formerly and now, it is only dukkha I describe and the end of dukkha.

—The Buddha, *Samyutta Nikaya* 22.86
(trans. John Peacock)

Western society increasingly sees human suffering as grossly abnormal and typically generated from outside sources; it is a state to be eliminated as soon as possible. We vigorously seek external remedies, such as medications, a variety of addictions, and transient external pleasures as cures for our unhappiness, over and above insight and understanding. These solutions to suffering are short lived, but we return time and time again to such supposed sources of happiness, as if they could possibly provide us with a stable state of well-being. Grasping at such remedies, however, simply increases our experience of suffering. Such a conundrum was also present at the time of the historical Buddha, and it was to this problem of human suffering that he devoted himself entirely for the final forty-five years of his life.

Over 2400 years ago,[1] Siddhartha Gautama Buddha, through a detailed investigation of his own mental process, devised a complex psychological understanding of the human condition, as well as a means of liberation from the ubiquity of human suffering. He did this without positing the intervention of deities and concerned himself not at all with philosophical and metaphysical investigations. His was an infinitely practical concern: understanding suffering and the end of suffering. During the last three decades, many aspects of Buddhist thought have infiltrated modern Western psychology. Buddhism is an empirical path based on the inescapable fact of human suffering. Essentially, Buddhism is a psychology of mind (e.g., Olendzki, 2010; Peacock, 2008), which proposes the possibility of overcoming suffering through one's own introspection and agency. This alone makes Buddhism quite appealing to Western psychologists.

This chapter will explore some of the similarities between Buddhism and contemporary Western psychotherapy, with an emphasis on psychoanalytic theory and practice. It will emphasize the way each perspective approaches the problem of human suffering and the recommendations each gives for how suffering can be overcome. How we view suffering determines, to some extent, how we propose to deal with it and whether or not we believe it can be surmounted. The psychoanalytic and Buddhist views of suffering are similar, but not the same; and while the techniques elucidated in both perspectives overlap considerably, they are not aimed at the same ends. These differences and their clinical meaning will also be addressed. In addition, case material will be presented in order to illuminate the complex, efficacious interaction of both meditation and psychoanalysis. But first, the long and occasionally conflicted history of the interface between psychoanalysis and Buddhism will be addressed.

---

1   The dates of the Buddha's birth and death are still debated; modern scholarship places his death later than originally thought, around 400 BCE (Gombrich, 2009).

Suffering in Buddhism

Birth is dukkha, aging is dukkha, sickness is dukkha, death is dukkha; encountering what is not dear is dukkha; not getting what one wants is dukkha; in brief these five bundles of clinging are dukkha.

—The First Discourse, *Dhammacakkapavata Sutta*
(trans. Stephen Batchelor)

The Pali word "dukkha" has most commonly been translated as "suffering." This translation is somewhat misleading, however. Suffering implies a response to the major traumatic events in life and evokes the experience of intense pain and angst. While the term encompasses the more dramatic renditions of suffering, "dukkha" also points to the more subtle, ubiquitous phenomena of daily life. Other translations of dukkha include "anguish," "unsatisfactoriness" (Peacock, 2008), "stress," "disturbance," "irritation," "dejection," "worry," "despair," "fear" (Story, 1973), "dissonance," and so on. No single word captures its essence entirely. The word dukkha derives from a compound of two Pali words that can be literally translated as "dirty space" or "bad space" (Peacock, 2008). It refers metaphorically to the axel of a wheel packed with dirt and grit, allowing it to work only with a constant grating and irritating inefficiency. Life is generally unsatisfactory (Gombrich, 2009), and our psychological distress is the result of the vicissitudes of life (Sucitto, 2010). This is due to the fact that everything is in flux, but we want our lives to be stable, consistent, and dependable. Since such stability can never be attained, everything falls short of lasting satisfaction. Dukkha is a mental or psychological phenomenon; it describes the anguish we bring upon ourselves. The actual experience of pain is inevitable. The sources are not, in themselves, transcendable. On the other hand, the psychological and pathological distress we engender by seeking and grasping at stability in a constantly changing world of phenomena is entirely curable.

Ennobling Truths

The most radical of the Buddha's teachings is that not only can dukkha cease, but that it can be stopped through our own personal insight. The Buddha's very first teaching dealt entirely with dukkha and his newfound insights into its causes, its cessation, and the path to its cessation. This *sutta*, "discourse," contains the description of the famous Four Noble Truths, which is foundational for all schools of Buddhism and is elaborated on or reiterated in multiple places throughout the Pali Canon. Buddhist scholar John Peacock greatly prefers the term "ennobling truth" over "noble truth," as this emphasizes the process of investigation; "you are not ennobled by 'truths,'" he writes, "you are ennobled by investigating truth" (2012a, p. 5; see also Peacock, 2008). These truths are often presented in the form of a medical metaphor. The disease is dukkha (the first ennobling truth). It has a cause: *tanha*, "craving" (the second ennobling truth). There is a cure: the elimination of craving (the third ennobling truth); and there is a treatment leading to the cure, the ennobling eightfold path (the forth ennobling truth).

THE FIRST ENNOBLING TRUTH

The first ennobling truth is simply the truth of suffering. Dukkha is impersonal and universal. Although it is likely to originate in the external realities of life, such as old age, illness, and death, it points entirely to the internal experience. We are the creators of our own suffering but are also uncannily expert at denying its existence. According to Ajahn Sucitto (2010), the Buddha, "is not implying that life is miserable; most things have a mix of pleasure and pain and neutrality in them. It's just that human experience is characterized by a constant restless quality of disquiet" (p. 34). Additionally, happiness can also be a source of suffering, given our tendency to cling to pleasurable states, which are impermanent, fleeting, and ultimately insubstantial.

Types of Suffering. There are three types of dukkha identified in the Pali Canon. *Dukkha-dukkha* describes ordinary dukkha, such as physical pain, injury, aging, and death, and encompasses all the things that occur in the physical body that give rise to distress. *Viparinama-dukkha* refers to the suffering that arises through confrontation with change.

Finally, *sankhara-dukkha* is constructed, conditioned, or compounded dukkha (Peacock, 2008). It has to do with the basic unsatisfactoriness of life because of our need to cling to the idea of permanence in a world where everything is changing. A hallmark of the problem with the fact of impermanence is that we persist in seeing the psychological and physical self as substantive, immutable, and continuous across time and space. This reification of the self gets us into a huge amount of trouble, in terms of dukkha. In reality, the self and its objects have no inherent permanence and are as much momentary construc-tions—as will be addressed below—as are all objects in the world (Engler, 2003). It is the attempt to seize and fix that which is inher-ently changeable that leads to frustration and despair.

Humans believe that suffering can be overcome, but we are utterly confused as to how this can happen. We impulsively grasp at pleasure and avoid that which causes pain in a misguided belief that we can maintain a pleasurable homeostasis. Yet the cessation of suffering is not rooted in any external phenomenon. It is the elaborate ways in which we turn away from pain through psychological defenses that lead to the increase and elaboration of pain.

THE SECOND ENNOBLING TRUTH

The second ennobling truth points to the source of dukkha: the human tendency to crave. The Pali word for "craving" is "tanha," commonly translated as "thirst"; it describes the state of endless want or desire. Craving is driven by desire and is a pathological state, not to be confused with the basic life drive, known as "libido" in common psychoanalytic parlance. When we grasp at pleasure, resist unpleas-antness, or misapprehend the nature of reality, dukkha is the outcome. We are deluded into believing that by seeking sensual pleasures, we can achieve and maintain a pleasurable state of being. It is a view of reality shaped and driven by internal beliefs and wishful fantasies, and it is mostly unconscious. Seeing things as they really are means letting go of this delusion, this desire for things to be other than they are. Ironically, it is our desire to eliminate suffering that initiates the problem of dukkha. The pursuit of pleasure is never ending, as it is ultimately ephemeral. Avoiding what is not pleasurable is similarly futile, and such experiential avoidance can ultimately result in increased misery.

Kama-tanha **and Freud's Pleasure Principle.** Tanha is reflexive, compulsive, and repetitive. From a psychoanalytic perspective, it is a manifestation of the repetition compulsion, an irrational and unconsciously driven tendency to re-create events that lead to the same distress. Traditionally, tanha is thought of as threefold. The first form of craving, "kama-tanha," or "sense craving," is the easiest to understand. It represents the endless craving for sensual stimulation (Peacock, 2008; Ajahn Sucitto, 2010). This is almost an exact description of Freud's pleasure principle. We seek pleasure and avoid that which is unpleasant. At its most pathological, this form of craving manifests as compulsive overeating, spending, or sexual behavior; but it is also present on a subtler, less obviously self-destructive level in the myriad of ways we lean into the experience of pleasant sounds, tastes, and sensations. Psychoanalytic thought would not hold such experience as problematic unless extremely distorted. We simply seek pleasure; it is a biological imperative. However, the Buddha understood such pleasure seeking as problematic precisely because that craving can never be fully satisfied and is based on the delusion that we can find an everlasting source of pleasurable experience.

Bhava-tanha **and the Development of the Self.** The second form of craving, "bhava-tanha," refers literally to the craving for becoming. It is the craving for an immutable sense of self. We hold tight to our sense of self, seeing it as a core that is unchangeable and continuous and responsible for guiding our activity. Buddhism suggests that our sense of self, like everything else in the world, is constructed, multiply determined, and in flux. It is not that we have no self in the Western psychological sense, of course. The ability to work, delay gratification, think logically, contain affect and impulses, organize oneself, and generally function appropriately in the world are necessary preconditions for adult life in general. These are all important aspects of the healthy psychological self (Aronson, 2004). It is simply that a solid, unalterable self, which is a guiding force in creating our experience, is not a reality from a Buddhist perspective; to continually and reflexively grasp at such a self-definition is bound to end in dukkha.

Vibhava-tanha **and Freud's Death Instinct.** The final form of craving is "vibhava-tanha," or desire for not being, for not becoming. This concept is not well elucidated in the literature but appears to refer to self-destructive, suicidal, and aggressive tendencies. It has some parallels with Freud's concept of the death instinct, which he posited as the counterpart of the life instinct in order to explain the problem of aggression and self-destructive tendencies, as well as war and the universal tendency to repeat old traumas from childhood. Vibhava-tanha describes the wish to opt out of the angst and complexity of life. It can also be seen in drug and alcohol abuse and the use of self-injurious behavior.

THE THIRD ENNOBLING TRUTH

The third ennobling truth states that there is a treatment for dukkha. "The end of dukkha is a reality" (Peacock, 2012a), and the treatment is not simply palliative. To overcome dukkha one must undermine craving. So how do we let go of craving? Suppression or repression is not advisable and, psychologically speaking, will not work anyway. One is instructed instead to become aware of craving as it arises in consciousness. But noticing the arising of craving can be extremely arduous and complicated, because our reflective defensive responses protect us from awareness of it before it even reaches consciousness. This is a place where psychoanalytically based treatments can interact most effectively with Buddhist practice, as will be addressed later. As we know, insight is often difficult to come by, and insight alone is not always sufficient for eliciting change. The Buddha thus also proposed a distinctly behavioral and environmental solution to the problem of craving. In Buddhist practice, one creates the conditions under which craving will not arise. Eventually, seeing dukkha clearly means seeing that there is really no pleasure in tanha, the effects of which keep us stuck in endless rounds of unhappiness and frustration.

THE FOURTH ENNOBLING TRUTH

The path or treatment for dukkha is the ennobling eightfold path. This path is comprised of eight interconnected factors and behaviors, which consist of ethical factors, mind cultivation, and the development of wisdom. These eight factors are right understanding, right thought, right speech, right action, right livelihood, right effort, right concentration, and right mindfulness. Western psychologies have appropriated only the concept of mindfulness into their treatment approaches. Acceptance and commitment therapy (ACT), however, incorporates therapeutic processes related to speech, action, livelihood, and effort (i.e., change or commitment processes) in addition to perspectives on concentration and mindfulness (i.e., acceptance processes).

Mindfulness and Suffering

The universal, transdiagnostic insight gained from engaging in a psychological perspective based on the four ennobling truths is that suffering can be overcome. To stop craving, one must learn to notice it arising, and notice too its self-defeating nature, impermanence, and insubstantiality. However, we need a special technology for doing this, a perspective from which to examine the nature and contents of the mind and observe what about our habitual tendencies keep us melded with our dukkha.

In Buddhism, the mind is seen as a process, not a thing, and is thus malleable and amenable to change (Olendzki, 2012b). We construct experience moment by moment. Since experience is constructed, the causes of suffering can be observed, and the reflexive response of grasping and craving can be caught as it arises in consciousness. This is the essence of mindfulness. Such "experience-near" examination of phenomena does not happen easily in the course of ordinary human experience, and it requires an atypical approach to slowing down and viewing the nature and workings of our minds. The Buddha delineated a system by which the mind could be comprehended and used as a means of understanding the very nature of reality, a system that can thereby help us transcend not just neurotic or pathological suffering but also the experience of suffering in its entirety. Mindfulness meditation is the primary technology for freeing one from the grip of dukkha.

Mindfulness and Insight

In the formal practice of insight meditation, we gradually come to see our grasping and craving as it arises, and we come to understand our tendency to reify our thoughts as actual "things." We learn that we can look at these thoughts and feelings unflinchingly and then unhook from them. Like psychoanalysis and psychodynamic psychotherapies, Buddhism is also concerned with the unconscious. In both traditions, that which lies outside of consciousness is seen as also giving rise to behavior and convictions, which become the source of suffering. The goal of uncovering what is unconscious—sometimes referred to as "latent dispositional tendencies" in Buddhist thought—is to understand its relationship to dukkha and to give rise to a new, healthier way of being in the world. According to Olendzki (2012b), through mindfulness meditation, we come to "reshape the automatic, unconscious structures of the mind....Aspects of experience to which we were entirely blind come into view, and the ability to choose one course of action over another becomes strengthened" (p. 125). This method is the ultimate one for the study of thoughts and emotions, but it is done alone, seated on a cushion. And, as will be described below, there are potential psychological pitfalls inherent in this practice and solitude, which can impede spiritual as well as psychological progress.

Psychoanalytic Views of Suffering

No doubt fate would find it easier than I do to relieve you of your illness. But you will be able to convince yourself that much will be gained if we succeed in transforming your hysterical misery into common unhappiness. With a mental life that has been restored to health you will be better armed against that unhappiness (Freud, 1893, p. 305).

It was Freud's belief that a successful psychoanalytic treatment resulted in a vestigial amount of dukkha, but it also empowered the individual with the tools with which to cope with these remnants. This belief is pervasive, I believe, in all forms of Western psychotherapy. Originally, Freud's aim was to develop a theory of mind broad enough to encompass the vicissitudes of human suffering. His project for a science of psychoanalysis saw its purpose as twofold: psychoanalysis as a science of mind, and psychoanalysis as a tool to help individuals overcome illness and suffering. His biologically grounded drive theory formed the foundation of classical psychoanalysis. From this perspective, individuals are seen as essentially hardwired to pursue pleasure and avoid pain. Our instinctual drives, both sexual and aggressive, are defining and essential and, as Freud eventually concluded, immutable. His was essentially a hedonic theory of motivation. We are driven to seek gratification of our instinctual drives through discharging them in our environment. These instincts or drives are essentially asocial. Through the course of development, the ego (here referring to the series of functions by which we adapt to our environment and maintain healthy functioning, not the narcissistic aspect of "ego" which is the meaning of this term in Buddhist literature) arises out of the murk of the id and wrestles the individual into adapting to the constraints of society. Some compromise is necessary, however, since these drives seek discharge and are often antithetical to the societal needs. Maximizing satisfaction while repressing the antisocial underpinnings of our instinctual forces becomes the psychic balancing act of all humans. Symptoms and compulsive behaviors result when the compromise is balanced too much on the side of repression.

From a psychoanalytic perspective, ignorance is unconsciously driven, but it is a blindness born from early conflicts and traumas believed too painful to bear in consciousness. Finding those conflicts and working through them in all of their manifestations is what frees the individual from their grip. Bringing the repressed into consciousness is one of the most important aims of classical psychoanalytic treatment. According to this view of human nature, suffering could be alleviated by making the repressed conscious though accurate and well-timed interpretation by a skilled therapist and by working through the nuance of its meaning. But suffering cannot be completely ameliorated.

Freud understood the limitations of his method: "The aim of treatment will never be anything else but the practical recovery of the patient, the restoration of his ability to lead an active life and of his capacity for enjoyment" (Freud, 1904, p. 253). He ultimately concluded, like the Buddha, that human beings are unable to live life fully in accordance to the pleasure principle. However, Freud's was a fundamentally tragic view of the world, not an insight that leads to psychological freedom. He saw a natural limit to the overcoming of suffering and pain; at best, we forge a compromise between id and reality, between the instincts and the pressures from society to conform and modify our desires for gratification. "Normal" functioning thus becomes a matter of "normal unhappiness." The compromise one achieves is adaptive, but freedom from suffering is never absolute. This is probably the most fundamental difference between Buddhism and early classical psychoanalysis.

Relational and Intersubjective Approaches to Psychoanalysis

Like Buddhism, psychoanalysis is far from a unitary construct. There have been multiple innovations in theory and technique since its inception. The most important current shift in psychoanalysis is toward relationality and intersubjectivity (Mitchell, 2000). People are seen not so much as motivated by immutable, biologically based drives, but by a complex network of relationships, beginning with the earliest attachments. Technically speaking, the relational approach represents a reaction against the notion of the analyst as the revealed source of knowledge, as the individual in the room who possesses the "truth" about the patient. From this perspective, suffering does not arise from conflict between drives and defenses, but from the failure to adequately establish and sustain relationships with others (Mitchell & Black, 1995).

A relational view of suffering sees it as constructed within an ongoing relational matrix. These approaches to psychoanalysis move away from genetic interpretations and uncovering of areas of psychic conflict and toward a more interpersonal understanding of our human experiences. Strikingly similar to the Buddhist notion that reality is constructed, the mind is also seen here as a *process*; it does not exist independent of other minds or the context in which it is embedded, and meaning is co-constructed through interactions with other minds. Suffering arises out of a suboptimal construction of the individual's experience, one that is overly impacted by early and ongoing conflictual relationships (Renik, 2007). The tendency toward re-creating early relational patterns is what gives rise to suffering in contemporary life. These patterns of relating arise in the consulting room and are the material with which the psychoanalyst and patient work in the here and now.

The primary vehicle of change in all forms of psychoanalytic treatment is the relationship between analyst and patient, and it is through this vehicle that insight and understanding are acquired

(Gabbard & Westen, 2003). From this perspective, change arises through the experience of a new type of relationship with the analyst. Reality is cocreated, as opposed to being understood via the vehicle of interpretations aimed at understanding hidden truths about the self. Here-and-now interactions are the focus of treatment, although reconstruction and understanding of personal experience is not de-emphasized (Greenberg, 2007).

By disconnecting the genesis of psychic pain and suffering from biologically rooted drives, the individual is seen as possessing a far broader opportunity to effect real change and release from suffering, which parallels Buddhist thought. Relational psychoanalysis, however, also stops short of positing a complete overcoming of dukkha.

Psychoanalytic Attention and Neutrality

The similarity between attention in psychoanalysis and in mindfulness meditation is quite striking (Epstein, 1988) and warrants discussion. Like Buddhism, psychoanalysis focuses on self-exploration and self-understanding, seeing for oneself what causes suffering. The "fundamental rule" of free association and the analyst's evenly suspended attention form the core of traditional psychoanalytic process. We ask the patient to give up conscious control over the presentation of his or her inner world. The patient is told to say whatever comes to mind, without censure. For this to occur, the analyst must maintain genuine open neutrality, a listening stance without judgment or goal, or else the patient will not risk venturing into the recesses of his or her mind and sharing whatever comes up with the analyst. In other words, the analyst "should simply listen, and not bother about whether he is keeping anything in mind" (Freud, 1912, p. 111).

Neutrality implies an openness, not siding with one side or another in the patient's internal process of bringing his or her conflicts to light (Hoffer, 2010). It is a crucial stance, with interesting parallels in the Buddhist concept of equanimity. This equanimity on the part of the analyst allows the true meaning of the conflict to manifest in the minds of the psychoanalyst and patient. From a relational perspective, however, this process is seen as more bidirectional. This process results in a form of exposure, which allows a more conscious working through of the core conflicts (see Wachtel, 2008). According to Hoffer (2010), neutrality means the analyst is neutral in terms of outcome, not indifferent to the patient's conflicts. The goal is providing an optimal environment for the free exploration of patients' conflicts without injecting the analyst's version of their resolution or foreclosing on their experience.

The form of attention emphasized in psychoanalysis has obvious parallels with *vipassana* meditation. Meditation requires a similar sort of evenly hovering attention and neutrality on the part of the meditator. In some ways, as meditators, we are taking on the role of both analyst and analysand: we are freely associating, which is precisely what begins to take place when we consciously decide not to control what is going on in our minds; and we are exercising a form of evenly hovering attention, which is what is required if one is to neutrally assess or simply note the contents of the mind. In meditation, however, we do not chase the contents or associations into every possible nook and cranny of our psyches in order to seek out the unconscious meaning of what arises. That type of exploration is most effective in the presence of another person. The exploration of the contents of our consciousness, the intensely personal process of uncovering and understanding the ways in which we have come to view personal conflicts, is not at all the goal in meditation.

Of course, analysis of thoughts can occur in meditation, especially if we are analytically inclined. But the ultimate goal of meditation is a step deeper than merely understanding personal conflicts. By attending to the *process* of what arises in consciousness, by noting its arising and falling away, we come to understand the constructed nature of our self-view and of all phenomena. The root causes of dukkha can be observed as we note the arising of desire and our tendency to reify experience. As Engler (2003) notes, "mindfulness leads to insight into the nature of all representations of self and reality as constructions only and as ungraspable in any real or definitive sense" (p. 68).

When all is going well, meditation has a positive impact on psychic functioning. It can strengthen adaptation, increase the ability to tolerate difficult affects, improve attention and concentration, and enhance psychological flexibility. But at times, particularly in the early stages of meditation practice or during times of personal turmoil, sitting with what arises is especially difficult. Once the mind is quiet, ego functions relax, and one involuntarily accesses previously repudiated aspects of experience (see Epstein, 1988, 1990). Meditation, like psychoanalysis, lifts the repressive barrier and allows access to that which we typically control by distraction, suppression, repression, and all the other defensive maneuvers we employ. To meet all content of mind in a nonjudgmental and equanimous manner requires a level of sustained maturity and a capacity for managing strong emotion and disturbing content. Such maturity is not always accessible to the meditator. On the other hand, when managed by a skilled therapist, the personal insights, psychological conflicts, and blocks that arise in the context of meditation practice can serve to further therapeutic gains.

Clinical Application

The following composite case illustrates the use of psychoanalysis and mindfulness meditation in tandem in assisting with the tolerance of strong, disavowed affect and in increasing insight into personal psychodynamics. Mary, a woman in her mid-thirties, entered treatment in order to address a lifelong struggle with anxiety. An industrious and intelligent woman, she had researched a number of valid means of helping herself. Her research into treatments led her to conclude that psychoanalysis would be the most efficacious approach, one that would lead her to the deepest and longest-lasting "cure." The year prior to entering treatment with me, she had enrolled in a mindfulness-based stress reduction (MBSR) course that was based on mindfulness meditation and techniques designed to address a wide variety of mental and physical difficulties, including anxiety (Kabat-Zinn, 1990). Subsequently, she developed a meditation practice and sporadically attended a local meditation group.

Mary possessed a surprisingly sparse understanding of her own dynamics. Dwelling on the past caused her so much pain that she avoided such exploration vigorously. She came from a particularly deprived childhood; very little attention had been paid to her individual accomplishments and abilities. Socially anxious, she learned social skills by carefully observing the behavior of others. Mary's father abandoned the family before she was a teenager, leaving in his wake a powerful longing, as well as unexpressed rage, tempered by her guilt. Her mother was an angry and bitter woman who either ignored Mary or subjected her to seemingly irrational criticism. The few happy memories from her childhood came from being alone, lost in her thoughts while walking, climbing trees, or gardening.

Mary's world had become increasingly small and circumscribed. Despite her intellect, she was marginally employed. Her world revolved around work, exercise, and her psychoanalysis. She saw her avoidance as destructive, felt exceedingly lonely, and wished to change. A responsible woman, Mary would not allow herself to avoid anxiety-provoking events altogether. She engaged socially, because she felt she had to, and muscled through events by turning on a well-rehearsed dose of charm and intellect. Our early sessions focused on her despair that despite all this effort, she was not experiencing a decrease in her anxiety. Initially, she was able to explore very little about her past. She was aware of her father's narcissistic investment in her intellect and its impact on her tendency to overutilize it defensively, but she could not go much further than this, much less explore its manifestation in our sessions.

Interpersonally, I noted a blunted aspect to her engagement. She was highly intellectual and serious. She eventually revealed her omnipotent belief that she could control others' responses to her through her intellect and her well-honed, but false, social demeanor. She was conscious of the fact that she engaged in this manner to keep people at bay, to avoid the intimacy she also longed for. In this initial stage of treatment, Mary presented with two profound problems: bearing witness to her own internal experience of pain and allowing me to witness it alongside her.

Mary's central insight from this stage of analysis came not directly in an analytic hour but arose in her meditation practice. After a year and a half of treatment, one day she shared a fantasy that occurred to her while attending her meditation group the previous evening. The teacher had used the term "container" in reference to the internal and external "space" that is needed for meditation to occur. It occurred to Mary that she saw me as trying to provide a similar container, but that she resisted engaging with it. She then realized that she believed my job was to create a space where her anxiety and her suffering would *not* arise and that, through the sheer force of my intellect, I would glean both the source and solutions to her problems and hand them over to her with a minimum of angst. I realized quietly that I was probably failing miserably at this, with my attempts to help Mary get in touch with her feelings and understand her past and its impact on her current functioning. I then remarked on the fact that this series of associations could occur on the meditation cushion, but not on the couch. Mary agreed and shared that she often found herself noticing more about herself in meditation than in the office. This led me, for the first time, to explore what actually was taking place in meditation for her. With some difficulty, Mary reported often feeling flooded by unwanted emotions in her meditation practice. She continued going, because she knew it was "good for her," and sometimes even experienced a relaxing effect from it; nevertheless, she found herself increasingly distracted and preoccupied by associations to her past while meditating. This work led her to the more conscious awareness of how she avoided truly engaging with me out of fear of being misunderstood, engulfed, and then presented with a restrictive, inaccurate view of her experiences, much as her mother had done. The psychodynamic reason for her seeking a meditation practice concurrent with psychoanalytic treatment was then open for exploration. She realized she sought aloneness as a means of avoiding being engulfed and overcome by another's mind, but in aloneness there was no one to help her comprehend her feelings, and she was left to face herself on her own. Meditation was initially satisfying and seductive, in that it allowed her, in solitude, to make space for her ruminations and perhaps to reach solutions without the terrifying reliance on another's interpretations. Mary became aware of how she privileged her own insights and solutions far above others'. But this had its limitations. Ironically, the more proficient she became at meditation, the more she was flooded by disavowed affects and memories. Thus, her meditation practice became the vehicle for allowing disavowed memories and affects into the analytic hour.

Mary realized that by engaging me primarily intellectually, she was attempting to maintain a deeply longed-for contact with me without the risk of being engulfed and criticized. We became aware that we were engaged in an enactment that recapitulated her relationship with her father, who valued her intellect and provided her with the only positive attention she could recall in her family. Mary found she could control the sessions—and me—through intellectual, but rather superficial, analysis of her difficulties. With these new insights, born out of her attempts to meditate, she began to share her associations more freely in session. Simultaneous exploration of the discomfort she experienced in allowing herself to trust me allowed her finally to accept her internal experience as valid—and potentially quite interesting—rather than threatening. Furthermore, as she became able to free associate in our sessions and work with her fear of me, her meditation practice improved, and she found it easier to simply observe her thoughts and feelings rather than be overwhelmed by them or compelled to work with them in solitude. She came to realize that this was analytic work and could be brought to her sessions. Mary began to glean the benefits from a more regular meditation practice. Primarily, she was more able to accept her thoughts and fears as things that maybe did not need to be invested with the power she gave them.

Conclusion

Buddhism and psychoanalysis share roughly the same goal—the alleviation of mental suffering—one working from a highly personal and individual perspective, the other from a more universal point of view. Both are radically experiential, rather than primarily philosophical or dogmatic. Both employ the technique of moment-to-moment awareness of our mental processes to reduce suffering. Psychoanalysis, however, by focusing on the personal, stops short of insight into our common humanity and does not posit the possibility of the end of all suffering. Perhaps the final view is that both ways of viewing the mind need to be considered synergistically. This is hardly an original conclusion, but it bears repetition and elaboration in light of the difficulties many have in personal meditation practice. There are clearly aspects of our contemporary existence that the original authors and compilers of the early Buddhist texts and commentaries were either not aware of or that carried little significance in their time. Buddhism and psychoanalysis investigate different aspects of functioning, and a complementary approach may, in the end, be the most realistic and useful.

References

Ajahn Sucitto. (2010). *Turning the wheel of truth: Commentary on the Buddha's first teaching*. Boston, MA: Shambhala.

Aronson, H. (2004). *Buddhist practice on Western ground: Reconciling Eastern ideals and Western psychology*. Boston, MA: Shambhala.

Batchelor, S. (2010). *Confessions of a Buddhist atheist*. New York, NY: Random House.

Batchelor, S. (2012). A secular Buddhist. *Journal of Global Buddhism, 13*, 87–107.

Engler, J. (2003). Being somebody and being nobody: A reexamination of the understanding of self in psychoanalysis and Buddhism. In J. D. Safran (Ed.), *Psychoanalysis and Buddhism: An unfolding dialogue* (pp. 35–79). Somerville, MA: Wisdom.

Epstein, M. (1988). Attention in analysis. In M. Epstein (Ed.). (2007), *Psychotherapy without the self* (pp. 101–122). New Haven, CT: Yale University Press.

Epstein, M. (1990). Psychodynamics of meditation: Pitfalls on the spiritual path. In M. Epstein (Ed.). (2007), *Psychotherapy without the self* (pp. 71–96). New Haven, CT: Yale University Press.

Freud, S. (1893). The psychotherapy of hysteria, from studies on hysteria. In J. Strachey (Ed. & Trans.), *The standard edition of the complete psychological works of Sigmund Freud* (Vol. 2). London, England: Hogarth.

Freud, S. (1904). On psychotherapy. In J. Strachey (Ed. & Trans.), *The standard edition of the complete psychological works of Sigmund Freud* (Vol. 7). London, England: Hogarth.

Freud, S. (1912). Recommendations to physicians practising psycho-analysis. In J. Strachey (Ed. & Trans.), *The standard edition of the complete psychological works of Sigmund Freud* (Vol. 12, pp. 109–120). London, England: Hogarth Press.

Freud, S. (1930). Civilization and its discontents. In J. Strachey (Ed. & Trans.), *The standard edition of the complete psychological works of Sigmund Freud* (Vol. 21). London, England: Hogarth Press.

Gabbard, G., & Westen, D. (2003). Rethinking therapeutic action. *International Journal of Psychoanalysis, 84,* 823–841.

Germer, C. (2005). Mindfulness: What is it? What does it matter? In C. Germer, R. Siegel, & P. Fulton (Eds.), *Mindfulness and psychotherapy* (pp. 3–27). New York, NY: Guilford Press.

Gombrich, R. (2009). *What the Buddha thought.* London, England: Equinox Press.

Greenberg, J. (2007). Therapeutic action: Convergence without consensus. *Psychoanalytic Quarterly, 76,* 1675–1688.

Hoffer, A. (2010). Passionate neutrality. *Pine Psychoanalytic Center Newsletter, 21*(3), 2–5.

Kabat-Zinn, J. (1990). *Full catastrophe living: Using the wisdom of your body and mind to face stress, pain, and illness.* New York, NY: Dell.

Mitchell, S. (2000). *Relationality: From attachment to intersubjectivity.* Hillsdale, NJ: Analytic Press.

Mitchell, S., & Black, M. (1995). *Freud and beyond: A history of modern psychoanalytic thought.* New York, NY: Basic Books.

Olendzki, A. (2010). *Unlimiting mind.* Somerville, MA: Wisdom.

Olendzki, A. (2012a). A classical future: Interview with *Insight Journal* editor Chris Talbott. *Insight Journal.* Retrieved from http://www.bcbsdharma.org/2012-12-28-insight-journal.

Olendzki, A. (2012b). Wisdom in Buddhist psychology. In C. Germer & R. Siegel (Eds.), *Wisdom and compassion in psychotherapy* (pp. 121–137). New York, NY: Guilford Press.

Peacock, J. (2008). Suffering in mind: The aetiology of suffering in early Buddhism. *Contemporary Buddhism, 9,* 209–226.

Peacock, J. (2012a, June 6). Mindfulness and the cognitive process: Part 1: The pathology of desire. *Insight Journal*. Retrieved from http://www.bcbsdharma. org/2012-06-05-insight-journal.

Peacock, J. (Aug. 1, 2012b). Mindfulness and the cognitive process: Part 2. *Insight Journal*. Retrieved from http://www.bcbsdharma.org/2012-8-31-insight-journal.

Renik, O. (2007). Intersubjectivity, therapeutic action, and analytic technique. *Psychoanalytic Quarterly, 76*, 1547–1562.

Safran, J. (Ed.). (2003). *Psychoanalysis and Buddhism: An unfolding dialogue*. Somerville, MA: Wisdom.

Safran, J. (2012). *Psychoanalysis and psychoanalytic therapies*. Washington, DC: American Psychological Association.

Story, F. (1973). II. Dukkha. (Vol. 2). In *The three basic facts of existence*. Wheel Publications. Kandy, Sri Lanka: Buddhist Publication Society.

Wachtel, P. (2008). *Relational theory and the practice of psychotherapy*. New York, NY: Guilford Press.

Westkott, M. (1998). Horney, Zen, and the real self. *American Journal of Psychoanalysis, 58*, 287–301.

CHAPTER 4

Before the Ass Has Gone, the Horse Has Already Arrived: Acceptance and Nonduality in Psychoanalysis and Buddhism

Jeremy D. Safran, PhD

In this chapter, I explore some of the implications of the Buddhist perspective on *nonduality* and acceptance for psychoanalytic practice. Nonduality is a mode of experiencing that breaks down the distinction between categories that are conventionally regarded as opposites (e.g., good versus bad, pure versus impure, sacred versus profane, heaven and hell). The Buddhist perspective on nonduality is that the natural human tendency to think about things in dualistic terms is at the heart of human suffering and that wisdom is the ability to experience things nondualistically. As long as we distinguish between things as they should be in some idealized state and things as they are, we are unable to be fully open to and appreciate the present situation for what it has to offer. I attempt to convey in this chapter a sense of the way in which the cultivation of a nondual perspective can lead to a radical and paradoxical perspective on the role of acceptance in the analytic process.

Acceptance As an Attitude

I am often asked how Buddhism influences my psychoanalytic practice. This is not an easy question to answer. I don't usually teach my patients to meditate, although I sometimes do. I don't usually talk about Buddhist concepts to my patients, although I sometimes do. So it is more a matter of attitude than anything else, and I think this attitude basically has to do with acceptance. I think that Buddhist practice helps me to cultivate a greater sense of acceptance of both my patients and myself. And in various ways, it helps me to enable my patients to become more self-accepting. I feel embarrassed to say this, because it feels like a modest claim, given my involvement in Buddhist practice for many years. And often when I say this to people, they say, "Well, doesn't psychoanalysis emphasize the importance of acceptance as well? For example, Freud cautioned analysts about the excessive zeal to cure. And what about Bion's admonition that we approach every session 'without memory and desire'?" And so on. My answer is "Yes, but…" Yes, psychoanalysis does emphasize acceptance, but at the same time, it doesn't. Or, yes, it does, but there is something more radical about the Buddhist perspective on the relationship between acceptance and transformation—a perspective that is paradoxical in nature. Moreover, in many ways this paradox lies at the heart of Buddhism, or certainly at the heart of some strands of Buddhism. There is a pithy Zen aphorism: "Before the ass is gone, the horse has already arrived." Now think about this for a moment. What does it mean? Trying to explain a Zen saying is like trying to explain a joke. You either get it or you don't. But given that the alternative of leaving it unexplained may be worse, I'll take a stab at it. The horse is a desirable state of being, associated with speed and gracefulness. The ass is a plodding beast of burden, the butt of jokes. Presumably most of us would rather be horses than asses. I know I would. And we imagine or hope that psychoanalysis will effect this type of transformation. But if we are looking to the future for the idealized horse to arrive and the maligned ass to depart, we are looking in the wrong place. The message of this aphorism is that the ass is already the horse, so to speak. If this is true, then why go into psychoanalytic treatment in the first place? This is the paradox to be grappled with. This is the paradox of acceptance.

Clinical Application

I have been seeing my patient Simon in analysis for five years now. He is thirty-three years old. He started treatment when he had just gotten into his first romantic relationship with a woman, and he sought treatment initially for a problem with impotence. It turned out that this impotence was also a metaphor for his experience of life in general: his feeling of not being strong enough, assertive enough, or masculine enough, not being master of his own destiny. Simon had fantasies of becoming a famous writer but rarely finished anything he began, because, in his mind, it wasn't good enough. He had fantasies of marrying a beautiful woman, but he didn't have the nerve to ask anyone out on a date. He was racked with self-doubt. He felt he was too quiet, too shy, too stiff, too aloof, too everything. Not assertive enough, not witty enough, not clever enough. And not spontaneous. Not anything enough.

Simon would typically begin sessions by announcing, "I've got nothing to say today." Then he would sit there in silence—a long, painful silence, during which he would utter only the occasional word. Exploration revealed that he felt pressured to produce something and was resentful of me because of this. And this was true of his life in general. In time, we came to explore his inability to produce anything in our sessions, his resentment of me, his self-criticism, and my frustration with him as an important enactment, thematically similar to his presenting problem of impotence.

A central feature of Simon's existence was a feeling of a "lack of being"—the feeling that, unlike other people, he was, in his words, "not at home in the world," and that he was always trying to be, rather than just being. It was impossible for Simon to be spontaneous. The fundamental questions in treatment were the following: Could he allow himself to just be, rather than trying to be something? Could he somehow let go of his self-induced pressure to produce something in our sessions? Could he let go of his fantasies of becoming a famous writer or marrying the perfect woman? And was it possible for me to let go of my desire for him to be more lively and engaging in our work together? Is it possible for someone to become more spontaneous by trying to be spontaneous? Is it possible for someone to fall asleep by trying to fall asleep?

There is an old Zen story about a teacher, who, upon seeing his student meditating, asked him, "Why are you meditating?" The student responded, "To become enlightened." The teacher picked up a tile and began to polish it. "Why are you polishing the tile?" asked the student. The teacher replied, "To turn it into a mirror." "How can you turn a tile into a mirror by polishing it?" asked the student. The teacher replied, "How can you become enlightened by meditating?" At this point, the student became enlightened.

From the worldview of nonduality, as long as Simon is waiting to become a famous writer before he gets on with his life, he is going to be stuck.

Nonduality and Psychoanalysis

There is an apocryphal story that Alfred Adler used to ask his patients, "What would you do if you didn't have your symptoms?" When they would tell him, Adler would then respond, "Well, then go out and do it." As long as Simon is waiting to become a famous writer, to marry the perfect woman, to become spontaneous—he will never be content. As long as he is waiting for me to be the perfect analyst, he is always going to be disappointed. Or another way of putting it is that it is the desire for things to be other than the way they are that is the cause of suffering. From a Buddhist perspective, life inevitably involves suffering—disease, loss, pain, death, and so on. But this suffering is not the problem. The problem is the attempt to avoid it. As Freud put it, psychoanalysis does not eliminate suffering; it transforms hysterical misery into ordinary unhappiness.

In early Buddhism, the emphasis was on eliminating suffering by letting go of attachment: letting go of the attachment to having things a certain way, letting go of the attachment to pleasure and the avoidance of pain, and so forth. Thus, enlightenment arises out of a certain type of renunciation. It arises out of the renunciation of our ordinary satisfactions and pleasures. What is intriguing here is that there is a certain parallel with Freud's thinking on the topic, in the sense that Freud emphasized the importance of renouncing one's instinctual strivings and of recognizing the impossibility of living life according to the pleasure principle. According to Freud, people need to recognize their illusions and fantasies as infantile strivings and learn to live life in accordance with the reality principle. Thus, in both Freud and early Buddhism (and also in important strands in contemporary Buddhism), the problem is desire. And the issue is what to do with our desire, given the fact that it will inevitably be thwarted and the fact that (as Freud believed) instinct is in conflict with civilization.

Both Freud's perspective on desire and the original Buddhist perspective can be seen in some ways as pessimistic ones. In Stephen A. Mitchell's (1993) words, "Freud was not a particularly cheerful fellow and his version of the rational scientific person is not an especially happy person. But that person is stronger, more grounded, more in line with reality, even if it's a somber reality" (p. 305).

The early Buddhist perspective absorbed some of the world-weary flavor characteristic of fifth-century BCE Indian culture. In this tradition of Buddhism, enlightenment consists of achieving liberation from *samsara*, the ongoing wheel of death and rebirth; or, for those of us who don't believe in reincarnation, it is ordinary worldly existence, with all its suffering and pain. The goal is to escape from this wheel of life, death, and rebirth and to attain the state of nirvana—that is, the extinction of desire or the extinction of self-centered craving. This is the Buddhist version of paradise. One could say that this is a more ambitious goal than Freud's insofar as Freud was not interested in the possibility of eliminating desire or self-centered craving, only in modulating desire in light of the reality principle. In that sense, Buddhists would say that their perspective is more optimistic, in that they believe that complete liberation from the pain of self-centered craving is possible—at least over a vast number of lifetimes.

Relational Psychoanalysis and the Problem of Desire

I now want to contrast a post-Freudian perspective on what can be referred to as the *problem of desire* with subsequent developments in Buddhist thinking. And in order to limit my scope, I focus on American psychoanalysis and, in particular, relational psychoanalysis. There has been a shift in contemporary psychoanalysis away from Freud's emphasis on the renunciation of instinctual strivings and the replacement of fantasy and illusion with rationality. This shift has been toward the creation of personal meaning and the revitalization of the self. As Mitchell (1993) puts it, "Many patients now are understood to be suffering not from conflictual infantile passions that can be tamed and transformed through reason and understanding, but from stunted personal development. Deficiencies in caregiving in the early years are understood to have contributed to interfering with the emergence of a fully centered, integrated sense of self, of the patient's subjectivity....What today's psychoanalysis provides is the opportunity to freely discover and playfully explore one's own subjectivity, one's own imagination" (p. 251).

If Freud's perspective can be characterized as a pessimistic one, I think it is fair to characterize this perspective, which many would argue is a particularly American take on psychoanalysis, as a more romantic one.

Now let us look at subsequent developments in Buddhist thinking. In the Mahayana tradition (which began to emerge in India around 100 BCE and subsequently became the dominant form of Buddhism in countries such as China, Japan, and Korea), the emphasis shifts away from the original goal—the attainment of nirvana, which is both the Buddhist equivalent of paradise and the extinction of desire—toward a different goal. And this goal can be described as paradoxical or ironic in nature, rather than romantic. One of the fundamental axioms in the Mahayana tradition is that samsara is nirvana. There is no difference between everyday worldly existence and paradise. And this is where nonduality comes into play. If you renounce samsara and dedicate yourself to attaining nirvana, you are falling into the trap of dualistic thinking. Once you start distinguishing between samsara and nirvana, your ordinary everyday existence becomes devalued. In Christianity, suffering will end when one dies and goes to heaven. In Judaism, suffering ends when the Messiah comes. Living this way can offer consolation, but what impact does it have on the texture of one's everyday existence? Freud (1927) made a similar point in his critique of religion, "The Future of an Illusion." One enters psychoanalysis in the hope of a positive transformation, but what impact does that hope have on one's experience? There is an old saying that the neurotic enters treatment in order to become a better neurotic. Harold Boris (1976), coming from a Kleinian-Bionian perspective, argues that hope interferes with the satisfaction of desire, because real satisfaction is always sacrificed in the hope of eventual fulfillment at some future point in time. One's present experience is always lacking in the shadow of one's idealized experience. As long as my patient Simon is waiting to become a famous writer or to meet the perfect woman or to become more spontaneous, his current life is devalued. In Zen they say that one has to give up hope in order to become enlightened. Or, returning to the psychoanalytic tradition,

Winnicott (1965) speaks about the important developmental task of optimal disillusionment—that is, giving up one's experience of omnipotence and coming to experience the independent existence of the other.

As I said earlier, it is not that psychoanalysis does not deal with this paradox of acceptance, but rather that this paradox is the central theme—or at least one of the central themes—in many forms of Buddhism, and it is linked to fundamental epistemological and ontological concerns. The originating text of the Mahayana tradition is called the *Prajnaparamita Sutra* (The Perfection of Wisdom Writings). The *Prajnaparamita Sutra* is thought to have been composed by a number of Indian scholars, although it is attributed to the Buddha. The central concern of the *Prajnaparamita Sutra* is with developing an understanding of the nature of reality, or at least an understanding of the limits of our ability to comprehend reality. Its intent is radically deconstructive in nature in that it challenges all knowledge claims, including its own. Its aim is to provide the reader with a glimpse of the way things appear to those who have reached some degree of spiritual attainment through long, intensive practice.

According to the *Prajnaparamita Sutra*, the essential nature of reality is what is referred to in Sanskrit as *shunyata*, which means "empty of inherent existence." Reality does not exist independent of our construction of it. This is a constructivist perspective, which anticipated the contemporary emphasis on constructivism in psychoanalysis by more than two thousand years. The *Prajnaparamita Sutra* is written in the form of inspirational poetry rather than logical discourse, and its recurrent message is that ultimate reality is indescribable, even inconceivable; the nature of reality cannot be grasped. This is not intended as a nihilistic formulation; rather it is an undercutting of all conventional ways of seeing things in order to clear a way for an opening—for an experience of awe in the face of the ultimate mystery of things. It is similar, in some respects, to the perspective conveyed in the *Book of Job*. As you will recall, Job is a wealthy and prosperous man with seven sons and three daughters and plenty of sheep, camels, and oxen. And Job is what is referred to as a God-fearing man. One day Satan challenges God to a wager. He wagers that if misfortune were to strike Job, he would lose his faith, and he would, as Satan puts it, "curse God." So God accepts the wager. He says, "Do anything you want. Just don't kill him." (Apparently this is a capricious God, but not without some conscience.) So Satan kills Job's children. He kills all his animals. He makes Job sick with boils "from his scalp to the soles of his feet" (Mitchell, 1979, p. 8).

Job's friends say to him, "You must have sinned," and they urge him to repent. They are convinced there is some way of understanding what has happened—that there is some order to the universe and some way of regaining control. If Job is suffering, there must be something he has done wrong. How do we understand our own misfortune? What is the nature of our responsibility when things don't work out?

But Job protests his innocence. He begs God to tell him what his crime is and how he has sinned. In Job's words, "If only God could hear me. State his case against me. Let me read his indictment. I would carry it on my shoulder, or wear it on my head like a crown. I would justify the least of my actions. I would stand before him like a prince" (Mitchell, 1979, p. 75). In other words, Job is asking, as we all do at times, "Why me?" And then God's voice thunders from the clouds (and here I have an image in my mind from Cecil B. DeMille's *The Ten Commandments*): "Where were you when I planned the earth? Tell me if you are so wise. Do you know who took its dimensions, measuring its length with a cord? What were its pillars built on? Who laid down its cornerstone, while the morning stars burst out singing and the angels shouted for joy?" And then he goes on to ask, "Does the rain have a father? Who has begotten the dew? Out of whose belly was the ice born? Whose womb labors with the sleet?" (pp. 79–81).

What is God saying here? Stephen Mitchell (the translator, not the analyst) makes the following comment: "Does the rain have a father? The whole meaning is in the *lack* of an answer. If you say yes, you're wrong. If you say no, you're wrong. God's humor here is rich and subtle beyond words" (1979, p. xxv, italics in original). In other words, the great cosmic joke is that there are no answers to the ultimate questions. The dialogue between God and Job continues in this fashion until finally Job has an epiphany. And at this point he says to God, "I know you can do all things and nothing you wish is impossible. I have spoken of the unspeakable and I have tried to grasp the infinite. I heard of you with my ears, but now my eyes have seen you. Therefore I will be quiet, comforted that I am dust" (Mitchell, 1979, p. 88). Now what kind of comfort can Job be experiencing? What we need to understand here is that Job is overcome with awe. He is overwhelmed with a feeling that falls on the boundary between reverence and fear. He is struck dumb by his revelation. Job experiences reality as infinite and beyond comprehension. And with this realization comes an experience of awe and surrender to the mystery of things. To use Ghent's (1990) distinction, he is not submitting to God's will; he is surrendering or letting go. He is not resigning himself to his fate; he is experiencing a profound sense of acceptance.

"Form Is Emptiness and Emptiness Is Form"

The most famous selection from the *Prajnaparamita Sutra* is called the "Heart Sutra." And one of the most memorable lines in it is as follows: "Form is emptiness and emptiness is form." Now what does this mean? It is a deconstruction of the dualism implicit in the notion that things are empty of inherent existence. If one takes the idea of "emptiness" too seriously, one ends up with a kind of nihilism, a kind of devaluing of everyday experience. It is fine to speak about things being empty of inherent existence, but if you jump off the top of a tall building, you die. If somebody you love dies, you suffer. So instead of saying that things are not as they appear or that they are as they appear, the Heart Sutra says that things both are as they appear and are not as they appear. The idea that things are empty of inherent existence is itself empty—empty of inherent existence. Ancient Buddhist philosophers said that the notion of shunyata (or emptiness) can be thought of as a type of medicine. It is a medicine for treating the disease of naive realism. If you take too much of it, like any medicine, it can make you sick.

In the *Prajnaparamita Sutra* there is an ongoing, radical deconstruction. Any assertion that is made is simultaneously undercut in a way that leaves us with no familiar bearings—an experience akin to Job's experience of reverence and awe in the face of the mystery of things. One of the most profound attempts to grapple with the Buddhist notion of nonduality can be found in the work of the thirteenth-century Japanese Zen master Dogen. Dogen struggled all his life with the question of why we need to meditate, if there is nothing to be attained. His resolution is that we sit and meditate not in order to attain something but as an expression of our Buddhahood, as an expression of our enlightenment. Here are a few quotes from Dogen:

83

It is the enlightened mind that arouses the thought of enlightenment....Arousing the thought of enlightenment means following the encouragement of others, doing good to even the slightest extent you are able, and bowing to the Buddha even while you are being annoyed by demons. (F. D. Cook, 2002, pp. 35–36)

When one first arouses the thought of enlightenment it is enlightenment. When one first achieves perfect enlightenment it is enlightenment. First, last and in between are all enlightenment. Foolish people think that at the time one is studying the Way one does not attain enlightenment. (F. H. Cook, 1989, p. 12)

Priest Pao-ch'e of Mount Ma-ku was fanning himself. A monk came by and asked, "The wind's nature is eternal and omnipresent. Why reverend sir, are you still fanning yourself?" The master replied, "You know only that the wind's nature is eternal. But you do not know the reason why it exists everywhere." The monk asked, "Well, why does it exist everywhere?" The master just fanned himself. The monk made a bow of respect. (F. H. Cook, 1989, p. 69)

The most important realization for Simon is that he is perfect the way he is. That is, he is perfect with all his faults and imperfections. He is perfect in his physical and psychological impotence and even in his lack of spontaneity. But if he is perfect the way he is, why does he need to be in psychoanalysis? This can be thought of as a type of koan. There are two major schools in Zen. One is referred to as the Rinzai tradition, and the other is the Soto tradition. In Rinzai, which was popularized in the West by the scholar D. T. Suzuki, there is an emphasis on the use of koan practice to help people break out of their dualistic ways of relating to experience. Koans are questions that cannot be solved logically: "What is the sound of one hand clapping?" "Show me your face before your parents were born" (which essentially means "be spontaneous right here and now"). "Why does the wind exist everywhere?" "Does the rain have a father?" One struggles with the question until something snaps inside, and one has a profound existential realization of "not-knowing"—a kind of pregnant and fertile void in which nothing and everything is possible. The use of koans as teaching devices was prompted by the realization that sitting and meditating for the sake of self-purification was buying into a dualistic perspective, the idea being that one is meditating in order to attain something.

The koan system evolved out of the recorded interactions of Zen masters and their students, in which the masters would ask their students insoluble questions to provoke them into a sudden insight, into a state of mind that cannot be attained in a linear way. In contrast to the *gradual path* of developing realization through ongoing meditation, the use of koans is associated with a type of *sudden path* to realization. The problem with the koan tradition, however, is that once it became institutionalized, it also became too goal oriented. The emphasis was on attaining these breakthroughs, these little glimpses of enlightenment. It is like having sex solely to achieve orgasm.

In contrast, the Soto tradition, which originated with Dogen, is in one sense a more *gradual path*. The emphasis is on meditation, but with a subtle difference from meditation as practiced in early Buddhism. The emphasis is on what is referred to as "just sitting." All one does is sit and watch the mind, without trying to attain anything. There are no good or bad meditation sessions. So, paradoxically, this too becomes a *sudden path*. Once the emphasis is placed on just sitting, the moment one sits down to meditate—the moment one begins to practice—one has attained one's goal.

There are some interesting similarities, in this respect, between the Zen tradition and the Dzogchen tradition in Tibetan Buddhism. The Dzogchen tradition emerged between the seventh and tenth centuries in the Tantric Buddhist tradition. Dzogchen emphasizes that fulfillment is forsaken the minute one buys into the myth of liberation. In this tradition, it is made clear that one should not—in any way—be trying to cut off one's thoughts or feelings or trying to transform them. The task is just to let the mind be. This is expressed, for example, in the words of the tenth-century Tantric teacher Saraha:

> If the truth is already manifest, what's the use of meditation?
> And if it is hidden, one is just measuring darkness. Mantras
> and tantras, meditation and concentration, they are all causes
> for self-deception. Do not defile in contemplation thought
> that is pure by its own nature. Whatever you see, that is it. In
> front, behind, in all ten directions, the nature of the sky is

always clear. But by gazing and gazing the sight becomes obscured (Watts, 1957, pp. 78–79).

Meditation in Dzogchen is similar to meditation in Zen in many ways. One sits and observes the arising and passing of thoughts, feelings, and sensations. The more one does this, the more one realizes that all phenomena arise from the mind and reemerge into it. All manifestations of the mind are empty of inherent existence. As the Heart Sutra puts it, "Form is emptiness and emptiness is form." There is no difference between the thoughts that emerge and the gaps between the thoughts. So it is not a matter of clearing or stilling the mind. Everything is perfect as it is.

Ordinary Magic

In Dzogchen, the student needs a teacher to do something referred to as introducing him or her to the nature of mind. This "introduction" is also referred to as "the pointing-out instruction." It is not sufficient to simply sit and observe one's own mind. One needs an advanced practitioner to point one in the right direction, to provide the student with a glimpse of awakened experience so that he or she will know what to look for. What does this mysterious initiation look like in practice? Here is a story from Sogyal Rinpoche (1992), a well-known Tibetan teacher, about the first time his teacher provided him with "pointing-out instructions."

> The first of these moments occurred when I was six or seven years old. It took place in that special room in which Jamyang Khyentse lived, in front of a large portrait statue of his previous incarnation Jamyang Khyentse Wangpo. This was a solemn, awe-inspiring figure, made more so when the flame of the butter lamp in front of it would flicker and light up its face. Before I knew what was happening, my master did something most unusual. What was it? He suddenly hugged me and lifted me off my feet. Then he gave me a huge kiss on the side of my face. For a long moment my mind fell away completely and I was enveloped by a tremendous warmth, confidence, and power. (pp. 41–42)

And here is an experience that stands out as memorable for me with my own Tibetan teacher. My teacher, Karma Thinley Rinpoche, the fourth incarnation of the sixteenth-century Lama Karma Thinley, once asked me in his broken, heavily accented English, "How does Western psychology treat nervousness?" "Why do you ask?" I responded. "Well," he replied, "I've always been a nervous person. Especially when I have to talk to large groups of people or to people I don't know, I get nervous." As was often the case with the questions that Karma Thinley asked me, I found myself drawing a complete blank. Part of it was the difficulty of finding the words to explain something to someone whose grasp of English was limited. But there was another more important factor. On the face of it, this was a simple question. But Karma Thinley was a highly respected lama. At the time, he was in his sixties. He'd spent many years mastering the most sophisticated Buddhist meditation techniques. Those who knew him well considered him to be an enlightened being. In the West, psychotherapists are increasingly turning to Buddhist meditation as a valuable treatment for a variety of problems, including anxiety. Who was I to tell him how to deal with anxiety? How was it possible that Karma Thinley, with all his experience meditating, could still be troubled by such everyday concerns? How could an enlightened person be socially anxious? Was he really enlightened? What did it mean to be enlightened? My head swirled with all these inchoate questions, and for a moment my mind stopped. I felt a sense of warmth coming from Karma Thinley, and I felt warmly toward him. I felt young, soft, open, and uncertain about everything I knew.

These are examples of what the Tibetan teacher Trungpa Rinpoche referred to as "ordinary magic." This ordinary magic is the magic of everyday life and relationships that we normally don't see, because we are looking for magic of a more dramatic nature. Now let me try to reconnect this to psychoanalysis and to my work with Simon. Simon has been seeing me in treatment for over five years. In some respects, he has made important changes. The woman he was involved with when I first met him ended their relationship shortly after the beginning of treatment. With my support, Simon recovered from his broken heart and got into another relationship, this time with a woman who was more interested in him than he was in her, but who was a kind and nurturing partner. In the context of this relationship, Simon overcame his impotence, although it would occasionally recur (and still does from time to time). After two years, Simon left this woman because he felt that she was not exciting enough and that she did not bring enough energy and initiative to the relationship. After a year, he started a relationship with a woman he considered to be stunningly attractive and whom he had to pursue. Taking the risk of actively pursuing a woman whom he was really attracted to was a new and important growth experience for Simon. Although they stayed together for a few months, he eventually left her, because she turned out to be rather cold and self-centered. At the present time, he is dating, but still alone. Simon is also taking active steps to pursue a writing career and is making some progress in this respect. There are times when Simon is optimistic about the future. And at such moments, he is more spontaneous in our work together. But there are also many times when he feels destined to be alone for the rest of his life and to never feel gratified professionally. At times like this, he questions what he has gained from five years of analysis. During these periods, our sessions are dead and monotonous. Simon feels pressured to produce and resentful of me for not being more helpful. And I feel impatient, frustrated, and unappreciated.

Sometimes it can be difficult to know how to end a chapter, in the same way that it can be difficult to know how and when to terminate an analysis. But I will attempt to pull some of the threads together by turning to a poetry collection called *Cold Mountain* (Watson, 1970). These poems were written by Han Shan, a ninth-century Chinese hermit and scholar considered to be enlightened, who, after a career as a farmer and a minor government official throughout which he was troubled by poverty and family discord, retired to a place called Cold Mountain. There he devoted himself to Zen practice and writing poetry. The striking thing about Han Shan's poems is their simplicity and honesty. Some talk about the profound and sublime. And some lament the difficulties of life and are filled with self-pity. They are characterized by a quality referred to in Zen as *suchness*. This is a quality of expressing things exactly as they are, in a direct, immediate, and uncontrived way.

I'm not so poor on reports and decisions—
Why can't I get ahead in the government?
The rating officials are determined to make my life hard.
All they do is try to expose my faults.

Everything, I guess, is a matter of Fate;
Still, I'm trying the exam again this year.
The blind boy aiming at the eye of a sparrow.
Might just accidentally manage a hit. (p. 37)

Aah! Poverty and sickness,
And me with no friends and relations.
There's never any rice left in the pot,
Dust often collects in the kettle.
A thatched roof that won't keep out the rain,
A broken-down bed I can hardly squeeze into,
No wonder I've gotten so thin—
This many worries would wear out any man! (p. 34)

The beautiful thing about these poems is that they deconstruct our ideas about what enlightenment or change are all about. They undercut any attempt to make a dualistic distinction between the state of having arrived and the state of struggling or searching. So I would like to close with a couple of short poems in the style of Han Shan, one for Simon and one for me. This is the one for Simon:

I've been in analysis for five years now.
Sometimes I feel as if I've made some progress.
But right now I'm wondering if I'll ever be happy;
My analyst is useless. Life sucks.

And here is a poem for me:

I've worked with Simon for five years now;
Sometimes I think I've helped him;
I feel happy for him and pretty good about myself.
But right now I wonder if he'll ever be happy;
I wish he'd have better luck.
Maybe I'm a lousy analyst.

References

Boris, H. N. (1976). On hope: Its nature and psychotherapy. *International Review of Psycho-Analysis, 3*(2), 139–150.

Cook, F. D. (2002). *How to raise an ox.* Somerville, MA: Wisdom.

Cook, F. H. (1989). *Sounds of valley streams.* Albany, NY: State University of New York.

Freud, S. (1927). The future of an illusion. In J. Strachey (Ed. & Trans.), *The standard edition of the complete psychological works of Sigmund Freud* (Vol. 21, pp. 5–56). London, England: Hogarth.

Ghent, E. (1990). Masochism, submission, surrender: Masochism as a perversion of surrender. *Contemporary Psychoanalysis, 26*(1), 108–136.

Mitchell, S. (Trans.) (1979). *The book of Job.* San Francisco, CA: North Point Press.

Mitchell, S. A. (1993). *Hope and dread in psychoanalysis.* New York, NY: Basic Books.

Rinpoche Sogyal. (1992). *The Tibetan book of living and dying.* San Francisco: Harper.

Safran, J. D. (2003). *Psychoanalysis and Buddhism: An unfolding dialogue.* Somerville, MA: Wisdom.

Watson, B. (1970). *Cold mountain: 100 poems by the tang poet Han-shan.* New York, NY: Columbia University Press.

Watts, A. W. (1957). *The way of Zen.* New York, NY: Vintage Books.

Winnicott, D. W. (1965). *The maturational process and the facilitating environment.* London, England: Hogarth.

CHAPTER 5

Compassion in Contextual Psychotherapies

Mark Sisti, PhD

In spite of its ancient origins, the concepts and practices associated with compassion are reemerging in a multidisciplinary way from psychoanalysis to functional contextual psychotherapies, evolution science to ethology, ethical philosophy to experimental ethics, behavioral economics to game theory, interpersonal neuroscience to sociology and political science. Among psychotherapies, compassion is explicitly prevalent among functional contextual therapies (i.e., third-wave behaviorism). Functional contextual psychotherapies share a contextual philosophical approach similar to that of relational psychoanalysis, which emphasizes nonmechanistic, acceptance- and mindfulness-oriented, value-based, interpersonal approaches that are empirically supported. Many of these factors are consistent with compassion-informed therapies. This chapter will review some of the history of compassion within its multicultural contexts. The primary focus, however, will be on introducing contemporary compassion conceptualizations, particularly as developed within functional contextual and relational psychodynamic approaches (e.g., compassion-focused therapy, Gilbert, 2009; compassionate mind training, Tirch, 2012; mindful self-compassion, Germer & Siegel, 2012). Inherent in compassion work are attachment theory and research born of interpersonal psychoanalysis and its underlying object relational conceptualizations (Bowlby, 1988; Beebe & Lachmann, 1998; Greenberg & Mitchell, 1983). In the interconnected spirit of compassion, it is hoped that this multidisciplinary dialogue will help these often insular but intellectually rich communities to recognize and participate with each other. Finally, it is also hoped that this chapter will promote the cultivation of compassionate values in a global culture that is increasingly individualistic, competitive, materialistic, driven by consumer consumption, and environmentally and personally alienated.

Compassion and Empathy: Historical Context

Before we briefly review some pre-contemporary theories of compassion, let us establish a basic working definition. "Compassion" comes from the Latin prefix *com-* (with) and the verb *pati* (to support, suffer, or endure). Thus, compassion is the act of feeling another's emotions or suffering with the intention and actual action of helping to alleviate that suffering. Utilizing this definition, this chapter will explore two interrelated concepts: compassion and self-compassion. Pro-social intentions and actions to ameliorate suffering are so fundamental to all forms of compassion conceptualization (if not to our fundamental nature) that they are sometimes referred to as the "fourth *F*" (friend— after fight, flight, and freeze) in the primary autonomic responses. It is "the tend and befriend response," the affiliative/attachment response. A common factor among many multicultural, ethical, and religious systems, compassion has many deontological (rule-governed) versions: "Do unto others as you would have them do unto you" or "Love thy enemy." Both secular and religious traditions (e.g., Confucian, Aristotelian, Judeo-Christian, Muslim, Hindu, and Buddhist traditions) have cultivated philosophies and practices around the compassionate principles of pro-sociality, mutual care, reciprocity, contemplation, fairness, and altruism. Some of these philosophies go as far back as nomadic and preagricultural civilizations (Armstrong, 1993; Ryan & Jetha, 2010). Current ethnological research is able to show primitive versions of such altruistic, self-aware, perspective-taking, and justice-oriented sensibilities, present even among certain primates, such as bonobos. On this more evolutionarily instinctual level, compassion relies on the basic ability to empathize (De Waal, 2009). Empathy, the fundamental ability to understand another's phenomenological (both thought and felt) experience, has long been recognized as an essential process across therapeutic approaches. The word "empathy," originally coined by Titchener in 1909, was a rough translation of the earlier German *Einfühlung*, an aesthetic-animistic concept in which a perceiver projects himself or herself into the object of perception, as if entering the other body and therefore feeling, as well as seeing, the other's experience (Lipps, 1903). This early theoretical work on empathy foreshadowed contemporary neurobiological discoveries regarding mirror neurons, neuronal resonance, and cognitive embodiment (Siegel, 2007). More cognitive-perceptual conceptualizations of compassion were developed in the Gestalt work of Kohler and eventually in the cognitive work of Piaget during the 1930s (Håkansson, 2003). *Einfühlung* and empathy arguably also foreshadowed seminal Kleinian object-relational countertransferential concepts such as "projective identification" and preoedipal (infantile) empathic failures, and subsequent adult cognitive-emotional attachment pathology (Mitchell & Black, 1995). Empathy as a separate but embodied awareness of the other's mind also prefigured psychoanalytic notions of mentalization (e.g., metacognitive relational awareness) and contemporary perspective-taking concepts such as theory of mind.

Two of the most influential promoters of the importance of empathic processes in psychotherapy are psychoanalyst Heinz Kohut and humanistic therapist Carl Rogers. Rogers was a seminal influence in pioneering the mutative powers of empathy as an essential and necessary therapeutic process (alongside the other two core processes he proposed: genuineness and positive regard). Rogers (1959) proposed that these three empathic processes, if provided by the therapist, would lead clients to wellness and self-actualization. Some of Rogers's key definitional elements of empathy—such as moment-to-moment awareness and the capacity to "sense the hurt or the pleasure of another as he senses it and to perceive the causes thereof as he perceives them, but without ever losing the recognition that it is as if I were hurt" (1959, 210; also see Håkansson, 2003)—foreshadow the mindful awareness and perspective-taking processes inherent in contemporary compassion work.

Kohut and subsequent self-psychologists also believed in the essential necessity of empathic attunement, described as a method of "vicarious introspection" through which to discover and repair unconscious representations and related transferences (Håkansson, 2003). Paradoxically, for Kohut, moments of empathic failure were crowned therapeutic opportunities for repairing the patient's pathological self-representations and transferences that resulted from prior empathic failures. Kohut's self-psychology went on to pursue an emphasis on self and intrapsychic defensive maneuvers, but it was subsequently followed by another trend of exploding interest in interpersonal early attachment (preoedipal) processes.

This short review of compassion's psychotherapeutic historical precursors would be remiss without a reference to the seminal empirical work of attachment theorists John Bowlby, Mary Ainsworth, and Mary Main (Wallin, 2007). Bowlby was one of the first to explicitly incorporate evolutionary theory into the understanding of social-emotional development. He proposed that attachment repertoires (e.g., proximity seeking, social monitoring, social maintenance, mirroring, communication, protecting, provisioning, and mutual emotional regulation) were selected by evolution, since they increased our reproductive and survival success; hence, attachment and mutual-care repertoires have become fundamental to our species. It has since been argued that compassion and all pro-social drives and behaviors (such as generosity, gratitude, love, pity, altruism, consolation, and sympathy) evolved from our condition of infant hypervulnerability, which necessitated an extended interaction with the so-called tender emotions such as mother-infant mirroring (Dovido, Piliavin, Schroeder, & Penner, 2006; Beebe & Lachmann, 1998). Such an interpersonally mood-regulated environment makes us exquisitely attuned to self-other perspective taking and other intersubjective processes (McHugh & Stewart, 2012). Allen, Fonagy, and Bateman (2008) and others have bridged interpersonal attachment styles (e.g., secure attachment histories) with an essential underlying cognitive mechanism of change: the ability to mentalize. They define "mentalization" as the capacity to flexibly and contextually see intersubjective perspectives, to mindfully "mind the mind" of both self and others (Allen et al., 2008). Such mindful and flexible perspective taking is also fundamental to the underlying processes proposed by compassion-informed clinicians and functional contextualists (e.g., Neff, 2011; McHugh & Stewart, 2012). The renewed interest in mindfulness (mentalization), perspective taking, and relational processes is emerging as an integrative nexus within contemporary psychoanalysis (Epstein, 2007; Allen et al., 2008), acceptance- and mindfulness-based approaches, and compassion-informed therapies. (For a review of central elements of functional contextualism, or third-wave behaviorism, see Hayes, Villatte, Levin, & Hilderbrandt, 2011.)

An Evolutionary and Neurobiological Road Map for Understanding Compassion

Gilbert (2009) and Tirch (2012) propose that there is psychotherapeutic power in an evolutionary, interpersonal, and neurobiological paradigm. They propose that the use of such a model in compassion-informed therapy is the beginning of a compassionate understanding of ourselves and others, the neutralization of self-blame, and the establishment of a mindful perspective toward self and others. They propose that our reactions are not entirely "our fault" but are an evolutionary artifact of our intergenerational, conditioned new brains (mammalian), which are built awkwardly right on top of our still operating old brains (reptilian). Gilbert (2009) and Tirch (2012) present human emotional reactions as resulting from the natural programming of an ancient evolutionary, prey-predator past, which is further conditioned by our more recent childhood and cultural contexts. This inherited conditioning is not under nearly the degree of self-conscious control we think it should be—an acknowledgment of the power of the unconscious, which psychoanalysts and functional contextualists both embrace.

Gilbert (2009) divides our nervous system into three emotion response systems: (1) threat, (2) approach/acquisition, and (3) affiliation/compassion. Evolutionarily speaking, our original reptilian "threat system" is still busy doing its job, scanning for threats and generally inhibiting us, just as it was designed to do millions of years ago. When our "threat system" gives us a break for a minute, the other old portion of the brain may take over and reflexively activate our "resource-acquisition system" (the dopaminergic reward system). Unfortunately, such fast-acting, automatic, unconscious, take-over systems are not always so well adapted to today's societies. Most of us are no longer functioning in small nomadic groups or a food-scarce and predator-ridden savanna, or in constant, lethal danger from being socially ostracized. To further confuse our old reptilian minds, we are bombarded daily by a fire hose of media images and messages perfectly designed to activate our threat and/or acquisition systems (Wilson,

2008). Our actual day-to-day world requires much more of our newer, primate brain and our tend-befriend, oxytocin- and opiate-based "social-affiliative compassion system." Compassion theory proposes that whether alone or together, humans' sense of safety is largely based on activating this evolutionarily newer affiliative system, and it is in that intrapsychic and interpersonal state that we *thrive* as individuals and communities. (For a more extensive review of these neurobiological evolutionary systems, see Gilbert, 2009; Porges, 2011.)

The Three Pillars of Compassion—A Contemporary Three-Process Model of Compassion: Mindfulness, Kindness, and Common Humanity

In recent years, there has been an increase of mindful and interpersonal processes in an array of psychotherapies, both within modern psychoanalysis and in functional contextualism. Analytically informed, but empirically oriented, attachment theorists and researchers (e.g., Ainsworth, Main, and Beebe) have been exploring attachment processes, intersubjectivity, mother-infant mood regulation, and mirroring. Fonagy has been exploring interpersonally aware processes of metacognitive, mindful, or "mentalized" states (Wallin, 2007). Simultaneously, there has been an increase in empirical research into both animal and human pro-sociality and altruism (De Waal, 2009; Dovido et al., 2006). In the behavioral community, there has been a trend toward integrating acceptance- and mindfulness-based ideas and flexible self-other perspective taking, while also addressing interpersonally intimate and loving repertoires directly (e.g., functional analytic psychotherapy, Tsai et al., 2009; acceptance and commitment therapy, Hayes, Strosahl, & Wilson, 1999). The accumulation of interpersonal knowledge in many fields (evolution science; interpersonal neurobiology; attachment; pro-sociality; mutual mood regulation; intersubjective recognition; self-awareness; and metacognitive, mindful, and mentalized processes) has reached a critical mass and has given way to a group of explicitly compassion-based psychotherapies (e.g., compassionate mind therapy, CMT, Tirch, 2012; compassion-focused therapy, CFT, Gilbert, 2009;

self-compassion therapy, SCT, Neff, 2011, Germer, 2009; mindful self-compassion, Germer & Siegel, 2012). While it remains to be empirically seen as to exactly what the underlying mechanisms of change may ultimately be among compassion therapies, the work of two or three influential researcher-clinicians currently dominates our understanding of compassion processes in psychotherapy. Gilbert (2009) and Tirch (2012), in their work on CFT, rely heavily on an evolutionary-neurologically based conceptualization, using imagery, perspective taking, relational inter/intrapersonal mood-regulation, and neurobiological activation as critical aspects of their framework. For Neff (2011) and Germer (2009), emphasis is placed on an interactive three-process model of compassion: (1) *mindfulness*, (2) *kindness*, and (3) *common humanity*. Both theories overlap and are compatible, incorporating Gilbert's evolutionary processes and structure as well as Neff's three processes. Neff's (2011) work has taken these three elements of compassion and applied them through the concept of "self-compassion"—that is, how we apply this triad of compassion in relation to ourselves and others. Germer (2009) proposes three complementary defensive maneuvers that function like dialectical counterparts to the three-core compassion processes proposed by Neff (2011). He refers to these threat-oriented responses as the "three poisons": (1) self-absorption, (2) self-criticism, and (3) self-isolation. When both Neff's (2011) and Germer's (2009) processes are combined, the triadic, polarized dialectics succinctly describe not only core pathological processes but also the affiliative, actualizing capacities inherent in human beings and communities. These compassion-oriented conceptualizations also overlap well with evolutionary models of so-called interpersonal neurobiology—for example, polyvagal theory, mirror neurons, and neuronal resonance (Siegel, 2007; Porges, 2011; Gilbert, 2009). I propose that contemporary compassion-informed therapy is explicitly and implicitly enriched by contemporary relational psychoanalysis. Such cross-fertilization occurs through compassion therapies' debt to attachment theories and research, its ongoing theoretical and clinical contributions of intersubjectivity, and its ongoing clinical elucidation of how we literally relate to our selves from within a "two-person" context, seminally described as the "relational matrix"—that is, self, other, and interactional poles (Greenberg & Mitchell, 1983).

Core Processes

Brach (2003) proposes that among the three core processes of compassion (mindfulness, kindness, and common humanity), the foundational process is mindfulness. More generally, acceptance- and mindfulness-oriented processes have become essential components of functional contextualism (e.g., acceptance and commitment therapy, ACT, Hayes et al., 1999; dialectical behavior therapy, DBT, Linehan, 1993; functional analytic psychotherapy, FAP, Kohlenberg & Tsai, 1991). "Mindfulness" is defined as paying attention on purpose, in the present moment, and in a nonjudgmental way (Kabat-Zinn, 1990). Mindful processes may also facilitate flexibility in attention, behavior, perspective taking, and action repertoires that decrease aversively controlled responses and experientially avoidant maneuvers (Hayes et al., 1999). In empathically engaging the varieties of suffering that therapists routinely face, the equanimity cultivated in mindfulness practices may be essential not only in conducting effective therapy but also in avoiding therapist empathy burnout.

Mindfulness and Psychoanalysis

Not only has mindfulness become integral to functional contextualism, it has shown an enduring and increasingly influential history among psychoanalysts. Early classical psychoanalytic mindfulness-like concepts are visible in Freud's use of a nonlinear, nonevaluative, moment-to-moment processing via "free association" and "evenly hovering attention" and in Jung's Eastern-influenced synthetic-dialectical union of opposites, described in his "transcendent function" (Epstein, 2007). Since Freud's now infamous comments describing meditative states as "oceanic feelings," much classical analytic ink has been spilled debating whether such meditative practices are, in fact, no more than "narcissistic attempts to regain an ideal infantile state" (Epstein, 2007). These classical analytic debates not only reflect a limited understanding of Eastern contemplative practices but can also be seen as early attempts to distance psychoanalysis from superstitious dogma and religious authority, aligning itself instead with the objective-positivistic science of the day (Epstein, 2007; Safran, 2003). Current mindfully informed therapists from both psychoanalytic and functional contextualistic approaches now have a vastly more complete understanding of mindfulness and other contemplative processes. We know that the stream of consciousness, open-focus mindfulness (*vipassana*) does not target entirely the same functions as the more singularly focused concentration methods, nor does either method engage entirely the same processes as compassion-focused practices (those traditionally referred to as *metta* or *tonglen*, "loving-kindness," practices in Eastern traditions; Chödrön, 2007; Salzberg, 1995). A mindful and compassion-informed therapist would engage both formal and informal variations on concentration, mindfulness, and compassion processes. Psychotherapeutic compassion interactions may or may not look like the traditional mindful or loving-kindness meditations in their original form and application. Mindful interactions may be so integrated into the fabric of therapist-client verbal and nonverbal interaction as to make their original cultural forms practically invisible.

Mindfulness and Mentalization

Contemporary psychoanalysts have been exploring a form of interpersonal mindfulness called "mentalization." It may be argued that mentalization concepts of mindfulness are particularly relevant to compassion since they explore the more interpersonal, intersubjective elements of mindfulness. Allen, Fonagy, and Bateman (2008) describe mentalization as "minding our mind" processes and propose that "mentalizing—attending to the mental states in oneself and in others—is the most fundamental common factor among psychotherapeutic treatments." Fonagy's comprehensive conceptualization of mentalization deconstructs the interrelations among attachment processes, mood regulation, perspective taking, social-emotional intelligence, metacognition, and mindfulness. Emphasizing the more interpersonal subtleties of mentalization, Stolorow (2011) introduced the related concept of the intersubjective into psychotherapy, describing it as a finely tuned awareness of mutual contingencies and mutual regulation. Research has shown that those who report secure attachment styles are more readily able to engage in mentalized states of mind, as if their minds have been regularly and effectively recognized, embodied, or contained by another (Wallin, 2007). Reflective awareness of this mentalized type is also consistent with the mindful equanimity and interpersonally mood-regulated states developed in compassionate relationships (Gilbert, 2009; Germer & Siegel, 2012). Stern and his colleagues at the Boston Change Process Study Group have identified intersubjectivity processes and their implicit moment-to-moment awareness (a key feature of mindfulness) as potentially producing the most significant psychotherapeutic change.

Kindness and Pro-Sociality

Kindness and pro-sociality are humanity's primate legacy of caring-related behaviors, such as "tend and befriend" instincts and "tender" emotions. On primitive emotional and instinctual levels, kindness can be tending, nursing, nurturing, holding, consoling, mirroring, synchronizing, healing, soothing, and repairing; and, at more advanced levels, it is forgiveness, reconciliation, cooperation, mediation, disarmament, reciprocity, intimacy, love, subjective recognition, gratitude, trust, sharing, fairness, justice, and morality. Accessing this response repertoire is particularly difficult—but necessary—when we are vulnerable and when we inevitably fall short, fail, or make a mistake. Compassionately informed neurobiologists have argued that it is compassion that often facilitates courage—that is, allowing ourselves to be open and vulnerable, relating in a caring, open, and flexible way in the face of threats (Chödrön, 2007). Activation of the attachment-affiliative system, our opiate/oxytocin system, functions as our most basic "safety system." It is in this sense that the activation of the compassion system may act quite literally as a neurobiological "antidote" to fight-or-flight fear activation (Siegel, 2007).

Interpersonally, kindness is described by attachment-oriented clinicians as the mutual recognition of suffering, loss, and imperfection accompanied by conscious and/or unconscious consolation and mood regulation (Wallin, 2007). This interpersonal mechanism of action has also been described within the therapeutic cycle of rupture and repair—that is, threat or disappointment and disconnection, followed by mutual acknowledgment, consolation, reconciliation, and reconnection—a cycle capable of facilitating resilience and growth (Muran & Barber, 2010). Recent attachment research has demonstrated that securely attached individuals are more likely to engage in such compassionate repertoires (Neff, 2011).

Gilbert (2009) refers to some of the most difficult work of compassion therapy as the evoking and working through of "blockages."

Similarly, Germer (2009) refers to "backdrafts," which are various forms of paradoxical reactivity and resistance to "tolerating" compassion—for example, urges to experientially avoid, devalue, destroy, and annihilate any sense of fallibility, vulnerability, interdependence, and shame. This emphasis on evoking, mindfully working through, and replacing blockages with compassion shares elements of the "conflict model" of relational psychoanalysis: namely, that relationships—real or imagined—inevitably enter into moments of seemingly irreconcilable conflict or impasse. Compassion-informed therapy would cultivate mindful and kind reactions to these inevitable dissonant self-states—idealized selves, the actual self, shadow selves, undesired selves, and disowned or dissociated so-called no-self states (Mitchell, 1991; Stern, 2003). Conditioning compassionate reactions to dichotomized, shameful, narcissistic-superior, guilt-ridden, self-other-loathing, self-absorbed, self-isolating repertoires is central to compassion work (Gilbert, 2009, p. 316).

Clinical Application

The patient is a fifty-three-year-old married male who is highly intelligent, was well educated in Ivy League universities, and is an entrepreneur who has developed successful businesses for others. His presenting problem was severe depression, anger, and recent erratic employment and income.

Therapist: I can understand how it must be devastatingly difficult, especially being a guy in our culture...not being able to find and maintain a job, not making more of a contribution to making ends meet....It's a very real problem....We have talked about the feelings of shame it triggers before.

Client: Yeah...it does....*[silence]*

T: Together we have noticed how some part of your mind makes *punishing* demands each time you have trouble maintaining work; it claims that if you do not earn more money, then you can *do* nothing of value, *be* nothing of value to anyone. [*The therapist is attempting to mindfully note the narrow "if-then" conceptual sense of self, while implicitly evoking a more expansive sense of common humanity,*

101

implicitly offering flexible rules regarding what brings value to life, and activating affiliative values and networks beyond acquisition networks.]

C: So I'm just supposed to make believe everything is just fine and what...?'What the hell are you saying?...What are you suggesting?...Tell me exactly what the fuck you mean. *[Volume increasing, shoulders pushed forward, leaning on edge of his seat.]*

T: Not working *is* a very real problem...as are society's judgments about it....The shame you feel about not successfully acquiring work *is* perfectly understandable....It's activated your threat fight-flight-freeze system.... We've talked about freezing in your work efforts...then punishing yourself, even being punished by your family for it....This also leads to a very old pattern of trying to change yourself by threatening and punishing yourself...because your approach-and-acquire system did not work out as planned....Is that happening right now?...You now seem stuck in-between those two choices...rather than sometimes going for your self-kindness, socially supportive, or mindful options. *[Offering social connection and validation as well as kindness as a motivating alternatives.]*

C: So what am I supposed to do instead...some namby-pamby bullshit and let myself off the hook, what kind of pussy bullshit is that? You are full of shit. Who believes that shit?...Is this what I pay you for? Give me some real fuckin' answers about work. *[Even louder volume now, very red in the face, hunched over and fixedly staring at me. Blockages, backdraft, and blowback to compassionate alternatives being interpersonally evoked.]*

T: *[Pausing, slowing my speech.]* As we have seen before in session...when I try to be genuinely understanding and compassionate and to try and join with you to explore a less punishing way of motivating yourself...to unfreeze your ongoing efforts to work...and...to explore what may be of value to you or your loved ones while you continue to find work...then you often get even more agitated and aggressive...like what we are engaged in right here and now....Can we pause and look at what is happening right now between us. *[Offering mutual kindness, mindfully noticing "if-then" interpersonal contingencies and blockages, mindfully eliciting in-moment awareness.]*

C: You fuckin' asshole, what do you fuckin' expect?... *[Now literally spitting mad, nearly out of his seat, screaming his words, face totally reddened, breathing very hard.]*

T: *[Attempting to compassionately notice my own distress with a longer silent pause now....Engaging in my own silent, interpersonally focused attempt to "breath in compassion for myself," while "breathing out compassion for the client," a phrase repeated silently, somatically evoking my own affiliative and kindness network.]* You know how fast and automatic both my and your reactions can be...so can I practice just pausing?... *[I pause and breathe, gently meeting his eyes, exaggerated breathing together.]*...Now can we just privately notice our own thoughts and sensations, feelings...simply labeling them to ourselves as they pass, just like we've mindfully practiced before....Bear with me please....We can always pick up on where we left off in our discussion. [Pausing, waiting...breathing together. Evoking mindful processing and shared common humanity in our mutual distress and mutual attempt to kindly coordinate efforts, all in the context of shame and intolerance for interpersonal compassion.]*

C: *[After a minute or so, now sitting back in his seat, less red in the face.]* So are you saying that when people try to be kind or understanding with me...I...what...don't want them to? I blast them....That's just bizarre....Why?

T: Perhaps...perhaps given the highly unpredictable, intensely judgmental, and aggressive history you have with your family, perhaps pushing that highly unpredictable kindness away...not opening up to it and trusting it...made sense *at that time. [Compassionately validating history of erratic family conditioning, contrasting mindful awareness of past-present, and evoking a mindful awareness of present contingencies and persons.]*

Common Humanity: Self and the Mother of Illusions?

Neff (2011) proposes that the fundamental compassion process may be "common humanity" (p. 61). The *com-* in "*com-*mon humanity" and "*com-*passion" means "with"—with the universal experience of suffering, loss, imperfection, separateness, inter-being, and impermanence. The fact that this universal suffering is part and parcel of our separateness while simultaneously providing one of our most common experiences of belonging and interconnection is a dialectical paradox. It is only from this shared sense of intersubjective embodiment that other compassion elements, such as kindness, become a natural response. "Common humanity" refers to having both a conceptual understanding of intersubjectivity and interdependence, but perhaps more importantly, an emotional understanding of the same— an embodied, mutual sense of suffering and, hence, emotional interdependence. Evolutionary scientists conceptualize this ability to literally feel another's suffering, at least on its most primitive "embodied" emotional levels, as a form of "emotional contagion," and on a more developmentally advanced cognitive level, as the formal operation of perspective taking (e.g., temporarily adopting the perspective of "you as if I"; McHugh & Stewart, 2012). Historically, Mahayana Buddhist philosophy would describe compassion's "common humanity" as a reflection of our most fundamental, interconnected, interdependent nature, based on the interrelated philosophical concepts of "emptiness" and "no-self." These seminal Eastern concepts refer to a pre-Cartesian, nondualistic viewpoint in which no two things are absolutely separate; "objects" and "selves" are said to be inherently empty of their own independent existence; instead, all things are causally "interdependent" (i.e., *pratītyasamutpāda*, commonly translated "dependent origination"; Hahn, 1999). Contemporary contextualist philosophy has de-reified "self," not as the classic drive-oriented, individual closed system, but as a contextualized, interactive, intersubjective open system.

Much debate has taken place about the merits of an entirely individuated concept of self relative to "no-self" concepts and contextualist-constructionist concepts of self as multiplicity (see Engler's review in Safran, 2003). Pragmatically speaking, the nature of self is not approached as a question about some absolute, "real," ontological self, but as a question of what is the most effective way to self-identify—relevant to particular sets of values—for a given client, at a given point in time (McHugh & Stewart, 2012). Relational-cultural theory (RCT) has proposed that we grow toward relationships throughout the lifespan and that an alienated, separate sense of self is at the core of most psychological disorders (Surrey & Jordan, 2012). Contemporary relational psychoanalysts have referred to the concept of a fixed and separate self as the "myth of the isolated mind," a construction that brings us one step closer to modernity's crisis of alienation (Stolorow, 2011; Safran, 2003, p. 267). Similarly, ACT therapists refer to defusing the conceptualized self, deliteralizing self-as-content, and therefore facilitating flexible perspective taking as self-as-context (Hayes et al., 1999). This acceptance of "selfing" as flexible perspective taking (not reifying self into a noun) shares many features with contemporary relational psychoanalytic ideas about self as a construction and self as a multiplicity of self-states whose inherent multiplicity is entirely natural and normal in day-to-day functioning (Bromberg, 1996; Mitchell, 1991; Aron, 2006). Flexible perspective taking (self-as-context) processes may be engaged by ACT therapists in a variety of experiential ways, such as the use of metaphors or imagery and the practice of imagining a contextualized/interactive, less over-conceptualized, less over-identified, less isolated sense of self.

A fundamental Buddhist imagery meditation (circa eighth century), which experientially engages common humanity, is aptly called "exchange and equalize" (Santideva, 1997). "Exchange and equalize" beautifully foreshadows contemporary functional contextual and relational psychoanalytic attempts to interpersonally engage flexible, non-dichotomized perspective taking through imagining a variety of others (from easy to difficult persons) and exchanging yourself with them, feeling their being equal to you in wanting to be happy and wanting to not suffer. Relational analysts such as Benjamin (2004) describe breaking rigid, overidentified complementarities and sensing the commonality of a rhythmic third—such as feeling a larger pattern, a dance, a three-dimensional space rather than a two-dimensional one. Within these contemporary dialectical-synthetic concepts, one can also see the earlier object relations concepts of Klein's developmental spectrum. A maturating individual eventually synthesizes both good and bad objects or selves, moving from the very dichotomized experience of self or other as bad or good—that is, the "paranoid-schizoid position"—toward the more mature and compassionate "depressive position" reflecting awareness of common humanity, in which we see the rhythmic oscillation of good and bad in both ourselves and others (Benjamin, 2004; Mitchell & Black, 1995).

Common humanity provides a flexible and interconnected model from which to reexperience self and other; however, it also provides a therapeutic opening to explore, contact, and construct values. It is an inherently socially conscious concept and is therefore not unrelated to theories of moral development (Bar-Tal, 1982; Arnette, 2011). Compassion therapies' renewed scientific reexploration of kindness, ethics, values, social justice, social-consciousness, and existential identity is one of many forms of a resurgent humanistic interest in psychotherapy and beyond (Comas-Diaz, 2012). Values engagement and construction may be clinically accessed through guided imagery, or existential, Socratic questions such as "vertical ascent" questions or variations of the Gestalt "magic wand" or "miracle question"—"If a miracle happened and you were no longer depressed (anxious, etc.), what would you do? And then? And then?"; or "what would you do in your day-to-day life if you achieved X (insert client fantasy or wish)?" These are attempts to experientially contact and construct long-term sustainable values and the action patterns involved in actualizing them. This type of conscious, agent-driven, valued living is contrasted with reflexively escaping pain (threat system) or perusing pleasure (acquisition system). This value-based sense of self is not dissimilar to the recent relational psychoanalytic reformulations, which have moved away from classic drive-discharge and/or pleasure-principle models. Social relations are not merely a means to tension reduction; social interconnection and mutual recognition are exponentially and reciprocally adaptive and rewarding—they are the context in which we thrive, not just survive (Greenberg & Mitchell, 1983). Neff (2011) proposes that it is the explicit activation of attachment process, the activation of a more interpersonal mindfulness of "experience and experiencer," that common humanity and kindness components add to the effectiveness of singular mindfulness-based treatments (Neff, personal communication, April 13, 2013).

Not only is common humanity a viable alternative to the poisons of self-absorption and overidentification, it also takes compassion beyond the limitations of prior positive-humanistic concepts such as unconditional positive regard, self-acceptance, and the ubiquitous holy grail: self-esteem. It is important to make a fundamental distinction between compassion and self-esteem. Western culture is well known for its cultivation of self-esteem, feel-good positivism, individuality, and self-reliance. The self-esteem movement in psychology has turned out Americans who have scored top in the world at self-esteem surveys, while their quality of life measures have not increased proportionally. Academic performance, marital satisfaction, job satisfaction, leisure time, and social satisfaction have been either flat or negatively correlated with self-esteem's rise, while measures of pathology (teen suicide, depression/anxiety rates, incidence of attention/impulse disorders, narcissism) have risen exponentially (Baumeiser et al., 2003). Standard measures of self-esteem and compassion are inversely correlated; compassion is inversely correlated with narcissism—and these inverse correlations continue to hold true with measures of self-compassion (Barnard & Curry, 2011). Standard measures of self-esteem are based on social comparison; one must be superior in some way to another (even if only in relation to self-performance)—despite the statistical impossibility of most of us being better than average. Superiority often generalizes into "in-group" superiority, a tribalism in which the objectification of the inferior-outside group dominates the in-group perspective. Paradoxically, self-esteem can lead to envy rather than joy for the welfare of others, as well as isolation, extremes of narcissism or loathing for self or other (when we fall short of expectations), and aggression. Even so-called noncontingent self-esteem (self-acceptance or true self-esteem) can be individualistically self-absorbed. Compassion's common humanity, on the other hand, is based on intersubjectivity, commonality, and on reciprocal care for mutual suffering. Unlike compassion and self-compassion, self-esteem fails us exactly when we need it most, when we are vulnerable, when we have experienced the inevitability of failure and loss (Neff, 2011).

Summary

If we continue to idealize the personal pursuit of happiness for its own sake and pathologize vulnerability, compassion, common humanity, and emotional suffering, we will begin to ignore other forms of virtuous and valued living at our own iatrogenic peril (Whitaker, 2011). Compassion-focused therapies (e.g., CMT or mindful self-compasstion [MSC]) and compassion-informed therapies (e.g., ACT, FAP) address such problems of alienation and interconnection. A compassion-informed culture may be an increasingly relevant social necessity as we reach a tipping point in our increasingly globally interconnected society. If we can cultivate and embody our pre-Kantian compassion-based feelings, our implicit pro-social morality, we may be able to access the big rewards of cooperation versus the small rewards of individual action (De Waal, 2009, p. 163).

References

Allen, J. G., Fonagy, P., & Bateman, A. (2008). *Mentalizing in clinical practice.* Arlington, VA: American Psychiatric Publishing.

Armstrong, K. (1993). *A history of God.* New York, NY: Ballantine Books.

Arnette, J. (2011). *Human development: A cultural approach.* Upper Saddle River, NJ: Pearson.

Aron, L. (2006). Analytic impasse and the third: Clinical implications of intersubjectivity theory. *International Journal of Psychoanalysis, 87,* 349–368.

Bar-Tal, D. (1982). Sequential development of helping behavior: A cognitive-learning approach. *Developmental Review, 2,* 101–124.

Barnard, L. K., & Curry, J. F. (2011). Self-compassion: Conceptualizations, correlates, and interventions. *Review of General Psychology, 15,* 289–303.

Baumeiser, R. F., Campbell, J. D., Kruger, I., & Vohs, K. D. (2003). Does high self-esteem cause better performance, interpersonal success, happiness, or healthier lifestyles? *Psychological Science in the Public Interest, 4,* 1–44.

Beebe, B., & Lachmann, F. M. (1998). Co-constructing inner and relational processes: Self- and mutual regulation in infant research and adult treatment. *Psychoanalytic Psychology, 15,* 480–516.

Benjamin, J. (2004). Beyond doer and done to: An intersubjective view of thirdness. *Psychoanalytic Quarterly, 73,* 5–46.

Bowlby, J. (1988). *A secure base: Parent-child attachment and healthy human development.* New York, NY: Basic Books.

Brach, T. (2003). *Radical acceptance: Embracing your life with the heart of the Buddha.* New York, NY: Bantam Books.

Bromberg, P. M. (1996). Standing in the spaces: The multiplicity of self and the psychoanalytic relationship. *Contemporary Psychoanalysis, 32,* 509–535.

Chodron, P. (2007). *Practicing peace in times of war.* Boston, MA: Shambhala.

Comas-Diaz, L. (2012). Psychotherapy as a healing practice, scientific endeavor, and social justice action. *Psychotherapy, 49,* 473–474.

De Waal, F. (2009). *The age of empathy: Nature's lessons for a kinder society.* New York, NY: Three Rivers Press.

Dovido, J. F., Piliavin, J. A., Schroeder, D. A., & Penner, L. A. (2006). *The social psychology of prosocial behavior.* East Sussex, England: Psychology Press.

Engler, J. (2003). Psychoanalysis and Buddhism as cultural institutions. In J. D. Safran (Ed.), *Psychoanalysis and Buddhism: An unfolding dialogue* (pp. 35–79). Somerville: Wisdom.

Epstein, M. (2007). *Psychotherapy without the self: A Buddhist perspective.* New Haven, CT: Yale College.

Germer, C. K. (2009). *The mindful path to self-compassion: Freeing yourself from destructive thoughts and emotions.* New York, NY: Guilford Press.

Germer R. D., & Siegel, C. (2012). Wisdom and compassion: Two wings of a bird. In *Wisdom and compassion in psychotherapy* (pp. 7–34). New York, NY: Guilford Press.

Gilbert, P. (2009). *The compassionate mind: A new approach to life's challenges.* Oakland, CA: New Harbinger.

Greenberg, J. R., & Mitchell, S. A. (1983). *Object relations in psychoanalytic theory.* Cambridge, MA: Harvard University Press.

Hahn, T. N. (1999). *The heart of Buddha's teaching: Transforming suffering into peace, joy, and liberation.* Berkeley, CA: Broadway Books.

Håkansson, J. (2003). *Exploring the phenomenon of empathy.* (Doctoral dissertation). Stockholm University, Sweden.

Hayes, S. C., Strosahl, K. D., & Wilson, K. G. (1999). *Acceptance and commitment therapy: An experiential approach to behavior change.* New York, NY: Guilford Press.

Hayes, S. C., Villatte, M., Levin, M., & Hildebrandt, M. (2011). Open, aware, and active: Contextual approaches as an emerging trend in the behavioral and cognitive therapies. *Annual Review of Clinical Psychology, 71,* 141–168.

Kabat-Zinn, J. (1990). *Full catastrophe living: Using the wisdom of your body and mind to face stress, pain, and illness.* New York, NY: Bantam Dell.

Kohlenberg, R. J., & Tsai, M. (1991). *Functional analytic psychotherapy: Creating intense and curative therapeutic relationships.* New York, NY: Plenum Press.

Linehan, M. M. (1993). *Cognitive-behavioral treatment of borderline personality disorder.* New York, NY: Guilford Press.

Lipps, T. (1903). *Aesthetik.* Hamburg, Germany: Leopold Voss.

McHugh, L., & Stewart, I. (2012). *The self and perspective taking: Contributions and applications from modern behavioral science.* Oakland, CA: New Harbinger.

Mitchell, S. A. (1991). Contemporary perspectives on self: Toward an integration. *Psychoanalytic Dialogues, 1,* 121–147.

Mitchell, S. A., & Black, M. J. (1995). *Freud and beyond: A history of modern psychoanalytic thought.* New York, NY: Basic Books.

Moacanin, R. (2003). *The essence of Jung's psychology and Tibetan Buddhism: Western and Eastern paths to the heart.* Somerville, MA: Wisdom.

Muran, J. C., & Barber, J. P. (2010). *The therapeutic alliance: An evidence-based guide to practice.* New York, NY: Guilford Press.

Neff, K. (2011). *Self-compassion: Stop beating yourself up and leave insecurity behind.* New York, NY: HarperCollins.

Porges, W. P. (2011). *The polyvagal theory: Neurophysiological foundations of emotion, attachment, communication, and self-regulation.* New York, NY: W. W. Norton.

Rogers, C. (1959). A theory of therapy, personality and interpersonal relationships as developed in the client-centered framework. In S. Koch (Ed.), *Formulations of the person and the social context.* New York, NY: McGraw Hill.

Ryan, C., & Jetha, C. (2010). *Sex at dawn: How we mate, why we stray, and what it means for modern relationships.* New York, NY: HarperCollins.

Safran, J. D. (2003). *Psychoanalysis and Buddhism: An unfolding dialogue*. Somerville, MA: Wisdom.

Salzberg, S. (1995). *Lovingkindness: The revolutionary art of happiness*. Boston, MA: Shambhala.

Santideva. (1997). *A guide to the Bodhisattva way of life*. Ithaca, NY: Snow Lion.

Siegel, D. J. (2007). *The mindful brain: Reflection and attunement in the cultivation of well-being*. New York, NY: W.W. Norton.

Stern, D. B. (2003). The fusion of horizons: Dissociation, enactment, and understanding. *Psychoanalytic Dialogues, 13*, 843–873.

Stolorow, R. D. (2011). Toward a renewal of personology in psychotherapy research. *Psychotherapy, 49*, 442–444.

Sullivan, H. S. (1953). *The interpersonal theory of psychiatry*. New York, NY: W. W. Norton.

Surrey, J., & Jordan, J. V. (2012) The wisdom of connection. In C. K. Germer & R. D. Siegel (Eds.), *Wisdom and compassion in psychotherapy: Deepening mindfulness in clinical practice* (pp. 163–175). New York, NY: Guilford Press.

Tirch, D. D. (2012). *The compassionate-mind guide to overcoming anxiety: Using compassion-focused therapy to calm worry, panic, and fear*. Oakland, CA: New Harbinger.

Titchener, E. B. (1909). *Lectures on the experimental psychology of the thought-processes*. New York, NY: Macmillan.

Tsai, M., Kohlenberg, R. J., Kanter, J. W., Kohlenberg, B., Follette, W. C., & Callaghan, G. M. (2009). *A guide to functional analytic psychotherapy: Awareness, courage, love, and behaviorism*. New York, NY: Springer Science + Business Media, LLC.

Wallin, D. J. (2007). *Attachment in psychotherapy*. New York, NY: Guilford Press.

Whitaker, R. (2011). *Anatomy of an epidemic: Magic bullets, psychiatric drugs, and the astonishing rise of mental illness in America*. New York, NY: Broadway Books.

Wilson, K. G. (2008). *Mindfulness for two. An acceptance and commitment therapy approach to mindfulness in psychotherapy*. Oakland, CA: New Harbinger.

Winnicott, D. W. (1971). The use of an object and relating through identifications. In *Playing and reality* (Vol. 13). New York, NY: Routledge.

CHAPTER 6

Mentalization: An Interpersonal Approach to Mindfulness

Geoff Goodman, PhD, ABPP

Mentalization and mindfulness are processes believed to produce therapeutic change in patients' symptoms and emotional well-being (Fonagy, Gergely, Jurist, & Target, 2002; Goodman, 2010; Kabat-Zinn, 2003). This chapter underscores the points of convergence and divergence between these two constructs. I argue that mentalization and mindfulness overlap in two key areas of therapeutic experience—observing mental phenomena, and labeling and/or describing mental phenomena—but that mentalization transcends these key areas by adding an interpersonal component that includes the minds of both the patient and the therapist. The chapter ends with two clinical vignettes from the treatment of a ten-year-old boy diagnosed with encopresis and a brief discussion of the methods used to enhance mentalization in this treatment, contrasted with a mindfulness approach.

Mentalization

Fonagy and his colleagues (2002) consider mentalization to be a developmental process in which the primary caregiver simultaneously communicates (1) an empathic understanding of the child's mental states and (2) a separateness from the child that helps facilitate the symbolization of emotional phenomena as mental states to be observed, as well as experienced. These communications occur within a secure attachment relationship in which the child feels secure in exploring his or her own mind, as well as the mind of his or her primary caregiver.

Fonagy (1991) defined "mentalization" as "the capacity to conceive of conscious and unconscious mental states in oneself and others" (p. 641). The defining feature of a mental state, according to Fonagy, is its intentionality, which includes "beliefs, thoughts, desires, expectations, etc." (p. 640). Fonagy also referred to this capacity as a theory of mind, which a person uses to understand and predict the behavior of oneself and others.

Fonagy et al. (2002) also used another term, "reflective functioning," to describe "the operationalization of the psychological processes underlying the capacity to mentalize" (p. 24). Reflective functioning, according to these authors, is "the ability to give plausible interpretations of one's own and others' behavior in terms of underlying mental states" (p. 26).

What does mentalization look like? You are walking down the street, and a runner is approaching you. About fifty yards away from you, he suddenly crosses the street. Why did he cross the street? You turn around and see that he has crossed back over onto your side of the street to continue his run. Why did he do that? You remember that you are walking your scary-looking German shepherd and reason that the runner must have been afraid of being bitten and crossed the street to avoid a possible altercation. You attribute the man's crossing the street to the possibility that he was experiencing an underlying mental state of fear in relation to your dog's menacing appearance.

Fonagy et al. (2002) argued that deficits in this mentalizing process are related to underlying psychopathology. For example, in the previous scenario, you might notice the runner crossing the street and say to yourself, *That's weird,* and continue walking—not realizing that your German shepherd might look scary to someone. You failed to mentalize the experience of the other person and your own influence on the other person's behavior.

Fonagy's writings on mentalization emphasize (1) the intersubjective nature of mental states and (2) the connection between the mental states of self and others and the behavior of self and others. The fact that the mental states of self and other people influence each other and underlie the mutual influence of the behaviors of self and other people represents a key ingredient in the regulation of affects, the predictability of interactions, and the organization of the self (Fonagy et al., 2002).

Explicit and Implicit Mentalization

Fonagy and Target (1997) defined two forms of memory—explicit, autobiographical, declarative memory and implicit, nonreflective, procedural memory. Emotional and impressionistic information dominates implicit or procedural memory and is accessible only through performance. Schematic representations of object relations are examples of procedural memories. Mentalization can rely on explicit (declarative) or implicit (procedural) memory (Allen, 2003). Mentalizing about the runner in the illustration above occurred in conscious awareness in a deliberate manner—explicit mentalization. Instinctively holding your German shepherd's leash more tightly when you first spot the runner occurs in a nonconscious, procedural, nonreflective manner. Such mentalizing illustrates intuitive empathy for what the runner might be feeling as he approaches your dog. No thoughts need appear in your conscious awareness to grasp the leash more firmly. In psychotherapy, "implicit and explicit mentalization are brought together" (Bateman & Fonagy, 2004a, p. 48). Explicit mentalization seems to be the therapeutic process by which implicit and explicit mentalization are brought together: "The explicit content of interpreting is merely the vehicle for the implicit process that has therapeutic value" (Bateman & Fonagy, 2004a, p. 47). On the other hand, "the foundation of any therapeutic work must by definition be implicit mentalization" (p. 47).

Mentalization-Based Treatment for Borderline Personality Disorder

Bateman and Fonagy (2004a, 2004b) have embedded the concept of mentalization in an empirically supported treatment for patients suffering from borderline personality disorder (BPD) called mentalization-based treatment (MBT). According to the authors (Bateman & Fonagy, 2004a), "Treatment focuses on increasing mentalization in borderline patients" (p. 36). "Retaining mental closeness" (p. 44) is the therapeutic principle used to accomplish the enhancement of mentalizing capacities. Specific therapeutic interventions include "representing accurately the current or immediately past feeling state of the patient and its accompanying internal representations," and "strictly and systematically avoiding the temptation to enter conversation about matters not directly linked to the patient's beliefs, wishes, feelings, etc." (p. 44). Empathic attunement to changes in mental states, active differentiation of mental states, and discussion of the patient's mental states in relation to the therapist's and others' perceived mental states in the here and now are other specific interventions that facilitate mental closeness.

Mindfulness in Psychotherapy

Hayes (2004) has called the recent proliferation of mindfulness-based treatments "the third wave" of behavior therapy, which could not have occurred if cognitive behavioral techniques could account for the effective track record of cognitive behavioral therapy (CBT). Hayes (2004), a researcher trained in the cognitive behavioral tradition and the founder of acceptance and commitment therapy (ACT), has concluded that the evidence against the unique effectiveness of cognitive behavioral techniques propelled the search for other techniques that might account for positive outcomes associated with CBT more consistently. Specifically, clinical improvement often occurs before cognitive techniques have been implemented (Ilardi & Craighead, 1994, 1999; Wilson, 1999), a fact that prompted two cognitive behavioral experts to conclude that there is "no additive benefit to providing cognitive interventions in cognitive therapy" (Dobson & Khatri, 2000, p. 913).

According to Hayes (2004), the solution for the CBT field was to move away from direct, first-order change strategies of specific thoughts and cognitive schemas and to embrace an indirect, "principle-focused" (p. 5) approach that would "considerably broaden the focus of change" (p. 6) to emphasize patient experience. This shift paved the way for the third wave of mindfulness-based treatments. If the reader doubts that the third wave signifies a shift toward a more psychoanalytic understanding and approach to treatment, he or she might be convinced by what some might find an ironic quotation from Linehan and her colleagues (Robins, Schmidt, & Linehan, 2004): "In contrast to the experimental evidence required by psychology, Zen [mindfulness practice] emphasizes experiential evidence as a means of understanding the world" (p. 39). Of course, over the past fifty years, members of the CBT community have sharply criticized psychoanalysts for privileging just this kind of evidence in their clinical work (e.g., Wolpe & Rachman, 1960).

Components of Mindfulness

In an important study to determine the various facets of mindfulness measured by five different questionnaires, Baer, Smith, Hopkins, Krietemeyer, and Toney (2006) conducted both exploratory and confirmatory factor analyses on all the items of these five questionnaires, using two samples of undergraduate students (one of 613 students, the other of 268). The results confirmed the presence of five facets of mindfulness: observing, describing, acting with awareness (concentration), accepting without judgment, and nonreactivity to inner experience. The first component, observing, is the observation of all thoughts, feelings, and sensations within the spectrum of awareness. The second, describing, is the labeling of these observed mental phenomena with words. The third, acting with awareness, is the focusing of awareness without distraction. The fourth, accepting without judgment, is refraining from applying evaluative labels to experience in the present moment and being open to all experiences, whether pleasant or unpleasant. The fifth, nonreactivity to inner experience, is not reacting impulsively to emotions.

Conceptual Problems with Mindfulness

The construct of mindfulness omits any recognition of an interpersonal component. Even as psychoanalysis has increasingly embraced a two-person psychology in which the therapist and patient are mutually influencing each other in ways that promote therapeutic change (Aron, 1990), the third wave of behavioral therapy seems to be mired in a one-person psychology. Almost nothing in the mindfulness literature suggests that the interaction between the therapist and patient influences the patient's capacity to engage in a state of mindfulness, sustain it, or practice it outside of psychotherapy sessions. The emphasis is on the private experience of the patient, not on a relationship (Bishop et al., 2004). In mindfulness-based treatments, it is the exposure to "disturbing emotions" that is the essential ingredient (A. M. Hayes & Feldman, 2004, p. 258), not an understanding of what these emotions might mean or might be communicating within the context of relationships (Malatesta-Magai, 1991). Commenting on the positive results of his outcome study of psoriasis patients randomly assigned to two conditions—with and without guided meditation instructions delivered by audiotape—Kabat-Zinn (2003) concluded that "social support [removed by the use of audiotape]...cannot be a major factor in the observed outcome" (p. 152), as though the therapist's audiotaped voice could not serve this very function.

What is glaringly absent is the therapist's use of mindfulness as a tool to help understand the patient in his or her totality. Freud (1912) envisioned the therapist's unconscious as a perceptual tool used to make a connection with the unconscious of the patient—what Schore (2006) referred to as a connection between the right hemispheres of two brains. This deep, intuitive connection, facilitated by the psychoanalytic process, is believed to promote a number of therapeutic changes, some of which occur outside the rational domain of the left hemisphere. In mindfulness-based treatments, the therapist's practice of mindfulness does not serve the purpose of modifying the intervention technique to facilitate mindfulness in the patient, or containing and metabolizing the patient's unbearable internal experiences, or even facilitating the patient's affect regulation. Mindfulness-based treatments focus strictly on the patient's relationship to mental phenomena—observing these phenomena and letting them go. Related to this point, mindfulness researchers underscore self-regulation rather than interactive regulation. And people who train their minds to become mindful develop relationships with their thoughts and feelings, not with others. Consider the anthropomorphization of emotions in this Buddhist monk's description of a mindfulness exercise: "Look straight in the eye of the disturbing emotion and understand what it is and how it works....When one genuinely looks at it, it suddenly loses its strength" (Goleman, 2003, p. 81). One might draw the conclusion that in this therapeutic model, one's relationships to one's emotions replace one's relationships to real people.

Points of Convergence and Divergence

Mindfulness and mentalization are neighboring constructs. Mindfulness promotes differentiation between the self and the mental activity of the self, thus facilitating the symbolization process. Mindfulness researchers call this process "decentering" (Lau et al., 2006; Teasdale et al., 2002): "awareness of one's experience with some distance and disidentification rather than being carried away by one's thoughts and feelings" (Lau et al., 2006, p. 16). Mentalization consists of taking an inventory of one's thoughts, feelings, and desires, which also promotes differentiation and facilitates symbolization. Both constructs also define openness and curiosity about one's own mental states as hallmark qualities of their respective constructs.

The constructs of mindfulness and mentalization are conceptually distinct in two ways. First, while mindfulness consists of paying attention only to one's own mental states (one-person psychology), mentalization consists of formulating hypotheses of others' mental states (two-person psychology) as well one's own mental states. Second, the goal of mentalization is to discover the meaning of mental states in interaction with others' mental states, whereas mindfulness has no stated goal (Kabat-Zinn, 2003). The decentering inherent in the mindfulness process, by contrast, is to liberate the person from the domination of literal language and, consequently, the literal meanings associated with language (Hayes, 2004; Hayes & Wilson, 2003). Related to this idea is the role of causality in the two constructs. Central to mentalization is the idea that mental states mutually influence each other, a process of causality that facilitates the formation of behavioral expectations of self in relation to others. By contrast, central to mindfulness is the suspension of belief in causality—that all internal and external experiences exist only in this moment, not in any past or future moments. Causality implies the passage of time; therefore, any process of exploring causal relationships between mental states would be considered mindless, not mindful. Thus, mentalization and mindfulness are neighboring constructs with some conceptual overlap, yet in some ways they also have differing therapeutic objectives.

This liberation of the self from the mental activity of the self—thoughts, feelings, wishes, and sensations—serves the purpose of psychic differentiation and separateness. One could conceptualize the holding on to versus the letting go of mental phenomena within an attachment paradigm. Perhaps patients categorized as having a preoccupied/entangled attachment pattern—emotionally hyperactivated, lacking differentiation from parental relationships, and embroiled in past experiences (Goodman, 2002; Kobak, Cole, Ferenz-Gillies, Fleming, & Gamble, 1993; Main & Goldwyn, 1994; Main, Kaplan, & Cassidy, 1985)—could benefit from a therapeutic approach designed to promote separation of self from feelings. Based on her empirical work, Dozier (2003) suggested that clinical intervention is most effective when the therapist provides a "gentle challenge" (p. 254) to the patient. In other words, separation-promoting interventions are provided to patients with preoccupied states of mind that reflect discomfort with autonomy. Perhaps the therapeutic success of dialectical behavior therapy (DBT) in treating patients with BPD (Linehan et al., 1991; Linehan, 1993a; Linehan, 1994)—previously associated with a preoccupied attachment pattern (Agrawal, Gunderson, Holmes, & Lyons-Ruth, 2004; Bateman & Fonagy, 2004b)—is related to the gentle challenge to these patients to detach from their hyperactivated emotional states. This detachment would promote a more modulated regulation of emotional states that could reduce the impulsive behaviors typically associated with BPD.

How would a mindfulness-based treatment approach work for patients who feel disconnected from interpersonal relationships—those patients categorized as having a dismissing attachment pattern? Dismissing individuals "limit the influence of attachment relationships and experiences in thought, in feeling, or in daily life" (Main & Goldwyn, 1994, p. 126). Mindfulness lacks the interpersonal dimension that could provide the gentle challenge that dismissing patients need to resolve their fears of closeness and dependence on others. In fact, it seems plausible to suggest that mindfulness reinforces a dismissing attachment pattern, characterized by defensive exclusion (Bowlby, 1973) of attachment needs. Consider the words of the practice's originator, the Buddha (Siddhartha Gautama): "He who loves fifty people has fifty woes; he who loves no one has no woes" and "Do not depend on others" ("Buddha quotes," n.d., pp. 2, 6). These words reflect the attitude of the prototypical dismissing person. Achieving distance between the self and the self's thoughts and feelings might prove beneficial for someone struggling with issues of separation and differentiation, but this approach might strengthen the defenses of a patient walled off from dependence and intimacy.

Kabat-Zinn (2003) has denied the importance of social support in his audiotaped mindfulness instruction; however, I would argue that the fantasy of a listening, nonjudgmental, supportive therapist ready to contain whatever unbearable material emerges is simultaneously alive in the patient's mind and empowering the patient to sustain a mindful state of consciousness. Mentalization-based treatment presents an interpersonal component that can increase the effectiveness of mindfulness-based treatments. Specifically, mentalization-based approaches explicitly identify the therapist-patient relationship as the fulcrum of therapeutic change.

Figure 1 is a Venn diagram of the common and distinctive features among these two constructs. According to exploratory and confirmatory factor analyses conducted by Baer et al. (2006), mindfulness consists of five factors: (1) observing mental phenomena, (2) describing or labeling mental phenomena, (3) acting with awareness or concentration, (4) nonjudging of mental phenomena, and (5) nonreactivity to mental phenomena. Although the Reflective Functioning Scale (RFS) developed by Fonagy and his colleagues (Fonagy, Target, Steele, & Steele, 1998) cannot be factor-analyzed, one can extrapolate four components from their operational definition of reflective functioning: (1) observing mental phenomena, (2) describing or labeling mental phenomena, (3) describing the meaning and motivation of one's own and others' behavior as the product of mental states, and (4) understanding the intrinsic linkage and mutual influence of mental states in self and others. Figure 1 demonstrates that the two constructs conceptually overlap on two features, (1) observing mental phenomena and (2) describing or labeling mental phenomena. Research is needed to determine (1) whether observing mental phenomena and describing or labeling mental phenomena are the two specific features shared by mentalization and mindfulness responsible for producing therapeutic change across theoretical orientations or (2) whether describing the meaning and motivation of one's own and others' behavior as the product of mental states and understanding the intrinsic linkage and mutual influence of mental states in self and others are two additional specific features implicitly responsible for producing therapeutic change.

Figure 1.
Common and Distinctive Features Between Mindfulness and Mentalization

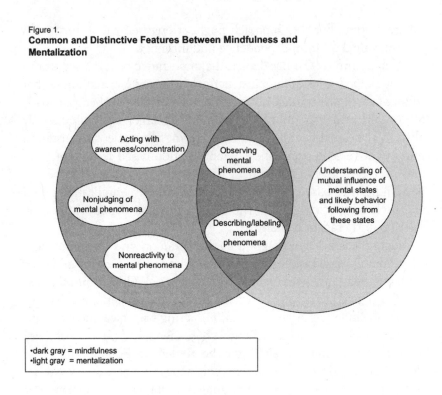

•dark gray = mindfulness
•light gray = mentalization

Enhancing Mentalization in Children

Fonagy and Target (2000) highlight three aspects to enhancing mentalization in child therapy: (1) enhancing reflective processes, (2) providing opportunities for play, and (3) working in the transference (see also Bleiberg, Fonagy, & Target, 1997). First, enhancing reflective processes consists of the therapist helping the child to observe his or her own emotions (this resembles the observing facet of mindfulness; Goodman, 2010). This process also includes understanding and labeling the child's emotional states, including physiological and affective cues (this resembles the describing/labeling facet of mindfulness; Goodman, 2010). Noticing how these mental states change over time in the here and now of therapy is crucial to enhancing mentalization in child therapy.

Second, play within the therapeutic relationship provides the child with opportunities to symbolize his or her dysregulated emotional states. This facilitates impulse control, delay of gratification, and affect tolerance—key outcomes for children who tend to externalize their affects. Play provides a potential space (Winnicott, 1968) or pathway to explore relationships one step removed from reality (Mayes & Cohen, 1993) by testing out new ways of relating to the therapist and regulating affect through the therapist, as well as by forming new expectations of affective responses from the therapist. The play process enables "feelings and thoughts, wishes and beliefs [to] be experienced by the child as significant and respected on the one hand, but on the other as not being of the same order as physical reality" (Bateman & Fonagy, 2004b, p. 84). This process naturally facilitates symbolic functioning, where words can encode unnamed affects and thus provide affective containment.

Third, working in the transference consists of allowing the child to explore inside the therapist's mind. The work of therapy takes place through observations of the therapist-patient relationship, focusing on the mental states of therapist and patient. Keaveny and her colleagues (2012) suggested two techniques that facilitate this mentalizing stance: "pause and review" and "Columbo-style curiosity" (the latter coined by Fowler, Garety, & Kuipers, 1995). In pause and review, the therapist invites the child to stop the interaction and reflect on what has just transpired between them, emphasizing what the therapist might have been thinking or feeling. Columbo-style curiosity facilitates the review process. The therapist investigates the interaction in a somewhat naïve way, which acknowledges that the child might have perceived the interaction in a way unanticipated by the therapist. The therapist demonstrates an interest in and understanding of the child's perspective without reflecting back the affective tone of the original interaction. The therapist works in the here and now, placing emotions stimulated by the therapeutic relationship in a context of sequential mental experiences.

Using humor in the therapeutic relationship to show understanding, without retaliating or withdrawing from the child, also clears a space for patients to own and disown threatening mental states while testing the therapist's attunement to the most vulnerable aspects of the child's self (Bleiberg, 2000). Working in the transference requires the therapist to "do something fresh and creative...which has as one component the real impact of the real patient on the [therapist], yet through its novelty reassures the patient that his [or her] attempt at control and tyranny has not completely succeeded....Without such creative spark the [therapy] is doomed to become an impasse, a rigid stereotypic repetition of pathological exchanges" (Fonagy & Target, 2000, p. 78). In the following clinical application, I hope to demonstrate the effect of a creative spark on the therapeutic process—retaining mental closeness to the child patient.

Clinical Application 1

Dennis Duress (a pseudonym), a ten-year-old only child, was referred to me for treatment by his parents because he was defecating in his pants at home and school. Dennis had been in full-time daycare since he was two years old because his parents both worked full-time jobs. At the time of these sessions (reported below), I was treating Dennis in outpatient therapy multiple times per week. At the outset of treatment, Dennis denied having feelings about anything. He seemed to put his unpleasant feelings into a compartment and leave them there for long periods of time, which gave him an illusory feeling of control—manifested by his ordering me around during sessions. He often behaved as though he were more powerful than I. Dennis had no friends at school and had alienated potential friends in his neighborhood. He seemed to be using encopresis as a highly effective mode of distancing himself from others and forcing others to distance themselves from him when he or they were getting too emotionally close and therefore making him feel too emotionally vulnerable. During the early treatment, Dennis erected roadblocks to the path of my discovery of his personhood: He incessantly played competitive board and card games in which he compulsively cheated to guarantee a favorable outcome. He often spent entire sessions talking about monster trucks—their designs, the drivers, the tricks they perform, the winners in various categories of monster truck contests, and their sponsors. He also demonstrated an encyclopedic knowledge of monster truck trivia. He was delighted and content to maintain a monotonous pattern of sharing facts about monster trucks. I felt marginalized in my relationship with Dennis, unable to reach him.

Toward this end, I sought to break up this in-session monotony. Dennis was making a Lego house for a monster truck driver to live in. I started building a Lego monster truck.

Dennis: Don't do that; it won't fit into the garage.

Me: I'm going to build a monster truck called The Duress Express. I'm going to make it out of aluminum, because it's an ultra-light metal. It's going to be super light, and I'm going to catch some really sick air *[a colloquial expression I learned from Dennis that indicates that during a jump, the truck stays in the air a long time].*

Dennis: You can't do that. Aluminum monster trucks were outlawed in 2000, and besides, monster trucks have to be a certain weight. You'll get disqualified.

Me: Well, I'm going to hide cinder blocks in my truck's secret compartment that the inspectors will never find, and then I'll just pop them out after the precontest weigh-in. And then I'll catch such sick air, the broadcasters will call it "diseased air"—and if you breathe it, you will die—that's how sick the air I'm going to catch will be.

Dennis: There can't be any secret compartments. You'll get disqualified, because your monster truck won't be regulation.

Me: Well, I'm also going to attach wings to my monster truck—The Duress Express—and it'll be able to fly.

Dennis: There's a monster truck sponsored by the Air Force that already has wings. And I'll sue you for using my last name. If you're so smart, how are you going to finance your monster truck?

Me: I have the American Psychological Association lined up as a sponsor.

Dennis: It's never going to happen.

In spite of its mildly antagonistic nature, we were engaged in a relationship. I was making emotional contact with him by using my own imagination and getting him to engage with my mind. In such cases where the child has experienced abuse or neglect and thus pho-bically avoids contact with an adult's mental world because of what he or she might find there, the therapeutic intent is "to facilitate the establishment of a beachhead, an area of self-other relatedness" (Fonagy & Target, 2000, p. 86). I was engaging Dennis any way I knew how, so that he could risk peering inside my mind and see that, not only was it harmless, but it was also favorably predisposed to his private interests. Every child in play therapy should be able to peer inside the therapist's mind and find a reasonable facsimile of his or her own authentic self—both its good and bad parts. The child observes that if the therapist can tolerate and survive the presence of the bad parts (the so-called alien self), perhaps the child can too. As illus-trated below, Dennis responded to this provocative interaction by showing me more of his internal world and permitting himself to enjoy our developing relationship.

Clinical Application 2

In the following session, Dennis brought his toy monster trucks in a customized suitcase, laid them out on the floor, set up ramps and obstacles, and directed each truck through the obstacle course with no variation—each truck performing identically to the previous one. I took a truck and began doing unconventional tricks with it—coun-teracting his ritualistic "play."

Dennis: That's impossible.

Me: You know that The Duress Express has already performed these very same tricks at Monster Jam.

Dennis: There is no Duress Express.

As I watched him run each truck through his obstacle course in monotonous succession, something novel happened—he began per-forming more unconventional tricks with his own monster trucks. I settled into the role of an arena announcer:

Me: Did you see that? That backflip was unbelievable! And then the slap wheelie followed by—I don't even know what you would call that, but it was incredible! What was that? A *double* backflip? Ladies and gentlemen, what you are witnessing here today is unprecedented in the history of Monster Jam!

Dennis allowed himself to smile when I pretended to be an arena announcer. He even joined me occasionally in the announcing duties:

Dennis: Here's Tom Meents attempting a *second* double backflip of the day. Can he save it? Oh, he saved it! He just completed the *second* double backflip of the day!

Me: Did you see him save it? Unbelievable!

We were collaborating for perhaps the first time in treatment. He was surreptitiously getting a taste of a relationship without having to defend against it. My efforts at engaging him—getting him to experience mental closeness to me—went unnoticed by him.

By making up stories, I was introducing myself as a person with my own intentions and feelings. Essentially, I was introducing Dennis to a separate person eager to engage with him on a series of adventures in fantasy, which he ultimately preferred to the monotony of his own ritualized play that, characteristically, shut me out. I chose story lines that mirrored his own stories, yet illustrated to him that I had a different understanding of them. For example, in my story, I too had a monster truck that competed with the others, yet my monster truck was built differently and performed unconventional tricks. According to Fonagy and Target (2000), "the capacity to take a playful stance may be a critical step in the development of mentalization as it requires holding simultaneously in mind two realities: the pretend and the actual....The [therapist] has to teach the child about minds, principally by opening his mind to the patient's explorations of the [therapist's] internal world" (pp. 86–87).

Just as a mentalizing caregiver communicates his or her understanding of the infant's mental states through the process of marking—using exaggerated facial and vocal expressions to indicate that the caregiver is aware of the infant's mental state but not experiencing what the infant is experiencing (Fonagy et al., 2002)—I used exaggerated storytelling to indicate to Dennis that I was aware of his mental state but was not experiencing what he was consciously experiencing. Thus, I was both attached to him as a secure base and separate from him. This stance simultaneously confirmed the existence of our relationship and challenged his need to dominate and control me, which deprived me of my subjectivity and thrust him back into his isolated, lonely position.

Commentary on Mentalization and Mindfulness in This Treatment

This treatment suggested the use of mentalizing interventions to make emotional contact with this emotionally remote ten-year-old boy. Specifically, I used play as a vehicle for interaction, which allowed Dennis to view the contents of my mind and determine that I valued the contents of his own. I believe that this experience and others like it will generalize to other relationships, in which he will begin to trust others enough to use them to regulate his emotions, just as other same-aged children do.

A sole reliance on mindfulness interventions, without the interpersonal component, would have doomed this treatment. Early in the treatment, I attempted an exclusively affect-labeling approach focused on Dennis's feelings—consistent with mindfulness principles. This strategy repeatedly failed, as Dennis emphatically stated that he did not want to talk about his feelings. He even complained to his mother (who reported it to me) that I asked the same five boring questions in every session—all having to do with feelings. I realized that an exclusively affect-labeling approach was not going to facilitate a therapeutic alliance. I shifted from an attitude of looking for opportunities to label affects to an attitude of looking for opportunities to make meaningful emotional contact with Dennis. Dennis was not interested in observing the contents of his own mind; on the other hand, observing the contents of my mind—which contained a facsimile of the contents of his mind—felt safer to him. He could feel secure exploring my mind and end up finding his own—an illustration of playing in displacement.

What made Dennis's treatment so difficult for me was his profound emotional isolation. I often felt that I could not reach him. Mindfulness facilitates differentiation between the self and the mental activity of the self. This approach might prove beneficial for someone struggling with issues of separation and differentiation but could strengthen a person's defenses against needs for dependence and intimacy. Although he was unwilling to discuss his feelings directly with me, it seems evident that Dennis's pattern of affect regulation consisted of compartmentalizing his feelings. A therapeutic strategy that facilitates dispassionate observation of thoughts and feelings could further isolate Dennis from emotional contact with himself and others.

Dennis's desire to avoid his emotional life at all costs suggests that he was not detached from suffering, as one would expect a mindful person to be, but instead had segregated his feelings of anxiety, rage, and loss and made them virtually inaccessible. Mindfulness-based interventions could exacerbate Dennis's tendency to act self-sufficiently and to be precociously autonomous, which necessitates a dismissal of unpleasant affect states and a consequent desire to control all relationship outcomes to avoid the emergence of such states. Dennis's primary symptom, encopresis, reflects a disconnection from unpleasant body-based sensations and a desire to isolate himself from others, while enraging his parents in the process. Encopresis insured Dennis some level of proximity to his parents, albeit with a hostile, sadomasochistic tinge.

The success of this treatment depended on my recognizing the latent needs for attachment and closeness and not allowing Dennis to deceive me (as he had deceived his parents) into listening to the manifest content of his presentation, which could easily be summed up by the command, "Get away!" Dozier (2003) suggested that therapeutic interventions are most effective when the therapist provides a "gentle challenge" (p. 254) to the patient. By relentlessly pursuing emotional contact and intimacy with Dennis (in a hyperactivating pattern) even though he signaled distance (a deactivating pattern), I was defying his expectation that I would be uncomfortable with his needs for closeness, protection, and comfort. I was letting him know instead that these needs were acceptable to me and, therefore, that *he* was acceptable to me. Dennis's defensive need to interact sadomasochistically was no longer necessary.

Because of Dennis's compromised symbolic capacity (i.e., using nonverbal channels of communication to act out his feelings rather than expressing them verbally), I chose to help him to mentalize his affects rather than act them out in a bodily function (encopresis) from which he was disconnected. I initially felt a need to engage in affect-labeling with Dennis but realized that this need was mine and was, in fact, getting me nowhere. Mentalizing affects with storytelling can facilitate the child's perspective taking and theory of mind (Mar, Tackett, & Moore, 2010) and eventually pave the way for later exploration of mental representations. A mentalizing approach (Fearon et al., 2006; Fonagy & Target, 2000; Midgley & Vrouva, 2012; Verheugt-Pleiter et al., 2008) can prepare nonmentalizing patients for later interpretive approaches that include transference interpretations and exploration of fantasy material.

Summary

The child needs to make contact with the therapist in a genuine, reciprocal relationship in which the child becomes aware that he or she has a mind with mental contents and that the therapist also has a mind with separate but related mental contents. Only then can the therapist proceed to explore fantasy material and try out more symbolically advanced intervention strategies. In a later treatment phase, the therapist can help the child understand the complexity of his or her internal conflicts—for example, that a symptom like encopresis exists because it protects the child from emotional vulnerability (specifically, from the risk of rejection and abandonment) by preemptively alienating others. In all treatment phases, the therapist is striving to make emotional contact with all parts of the patient's self, which eventually permits the patient's exploration of the contents of his or her mind as well as the therapist's mind. Through this empathic connection, the therapist provides a mental secure base from which the patient can explore unknown territory and to which the patient can return when the terrain becomes too frightening. Child therapists need to acquire a whole arsenal of artist's tools. In some situations, a therapist might need a chisel, while in others, a paintbrush will do. Our field needs fewer technicians and more artists.

References

Agrawal, H. R., Gunderson, J., Holmes, B. M., & Lyons-Ruth, K. (2004). Attachment studies with borderline patients: A review. *Harvard Review of Psychiatry, 12,* 94–104.

Allen, J. G. (2003). Mentalizing. *Bulletin of the Menninger Clinic, 67,* 91–112.

Aron, L. (1990). One-person and two-person psychologies and the method of psychoanalysis. *Psychoanalytic Psychology, 7,* 475–485.

Baer, R. A., Smith, G. T., & Allen, K. B. (2004). Assessment of mindfulness by self-report: The Kentucky inventory of mindfulness skills. *Assessment, 11,* 191–206.

Baer, R. A., Smith, G. T., Hopkins, J., Krietemeyer, J., & Toney, L. (2006). Using self-report assessment methods to explore facets of mindfulness. *Assessment, 13,* 27–45.

Bateman, A. W., & Fonagy, P. (2004a). Mentalization-based treatment of BPD. *Journal of Personality Disorders, 18,* 36–51.

Bateman, A. W., & Fonagy, P. (2004b). *Psychotherapy for borderline personality disorder: Mentalization-based treatment.* Oxford, England: Oxford University Press.

Bishop, S. R., Lau, M., Shapiro, S., Carlson, L., Anderson, N. D., Carmody, J., Segal, Z. V., Abbey, S., Speca, M., Velting, D., & Devins, G. (2004). Mindfulness: A proposed operational definition. *Clinical Psychology: Science and Practice, 11,* 230–241.

Bleiberg, E. (2000). Borderline personality disorder in children and adolescents. In T. Lubbe (Ed.), *The borderline psychotic child: A selective integration* (pp. 39–68). London, England: Routledge.

Bleiberg, E., Fonagy, P., & Target, M. (1997). Child psychoanalysis: Critical overview and a proposed reconsideration. *Psychiatric Clinics of North America, 6,* 1–38.

Bowlby, J. (1973). *Attachment and loss, Vol. 2: Separation: Anxiety and anger.* New York, NY: Basic Books.

Buddha quotes. (n.d.). *Brainy quote.* Retrieved from http://www.brainyquote.com/quotes/authors/b/buddha.html.

Dobson, K. S., & Khatri, N. (2000). Cognitive therapy: Looking backward, looking forward. *Journal of Clinical Psychology, 56,* 907–923.

Dozier, M. (2003). Attachment-based treatment for vulnerable children. *Attachment and Human Development, 5,* 253–257.

Fearon, P., Target, M., Sargent, J., Williams, L. L., McGregor, J., Bleiberg, E., & Fonagy, P. (2006). Short-term mentalization and relational therapy (SMART): An integrative family therapy for children and adolescents. In J. G. Allen & P. Fonagy (Eds.), *The handbook of mentalization-based treatment* (pp. 201–222). Chichester, England: Wiley.

Feldman, G., & Hayes, A. (2005). Preparing for problems: A measure of mental anticipatory processes. *Journal of Research in Personality, 39,* 487–516.

Fonagy, P. (1991). Thinking about thinking: Some clinical and theoretical considerations in the treatment of a borderline patient. *International Journal of Psycho-analysis, 72,* 639–656.

Fonagy, P., Gergely, G., Jurist, E. L., & Target, M. (2002). *Affect regulation, mentalization, and the development of the self.* New York, NY: Other Press.

Fonagy, P., & Target, M. (1997). Attachment and reflective function: Their role in self-organization. *Development and Psychopathology, 9,* 679–700.

Fonagy, P., & Target, M. (2000). Mentalization and personality disorder in children: A current perspective from the Anna Freud Centre. In T. Lubbe (Ed.), *The borderline psychotic child: A selective integration* (pp. 69–89). London, England: Routledge.

Fonagy, P., Target, M., Steele, H., & Steele, M. (1998). *Reflective–functioning manual, version 5: For application to adult attachment interviews.* London, England: University College London.

Fowler, D., Garety, P., & Kuipers, E. (1995). *Cognitive behaviour therapy for psychosis: Theory and practice.* Chichester, England: Wiley.

Freud, S. (1912). Recommendations to physicians practising psycho-analysis. In J. Strachey (Ed. and Trans.), *The standard edition of the complete psychological works of Sigmund Freud* (Vol. 12, pp. 109–120). London, England: Hogarth.

Goleman, D. (2003). *Destructive emotions: A scientific dialogue with the Dalai Lama.* New York, NY: Bantam.

Goodman, G. (2002). *The internal world and attachment.* Hillsdale, NJ: Analytic Press.

Goodman, G. (2010). *Transforming the internal world and attachment: Theoretical and empirical perspectives* (Vol. 1). Lanham, MD: Aronson.

Greenberg, J. R. (1986). Theoretical models and the analyst's neutrality. *Contemporary Psychoanalysis, 22,* 89–106.

Greenberg, J. R., & Mitchell, S. A. (1983). *Object relations in psychoanalytic theory.* Cambridge, MA: Harvard University Press.

Hayes, A. M., & Feldman, G. (2004). Clarifying the construct of mindfulness in the context of emotion regulation and the process of change in therapy. *Clinical Psychology: Science and Practice, 11,* 255–262.

Hayes, S. C. (2004). Acceptance and commitment therapy and the new behavior therapies: Mindfulness, acceptance, and relationship. In S. C. Hayes, V. M. Follette, & M. M. Linehan (Eds.), *Mindfulness and acceptance: Expanding the cognitive-behavioral tradition* (pp. 1–29). New York, NY: Guilford Press.

Hayes, S. C., Strosahl, K. D., & Wilson, K. G. (1999). *Acceptance and commitment therapy: An experiential approach to behavior change.* New York, NY: Guilford Press.

Hayes, S. C., & Wilson, K. G. (2003). Mindfulness: Method and process. *Clinical Psychology: Science and Practice, 10,* 161–165.

Ilardi, S. S., & Craighead, W. E. (1994). The role of nonspecific factors in cognitive-behavior therapy for depression. *Clinical Psychology: Science and Practice, 1,* 138–156.

Ilardi, S. S., & Craighead, W. E. (1999). Rapid early response, cognitive modification, and nonspecific factors in cognitive behavior therapy for depression: A reply to Tang and DeRubeis. *Clinical Psychology: Science and Practice, 6,* 295–299.

Kabat-Zinn, J. (2003). Mindfulness-based interventions in context: Past, present, and future. *Clinical Psychology: Science and Practice, 10,* 144–156.

Keaveny, E., Midgley, N., Asen, E., Bevington, D., Fearon, P., Fonagy, P., Jennings-Hobbs, R., & Wood, S. (2012). Minding the family mind: The development and initial evaluation of mentalization-based treatment for families. In N. Midgley & I. Vrouva (Eds.), *Minding the child: Mentalization-based interventions with children, young people, and their families* (pp. 98–112). London, England: Routledge.

Kobak, R. R., Cole, H. E., Ferenz-Gillies, R., Fleming, W. S., & Gamble, W. (1993). Attachment and emotion regulation during mother-teen problem solving: A control theory analysis. *Child Development, 64,* 231–245.

Lau, M. A., Bishop, S. R., Segal, Z. V., Buis, T., Anderson, N. D., Carlson, L., Shapiro, S., & Carmody, J. (2006). The Toronto Mindfulness Scale: Development and validation. *Journal of Clinical Psychology, 62,* 1445–1467.

Linehan, M. M. (1993a). *Cognitive-behavioral treatment of borderline personality disorder.* New York, NY: Guilford Press.

Linehan, M. M. (1993b). *Skills training manual for treating borderline personality disorder*. New York, NY: Guilford Press.

Linehan, M. M. (1994). Acceptance and change: The central dialectic in psychotherapy. In S. C. Hayes, N. S. Jacobson, V. M. Follette, & M. J. Dougher (Eds.), *Acceptance and change: Content and context in psychotherapy* (pp. 73–86). Reno, NV: Context Press.

Linehan, M. M., Armstrong, H. E., Suarez, A., Allmon, D., & Heard, H. L. (1991). Cognitive-behavioral treatment of chronically parasuicidal borderline patients. *Archives of General Psychiatry, 48*, 1060–1064.

Main, M., & Goldwyn, R. (1994). *Adult attachment scoring and classification systems* (6th ed.). Unpublished manuscript, University College London.

Main, M., Kaplan, N., & Cassidy, J. (1985). Security in infancy, childhood, and adulthood: A move to the level of representation. In I. Bretherton & E. Waters (Eds.), *Growing points in attachment theory and research. Monographs of the society for research in child development, 50*(1–2, Serial No. 209), 66–104.

Malatesta-Magai, C. (1991). Development of emotion expression during infancy: General course and pattern of individual difference. In J. Garber & K. A. Dodge (Eds.), *The development of emotion regulation and dysregulation* (pp. 49–69). New York, NY: Cambridge University Press.

Mar, R. A., Tackett, J. L., & Moore, C. (2009). Exposure to theroy-of-mind development in preschoolers. *Cognitive Development, 25*, 69–78.

Mayes, L. C., & Cohen, D. J. (1993). Playing and therapeutic action in child analysis. *International Journal of Psychoanalysis, 74*, 1235–1244.

Midgley, N., & Vrouva, I. (Eds.). (2012). *Minding the child: Mentalization-based interventions with children, young people, and their families*. New York, NY: Routledge.

Mitchell, S. A. (1988). *Relational concepts in psychoanalysis: An integration*. Cambridge, MA: Harvard University Press.

Robins, C. J., Schmidt, H., III, & Linehan, M. M. (2004). Dialectical behavior therapy: Synthesizing radical acceptance with skillful means. In S. C. Hayes, V. M. Follette, & M. M. Linehan (Eds.), *Mindfulness and acceptance: Expanding the cognitive-behavioral tradition* (pp. 30–44). New York, NY: Guilford Press.

Roemer, L., & Orsillo, S. M. (2002). Expanding our conceptualization of and treatment for generalized anxiety disorder: Integrating mindfulness/acceptance-based approaches with existing cognitive-behavioral models. *Clinical Psychology: Science and Practice, 9*, 54–68.

Salmon, P. G., Santorelli, S. F., & Kabat-Zinn, J. (1998). Intervention elements in promoting adherence to mindfulness-based stress reduction programs in the clinical behavioral medicine setting. In S. A. Shumaker, E. B. Schron, J. K. Ockene, & W. L. Bee (Eds.), *Handbook of health behavior change* (2nd ed., pp. 239–268). New York, NY: Springer.

Schore, A. N. (2006, June). *Neurobiology and attachment theory in psychotherapy: Psychotherapy for the 21st century*. Workshop presented by PsyBC, Mount Sinai Medical Center, New York, NY.

Teasdale, J. D., Moore, R. G., Hayhurst, H., Pope, M., Williams, S., & Segal, Z. V. (2002). Metacognitive awareness and prevention of relapse in depression: Empirical evidence. *Journal of Consulting and Clinical Psychology, 70*, 275–287.

Verheugt-Pleiter, A. J. E., Zevalkink, J., & Schmeets, M. G. J. (Eds.). (2008). *Mentalizing in child therapy: Guidelines for clinical practitioners.* London, England: Karnac Books.

Wells, A. (1999). A cognitive model of generalized anxiety disorder. *Behavior Modification, 23,* 526–555.

Wells, A. (2002). GAD, metacognition, and mindfulness: An information processing analysis. *Clinical Psychology: Science and Practice, 9,* 95–100.

Wilson, G. T. (1999). Rapid response to cognitive behavior therapy. *Clinical Psychology: Science and Practice, 6,* 289–292.

Winnicott, D. W. (1968). Playing: Its theoretical status in the clinical situation. *International Journal of Psychoanalysis, 49,* 591–599.

Wolpe, J., & Rachman, S. (1960). Psychoanalytic "evidence": A critique based on Freud's case of little Hans. *Journal of Nervous and Mental Disease, 131,* 135–148.

CHAPTER 7

The Development of the Ordinary Self: A Psychoanalyst's Professional and Personal Encounter with Mindfulness

Alan J. Stern, PhD

Several years ago, I experienced some distressing emotional problems that brought on familiar bouts of anxiety. This interfered with relationships I valued, and I judged myself harshly for having these feelings. I thought it would be wise to find a respected and seasoned therapist. This was not the first time I was in therapy. I had been in psychotherapy for a time as a young adult. And in the course of becoming a psychoanalyst, I had had a thorough personal analysis that I found extraordinarily helpful.

During this new period of therapy, I reaffirmed that I had a lot of self-understanding and that I often used self-analysis to advantage. But I also realized that I needed help in not losing sight of that understanding amid distress. And I needed help in living with some of the distress that came upon me unconsciously and did not vanish, even in the light of understanding.

Mindfulness-Based Stress Reduction

About a year earlier, a colleague had mentioned to me that she had just finished an eight-week course offered by the Duke University

Department of Integrative Medicine. The course was the mindfulness-based stress reduction (MBSR) program modeled after the pioneering work of Jon Kabat-Zinn at the University of Massachusetts. The next time the MBSR program was offered at Duke University, I enrolled. As I began to use mindfulness in my daily life, I realized that I was beginning to see another means for expanding psychological awareness and the maintenance of psychological equilibrium.

Mindfulness

Jon Kabat-Zinn (1990) describes mindfulness as paying attention on purpose and without judgment. The rationale behind MBSR is that painful symptoms are observed nonjudgmentally, in a way that simultaneously reduces the suffering those symptoms cause and gives space and new perspective for more effective behaviors to develop. It is the accepting engagement that, somewhat paradoxically, facilitates important emotional and behavioral changes.

Metta Meditation

Metta is the ancient Buddhist tradition of compassionate meditation, self-compassion, and compassion toward others. It is a core part of the Duke MBSR training program. "Compassion" is here defined as "basic kindness, with deep awareness of the suffering of oneself and other living beings, coupled with the wish and effort to alleviate it" (Gilbert, 2009). Initially, I was suspicious of such "soft" concepts. I questioned these notions during class meetings; the questions came up again, repeatedly, during my own now daily practice. Over time, however, I came to see that there is a tenderness and kindness in this practice that, when focused on the suffering of clients and oneself, can help the analyst guide patients toward new insights and behavior. From my perspective, compassion is a more receptive, perhaps more vulnerable, form of empathy.

Emotions as they arise under the circumstances of metta meditation are more frequently tenderly entertained than in other circumstances. The difference can be palpable. The tenderness and receptivity can often be felt in one's body, and it makes facing difficult emotions both more specific, by the mindful practice, and more endurable, by the loving-kindness mindset. I like the way the term "open-heartedness" seems to embody this attitude. Gradually I came to suspect that compassionate mindfulness—its theory and practice—can assist the psychoanalyst fashion a treatment plan and also work more effectively with difficult transference and countertransference experiences.

My Experience of Mindfulness

The initial impact of my experience with mindfulness through classes, retreats, readings, and my steady meditation practice yielded a number of benefits and methodologies.

- Mindfulness is a concrete tool with which to psychologically pause in a regular, rather ritualized way. This allows for more effective differentiation between aspects of subjective experience, so that I can choose which will most effectively manage behavior.

- Practicing it, I experience less reversion to automatic ways of thinking and a reduction of harsh judgments toward self and others. I can sometimes use the meditation to pause long enough to choose not to react to others and myself ineffectively or unkindly.

- It is a methodology that frequently reduces anxiety in the moment.

- It is a methodology that often increases self-acceptance, even amid painful emotions.

- It is a methodology that deepens and expands the self-understanding I had worked so long and hard to develop during years of therapy and self-analysis.

- Practicing mindfulness gave me a desire to apply the technique in appropriate clinical situations.

Clinical Application 1

A former patient (whom I will call Cathy) contacted me in the midst of major problems with a serious relationship and an intense recurrence of symptoms. She was feeling deeply depressed, attacking herself, and feeling self-hatred. After a few appointments, I thought I understood the current situation. I wanted to be helpful. I was somewhat concerned, however, about what I had to offer. I knew that as a result of years of hard psychoanalytic work, Cathy knew a great deal about her psychology and its problem areas. She had insight but was still encountering intense emotional struggles. Her efforts at helping herself, her versions of self-analysis, were not as effective as she and I both hoped them to be.

After her father's early death, Cathy grew up with a mother who intruded into Cathy's thoughts and feelings. Cathy's mother repeatedly said that she knew what Cathy was feeling more than Cathy did. Cathy's mother was a woman who typically told Cathy what to do and how to act, and took credit for Cathy's achievements.

It is easy to understand that a client with such a family background would often interpret a friend's or her analyst's efforts at helpful interpretation as a mental or emotional take-over. Not infrequently, when I presented well-supported transference interpretations, Cathy felt upstaged, like I had stolen her thunder or beaten her to the punch, much as her mother often did. Even small instances of misattunement or misunderstanding were often met with injured dismay that could quickly, unconsciously turn into angry, self-protective responses that we came to call "explosions" or "fits," using Cathy's words. Since then, I have come to understand these "explosions" better; I believe Cathy was experiencing contact with "invasive objects" (Williams, 2010), which she felt she had to retain at all cost in therapeutic interactions and that interfered with symbolization and reflective functioning.

Invasive Objects

After many attempts of transference interpretations and some instances when I raised my own voice in unhelpful, frustrated responses to her alarmed explosiveness, I suggested to Cathy that she meditate about these situations "with intention," with the aspiration of shedding light on how and why these outbursts arose in our analytic work. I gave Cathy some simple instructions on breath-focused meditation and the mindful body scan. I suggested selected chapters in *The Mindful Way through Depression* (Williams, Teasdale, Segal, & Kabat-Zinn, 2007). Soon thereafter, I suggested that Cathy read Sharon Salzberg's (1995) thin, classic volume *Lovingkindness*. I also suggested that she experiment with some of the compassionate meditation exercises that Salzberg introduces.

For Cathy, to have a way of making the insights borne of interpretation to be *her own* and expanding the insights *in her own way* in places of *her own choice* was emotionally significant. This provided a mirroring function for the consolidation and maintenance of a more stable self. Some of the time it helped. Discussing the meditations gave us both a new leverage with which to explore our enactments. My own "meditation with intention" helped me deal with the countertransference feelings of being unfairly accused of making things worse by trying too quickly and too hard to help.

Cathy needed protected space and time by herself to realize that those intrusions, take-overs, and induced fears are part of past patterns that she could not escape and that they had come to form an identification and sense of self that she has worked hard—and to a substantial degree, successfully—to alter. Cathy has been the victim of a particularly injurious form of parental early relationship, one that Paul Williams (2010) has graphically labeled "invasion." Her mother's invasion interfered with Cathy's capacity for symbolization and the early formation of a sense of self. So destructive was this form of intrusion that to survive, young Cathy had to incorporate a version of her mother's extreme sense of vulnerability, inadequacy, and entitlement into her own emerging self. In some nonverbal, unconscious part of her mind, Cathy deeply feared that changing fundamentally (deserting the introjected, invasive maternal object) would be disastrous in an unforeseeable but deadly way. This lack of symbolization often renders an intense conflict that results as bodily sensations rather than conscious thoughts. In times of extreme strain, Cathy had intense headaches centered in her forehead, which we related to such psychic conflict.

Cathy understood the benefits of self-analysis. She said meditation helped with her self-analytic process. Meditation can be conceptualized as a container, a rather safe container for the self-analytic effort. It can expand self-analysis, as it can expand free association. Cathy notes, "When I said, 'You were hard to ignore,' I meant that in a positive way...in the way that we talk about how I'm carrying you (the analysis, the work we've done) around in my head, I guess, as a partial replacement superego, rather than the one I had when I first walked into your office.... I also run into 'you' when I manage to do a little mindful meditation....You are hard to ignore because we have covered so much ground, so much of my personal inner history. The self-analysis is part you, part me, and part us in the office."

Epstein (1995) has written about how meditative states can be like periods of psychoanalytic free association. During retreats, I have often felt that the many periods of sitting and walking meditation in a day facilitated rather long stretches of free association, as in an effective period of self-analysis. In this, I think my reaction is very similar to the one Cathy expressed in the last paragraph.

Expanded Awareness

Expanded awareness is a fundamental contribution of the mindful approach to psychotherapy. From my experience, meditation, integrated with psychoanalytic therapy, works most effectively as a means of "refinding," refining, and expanding the insights often acquired in long-term therapy. These are insights that are often obscured by crises that evoke old narratives, maladaptive self-states, or impulsive behaviors. Meditation is a way to pause in a relatively contained private space. Within that space, if repeated over time in a rather ritualized manner, there is an opportunity—without pressure—to extend insights, to bring detail, to bring conviction to understandings, to make insights one's own, even to play with insights.

Transitional Space

Meditation can induce a sense of being in a safe place, a reliable refuge where new experiences can be tried out and played with. It has reminded many psychoanalytically oriented meditators of Winnicott's (1965) concept of "transitional space." Transitional space is an "intermediate" area of experience that is on the fringe of fantasy and reality. Epstein (1995) emphasizes the openness of this space, an openness that is not interfering, like the openness provided by a mother to allow a child to play uninterruptedly in her presence. This is also a space that enables some people to imagine new behaviors without almost instantaneous fear or discouragement or critical evaluation by an authoritative person such as a parent or therapist.

A Mindful Attitude Toward Dreamwork

In my clinical work, I try to help clients use a mindful perspective in their work with dream associations. Anxiety dreams often caused Cathy to feel overwhelmed by fears and anger, but one brought about a different response. Cathy remarked, "I am trying to answer these chronic visitors. I viewed the dream last night as a visitor, because I actually stopped and asked the question, why am I having this dream, why now?...In an odd way, it was sort of comforting that I could interrogate the dream and connect it to an old pattern. It's comforting to know I am facing my demons." A mindful attitude toward dream content—and private content in general—creates psychological distance from experience such that it can be engaged like a visitor and not an impingement on the self. Cathy remarked, "It is what I have to do this year: not let them get me or overtake me and scare me." Cathy's conceptualizing the dream and similar unbidden feelings as "visitors" allowed her to not identify with them or the formulation "I am such a fearful person" as the essence of her self-definition. This facilitated more flexible availability for other experiences to emerge and the enhancement of self-esteem. Often, Cathy was able to recognize, independently, in her own time and language (not just during the limited therapy hours guided by the words of the therapist), that she was slipping into a familiar negative pattern. This insight allowed her to engage with different aspects of her experience when managing her behavior, which allowed for a broader, more flexible behavioral repertoire.

Increasing Access to Difficult Internal Experiences

Mindfulness also helps facilitate awareness of difficult private content. As Cathy remarked, "One thought—event pattern I've picked up from mindfulness that won't surprise you is how much I do out of guilt...over troubling thoughts or judgments I make about others on the inside, my negative or angry thoughts, how much guilt over the past or myself in the past drives my present actions. Guilt is not actually new. I am sure we have talked about it a lot, but I don't think I was aware [of] how much it is a part of my daily thought stream."

Mindfulness as a Means to Effectively Use Transference and Countertransference

Cathy's brave commitment to truthfulness and full awareness or self-understanding in her life is built on years of psychoanalytic work and refined—in some cases, rediscovered—in extra-analytic situations. This process has been strengthened by her mindfulness practice. Reflecting on both the treatment experience and mindfulness meditation, Cathy remarked:

> One thing that has changed is my ability to keep the observing and experiencing mechanisms in me in play at the same time. I can't decide if the two are parallel or layered. I think it is layered when at [its] best, with the observing/understanding mode on top, the experiencing below or distant. At its worst, I think the two are parallel, competing modes in my mind, in which I must be more active in keeping the observing in action to check the experiencing. When the authors [Williams et al., 2007]...encourage a person to be intensely in the moment—that is, to start focusing in highly intense ways on parts of the body, the feet walking, the smell of one's surroundings, breathing—by the time one does that, a "long moment" has passed where one has actually sorted through the feeling state and seen it/felt it coming (if one is trained)

and understood the sequence enough to walk away from it.... It is as if the intense focus on the feet or the middle body in the present allows one's mind to go back or down to the distant or deep parts of the mind. It's very similar to the psychoanalytic idea of observing and experiencing emotions at the same time.

Cathy requires additional tools and means of "holding on to" (as she puts it) and refining and taking in as her own the analytic insights she worked so hard to achieve. She makes good use of a method of at least partially accepting parts of herself that she deeply wishes to change but has found stubbornly resistant.

Even with the meditation and reading added to our clinical work, her struggle to hold, build, and act on the deep insights is difficult. She often says that the long effort makes her "tired out," even though she knows she has made a great deal of progress. Mindfulness helps her persist effectively in her courageous efforts.

My clinical experience convinces me that mindful perspectives and practices can help both patient and analyst perceive, tolerate, and understand challenging transference and countertransference as they unfold during psychoanalytic treatments.

Anatta: No-Self

One of the central goals of advanced Buddhist practice is *anatta* (no-self). As Buddhist-influenced psychologists Jack Engler and Paul Fulton (2012) explain in a lucid article, anatta is usually considered an outcome of insight meditation at an advanced stage. They write, "At its root anatta is any moment of experience that is not organized around the representation of self as a separate, independently existing entity—any time I am not organizing myself as 'me' or 'mine' or as any representative or identity at all" (p. 178). The question of the "self" looms large from both Buddhist and psychoanalytic perspectives, because both practices share a central focus on disorders of the self— suffering caused by preoccupation with the ego and the extraordinary, often isolating efforts we go to in order to protect ourselves against imagined threats.

Continuous Self

The late Stephen Mitchell (2003) argued that the self can be refined and refashioned, but not eliminated, as an organizing psychological structure. Following Mitchell, I conceptualize the self as an array of self-states that shift and evolve over time but nonetheless lend a sense of continuity, individuality, and agency to a personality.

Ordinary Narcissism

Adding a mindfully informed perspective and mindful practices to more traditional psychoanalytic conceptions and therapeutic interventions can help patients achieve a sense of themselves that is more "proportional" or "ordinary." Engler and Fulton (2012) conceptualize "ordinary healthy narcissism" as an intermediate stage on the path to no-self. They describe this portion of the continuum of the self as "'ordinary' nonclinical narcissism—the daily egocentrism common in otherwise psychologically healthy individuals." (p. 179). In their view, "even the healthy narcissism characteristic of a well-adjusted mature individual is a cause for distress. When we relate to others through the perspective of self, we invite a subtle (and at times not so subtle) valuation of experience as good or bad for me. Our likes and dislikes become de facto yardsticks by which all experience is judged, resulting in a degree of restlessness" (Engler & Fulton, 2012, p. 178).

Is this restlessness inevitable? Is it often an expression of agency, of healthy goal-seeking ambition and assertiveness? Is it an example of what Buddhists call "skillful effort"? I suspect this proportionate egocentrism, or self-concern, is part of most clinicians' notion of health. It may also be possible that encouraging attention toward "no-self," however well intentioned, may cause substantial efforts along the pathway to reductions in narcissistic self-preoccupations to not be adequately recognized or reinforced.

It is not necessary to enter into an effort to resolve the paradoxes of Buddhist teachings about the self to get concrete psychological benefit from Buddhism's central message. The desired transformation is toward reduced self-preoccupation, fewer comparisons, fewer moments spent imagining supposed superiority or inferiority, and less time spent in the grip of envy or disdain. The narcissistically disturbed person is often convinced that only a limited set of circumstances in his or her life are tolerable. There is an attachment to the pursuit of these narrow outcomes in the often unconscious effort to avoid deep shame and depression. What Buddhist teachings and practices can do is act as tools to loosen such attachments, to help people experience in therapy and in their lives that such specific attachment situations and outcomes are not necessary for a sense of well-being.

Working with Self Disorders

I have worked with many patients who struggle with a deep sense of inauthenticity and instability of self-other representations. This corresponds to what Winnicott (1965) labels the "false self." Winnicott (1965) defines the false self as the part of the personality that develops in response to "impingements" that are beyond the child's capacity to manage or tolerate. The false self lacks creativity, authenticity, and vitality. This is similar to what Engler and Fulton (2012) call "narcissistic object relations." Movement from this perfectionistic, defensive stance—a position that brings both unstable grandiosity and depression—toward a more ordinary, stable self is an important part of the therapy process.

The Ordinary Self

Movement from a "false self" and the transformation of its unconscious defenses toward what I call an "ordinary self" generally requires painful downsizing. The downsizing can eventually bring great relief and a growing sense of authenticity and autonomy; but the cost, in terms of accepting a smaller space in the world and less attention and praise, is substantial and is often resisted. In addition, there are instances when the "ordinary self," which the analyst strives to help the patient construct, requires an expansion—a self-appreciation that encompasses more talents, more possibilities, more room for ambition, and innovative actions. Perhaps surprisingly, this expansion is typically also fiercely resisted.

Clinical work on the transformation of entrenched grandiose defenses is especially challenging, because these defenses—often some form of aggression toward others, as well as the self—have lent those with narcissistic sensibilities a sense of being powerful. Discussion and transformation of these defenses is helped by focused, mindful awareness and the subsequent psychological space with which to adjust gradually to such awareness.

Clinical Application 2

Paul began treatment with a self disorder—a "false self" drawn from and tied to the needs of early caretakers—and chronically unstable self-esteem defended by achievement and grandiosity. From the outset, however, he was very motivated to participate in therapy, which he had never tried before. He quickly agreed to twice-weekly therapy sessions, the maximum intensity he could fit into his budget and busy schedule. And he was determined to work hard in those sessions. I did not want to interfere with the ready flow of feelings or the slowly emerging transference. In this instance, I used mindfulness indirectly as a supplementary guide to my therapeutic strategy and as a way of dealing with my own feelings that emerged during the treatment.

Paul, a very accomplished professional, came to consult with me in great urgency and pain. His marriage was falling apart. A beloved grandparent was dying, and he was extraordinarily anxious and often strongly depressed. He was aware that his marriage had been unhappy for both him and his wife. He knew that he had met a woman who might offer a more satisfying relationship and that his grandfather was sick and very old, but somehow he felt that he could endure neither the end of the marriage nor the death of his grandfather. He felt intensely that both his wife and his grandfather were essential to his rapid and acclaimed professional success, and he felt that his professional success and its expansion was essential to his well-being.

Paul had been a precocious youngster. He had been told, especially by his father and his grandfather, that he had special talents and was destined for great things. He grew up pampered and unevenly. He often felt awkward physically and did not get along well with children his own age. Male peers frequently bullied and shamed him. Paul shone academically but internally felt insecure and inept, in constant need of reassuring achievements and dedicated help from his parents, grandparents, and eventually his wife. He devoted extraordinary hours and efforts in a successful, swift professional ascent.

As he contemplated a different kind of life, a less painful and less isolated one, Paul reviewed his past interactions and current important relationships. But the centrality of sadistic-masochistic defenses in both early family ties and current connections posed challenges to my empathy. Sadistic devaluations of siblings, colleagues, and, at some times, me stretched my empathetic resources and my capacity to remain within the difficult transference-countertransference situations. Silently evoking in myself the phrases and sensibilities of metta meditation gave me space to listen to the details of Paul's relentless self-attacks and his infliction of suffering on others.

To protect himself against deep shame, Paul needed to think of himself as a dangerous person. By keeping in mind Buddhist teachings about the suffering involved in rigid attachments, I could strengthen and expand my empathic listening to Paul's attachment to being a fearsome person. The additional theoretical lens of metta—Buddhist compassionate mindfulness—gave me an additional clinical tool with which to devise and revise a treatment strategy. Many times this new perspective helped me patiently reword interpretations that Paul could listen to and retain.

Acceptance and Commitment Therapy

Meaningful change usually requires new behaviors. Perhaps especially with those who have grown accustomed to narcissistic relationships and the often addictive quality of the emotional supplies that others provide in these profoundly uneven ties, there is deep resistance to new activities. Psychoanalysts need to help clients imagine and then try new behaviors.

At this point in Paul's treatment, I began to use the language of acceptance and commitment therapy (ACT: Hayes, Strosahl, & Wilson, 2012), which provided a bridge between the hard-earned insights of psychoanalytic treatment and new, innovative behavior patterns that increased his quality of life. To begin new behaviors, acceptance and commitment therapy emphasizes self-awareness enhanced by mindfulness, acceptance of the emotions uncovered, clarification of values, and committed action guided by those values. The ACT approach builds and extends the use of mindfulness in a creative way.

Paul was lucky in that his new girlfriend pushed him to relate to her more as a cooperating adult and less as an entitled child. To help Paul formulate the values associated with the changes he both wanted and fought against, and to help him gather the will to press ahead in a determined way, I drew upon the concepts, language, and track record of ACT. New behavior need not wait for a client's full new insight to develop and mature. In Paul's case, his new girlfriend demanded some changes in his habitual way of interacting. I felt that even small steps toward new patterns of interaction would encourage Paul and assist the deepening insight and the self-transformation. He wanted to be more reciprocal, more generous, and more sharing. At first we discussed taking small steps involved in being more open financially. Paul decided to tell his girlfriend about his exact income and his accumulated assets. He decided to move slowly toward paying for things on the basis of income rather than a strict formula of each of them paying all of his or her own bills. Similarly, he began to take small steps toward sharing his apartment in a way that gave pleasure to his partner, even though it caused him some discomfort. Also, he prepared meals in more cooperative, generous ways. With Paul, I used the language of "committed action based on considered values." For this highly intellectual, thoughtful man, the language made an impact and he used the language in our sessions. I talked about moving toward an "ordinary, freer, more grown-up self"; Paul felt these terms resonate as well. Paul also made major changes in his professional life. For many years, he had been proud of his reputation as a relentless critic of professional peers. His writing was known for its bite and rancor. During our work together, he began to apologize to colleagues for cruel, hostile writing and presentations.

The small and large changes in behavior I have noted took place over months, and there were plenty of setbacks, often provoking intense arguments with his girlfriend and some tense sessions with me. But Paul could feel the momentum of the change. He began, with some wonderment, to report that he felt "a lot less like a fraud." And he developed a sense of humor, which was more in evidence as he reported feeling happier, and that "ordinary was better," but he was "in no hurry to get there sometimes." Paul was reminded, he said, of a phrase he thought St. Augustine had written: "make me holy, but not yet."

Paul, unlike Cathy, did not come to employ a regular meditative practice in tandem with his psychoanalytic treatment. Knowing of my interest in mindfulness from my website and from the person who referred him to me, he cautioned me not to press him to become a daily meditator. But he learned about the mindful approach through our discussions and his own reading. He explicitly approved of the way I used the mindful perspective to help him evoke and tolerate painful memories, especially those involving shame and envy. He thought my consistent discussion of kindness helped him make big changes. As the treatment entered its third year, Paul told me that during his regular exercise runs, he often fell into what he imagined was a meditative state. During those times he liked to think over the relatively rapid pace of change he had made in his life and what he can do not to fall back into destructive relationships.

The Psychoanalytic Community

Although my gradual, growing involvement in the world of mindfulness felt natural, I experienced some tension and concern about how I was being perceived in the local psychoanalytic community, in which I had been deeply involved for more than thirty years. Would I be seen as moving too far from the "mainstream"? Would my referral base be affected by a shift in reputation? But I live and work in a psychoanalytic community that has become increasingly tolerant. In this community I have encountered broad support, considerable curiosity, and opportunities to teach about the integration of mindfulness and treatment, as well as some expression of skepticism about my utilization of mindfulness in clinical work. We now live in a pluralistic psychoanalytic universe (Safran, 2012). Adding another perspective or utilizing new clinical tools no longer faces routine opposition on the grounds that it violates some orthodox psychoanalytic axiom or technique.

Going Forward

The integration of mindfulness and psychotherapy as a general enterprise is relatively recent, and the use of mindful perspectives and practices in psychoanalytic treatments is more recent still. We need to learn from accumulated clinical experience and research how and for which patients using mindfulness in psychoanalytic treatment is most effective. Involvement in the world of mindfulness has changed me— as a person and a therapist—in beneficial ways. I am a psychoanalyst with an integrative disposition who looks forward to daily meditation and an expanded understanding of how to use mindfulness in clinical practice.

References

Engler, J., & Fulton, P. R. (2012). Self and no-self in psychotherapy. In C. K. Germer & R. D. Siegel (Eds.), *Wisdom and compassion in psychotherapy: Deepening mindfulness in clinical practice* (pp. 176–188). New York, NY: Guilford Press.

Epstein, M. (1995). *Thoughts without a thinker.* New York, NY: Basic Books.

Gilbert, P. (2009). *Overcoming depression* (3rd ed.). New York, NY: Basic Books.

Hayes, S. C., Strosahl, K. D., & Wilson, K. G.. (2012). *Acceptance and commitment therapy: The process and practice of mindful change* (2nd ed.). New York, NY: Guilford Press.

Kabat-Zinn, J. (1990). *Full catastrophe living.* New York, NY: Random House.

Mitchell, S. A. (2003). Commentary: Somebodies and nobodies. In J. D. Safran, *Psychoanalysis and Buddhism* (pp. 80–85). Somerville, MA: Wisdom.

Safran, J. D. (2012). *Psychoanalysis and psychoanalytic therapies.* Washington, DC: American Psychological Association.

Salzberg, S. (1995). *Lovingkindness: The revolutionary art of happiness.* Boston, MA: Shambhala.

Siegel, R. D., & Germer, C. K. (2012). Wisdom and compassion: Two wings of a bird. In C. K. Germer & R. D. Siegel (Eds.), *Wisdom and compassion in psychotherapy: Deepening mindfulness in clinical practice* (pp. 7–34). New York, NY: Guilford Press.

Williams, M., Teasdale, J., Segal, Z., & Kabat-Zinn, J. (2007). *The mindful way through depression.* New York, NY: Guilford Press.

Williams, P. (2010). *Invasive objects: Minds under siege.* New York, NY: Routledge.

Winnicott, D. W. (1965). Ego distortion in terms of true and false self. In *The maturational process and the facilitating environment: Studies in the theory of emotional development* (pp. 140–152). New York, NY: International Universities Press.

PART 2

The Evolution Continues:
Psychodynamic Psychotherapy in Action

CHAPTER 8

The Role of Mindfulness and Acceptance Within Assimilative Psychodynamic Psychotherapy

Jerry Gold, PhD, ABPP

Assimilative psychodynamic therapy is an integrative, psychody-namically based approach in which the basic psychodynamic framework has been enlarged to include and permit the use of cognitive behavioral, experiential, and systemic interventions, when indicated, resulting in the expected changes usually obtained from those techniques and, in addition, resulting in changes at the psychodynamic level that are not usually associated with those techniques. These potential changes include insight, a corrective emotional experience, a resolution of resistance, modification of a transference issue, and a way out of an enactment. Having assimilated this view of new change potentials, the theory of change around which the model is built must be changed as well. This last process might be described as the assimilative correlate to the assimilative process of absorbing active techniques.

Assimilative Psychodynamic Psychotherapy: A Framework for Integration

As I described in chapter 1 of this volume, assimilative integration begins with a single home theory, one that is selected from the variety of existing therapies. In this model, the home theory is a relational psychoanalytic model (Gold & Stricker, 2001), in which many processes of change—and many sources of change—are seen as equivalent in impact and in utility. These change processes include insight and the working through and reduction of intrapsychic conflict, anxiety, guilt, and other unresolved issues. Added to these, as a crucial change factor, is the "corrective emotional experience" (Alexander & French, 1946). This idea refers to the learning that follows new experiences in the therapeutic interaction that may lead to changes in conscious and unconscious processes, such as representations of self and of others.

The current model of assimilative psychodynamic psychotherapy is usually identical to standard psychodynamic approaches in that exploration and interpretation of unconscious conflict and structures usually predominate. However, this approach gives equal weight to those cognitive, behavioral, and emotional difficulties with which the patient is struggling, and the therapist is free to intervene actively and directly in these issues. When psychodynamic work is not sufficient or applicable in this regard, the therapist will use techniques drawn from cognitive, behavioral, experiential, and systems approaches.

This willingness to address the patient's problems directly within the context of a psychodynamic therapy has two advantages. First, and most obviously, the patient can be expected to make the same gains as he or she would in those therapies from which these active techniques are borrowed. Thus, cognitive restructuring leads to more accurate and adaptive ways of thinking, work on "unfinished business" through an empty chair technique yields closure and greater distance from past struggles, and exposure techniques can eventuate in lessened avoidance and anxiety. Mindfulness and acceptance techniques can be used in the same ways as they might in mindfulness-based cognitive therapy (MBCT; Segal, Teasdale, & Williams, 2004) and acceptance and commitment therapy (ACT; Hayes & Lillis, 2012) and, if successful, will lead to the same outcomes.

These changes—and others of their type—are highly desirable, regardless of the home theory upon which the therapy is based. As Gold & Stricker (2001, 2013) have emphasized repeatedly, however, the successful use of active interventions in this context can and does lead to changes in other spheres of psychological life, particularly at an unconscious level. This perspective states that psychological change is multidirectional and multidimensional, and that, as in normal processes of psychological development, the wishes, fears, fantasies, and images that make up our unconscious mental lives are the derivatives of lived experience and therefore may be changed by novel and corrective experiences.

After a description of the expanded, open-system version of psychodynamic theory that guides this approach, this chapter will focus specifically on the times and ways in which mindfulness and ACT techniques can be assimilated into a psychodynamic framework. In the next section, I will describe the "three-tier model" (Stricker & Gold, 1996) that guides assessment and case conceptualization in assimilative psychodynamic psychotherapy. I will explore the ways that expanded mindfulness and acceptance can be used therapeutically to promote and deepen psychodynamic exploration and change, as well as for their more typical results in alleviating the patient's experience of struggle and suffering. I will also explore the ways in which psychodynamic work can potentiate the use of ACT and mindfulness by identifying and reducing the patient's conscious and unconscious difficulties with those methods, especially those dynamically based resistances to those techniques. The final section of the chapter includes several clinical applications that illustrate this assimilative use of mindfulness and ACT within an integrative psychodynamic method.

The "Three-Tier Model": An Expanded Psychodynamic Perspective on Psychopathology

The "three-tier model" was originally introduced by Stricker and Gold (1988) as a way of describing the totality of psychological functioning in those patients who were diagnosed with personality disorders. As we turned our interests toward the development and description of what became assimilative psychodynamic psychotherapy, we found that this model was a very useful heuristic that allows us to make the necessary integrative shifts from psychodynamic exploration to active intervention and back again (Stricker & Gold, 1996; Gold & Stricker, 2013).

The tiers in the three-tier model refer to the different levels of experience at which a patient's functioning is being studied and at which his or her strengths, weaknesses, and characteristics can be identified. *Tier 1* refers to all overt behavior and to the patient's patterns of interacting with significant persons in his or her life. Clinically important phenomena, such as his or her avoidance of feared and anxiety-provoking situations and interactions, are assigned to tier 1. Problems in this tier are usually addressed through the use of behavioral and interpersonal interventions in addition to psychodynamic exploration of the motivational and developmental sources of these concerns. *Tier 2* refers to all cognitive, perceptual, emotional, and visceral experiences of which the patient is aware and is able to report and describe. *Tier 3* is the tier in which inferred psychodynamic (i.e., unconscious) processes are located and examined. These variables include wishes and other sources of motivation, conflict, defense mechanisms, and self- and object representations.

Once the patient's functioning at all three levels has been assessed as completely as is possible, a second, crucial step in the assessment and case conceptualization process begins. This step involves the search for causal relationships between variables in different tiers. A crucial assumption in assimilative psychodynamic psychotherapy is that problems may reflect issues that occur simultaneously in two or three of the tiers, while being displayed in only one of the tiers. This understanding of causality is, of course, fairly standard in many schools of psychotherapy. Cognitive approaches are built on the assumption that behavior (tier 1) is an outcome of thinking (tier 2), while psychoanalytic theory has always been identifiable by its insistence that behavior (tier 1) and conscious experience (tier 2) are the derivatives of unconscious processes (tier 3).

The three-tier model does not privilege any of these three spheres as primary in directing or causing the patient's problems. It assumes that while functioning in tier 1 (behavior and relatedness) and tier 2 (conscious experiences) often follows from tier 3 processes (psychodynamics), it may be just as likely that functioning in tiers 1 and/or 2 provokes or maintains tier 3 issues. If this is the case, then intervention in any of the tiers can be expected to have potential impact in any of the other tiers, as well as in the tier to which it is directed. Just as repairing a roof may prevent damage to the foundation of a building, we assume that helping the patient to establish new skills and strengths and to fill in psychological deficits in any of these levels of psychological life can have corrective results in any of the others.

The connections between psychological activity among the different tiers therefore guide the therapist in considering the need for an integrative shift from psychodynamic exploration to active intervention at some or several points in the treatment, as the patient's functioning in and out of sessions alerts the therapist to the need to use an assimilative intervention that will impact the patient at two or three of these levels of functioning. Often it is most useful to identify those social, behavioral, and experiential problems and concerns that might eventually become resistances or impediments to effective psychodynamic treatment. Psychodynamic work is often impeded or interfered with by the patient's focus on his or her immediate problems and pain, and/or by adaptive difficulties in coping with external demands. These tier 1 and 2 problems become resistances in the psychodynamic processes and often, if unaddressed, their continuance or exacerbation can lead to strains or ruptures in the therapeutic alliance and to negative transference reactions and destructive enactments of past, painful relationships. If these interactional, emotional, and cognitive problems are successfully addressed by the assimilative use of active intervention, change at all three tiers can occur, and the positive balance in the therapeutic alliance can be established, strengthened, or restored. The changes that accrue at tiers 1 and 2 are the most obvious, since they are directly connected to the standard ways the specific active interventions are used. But what happens at tier 3? This question addresses the unique value of this integrative model. The most important assumption upon which assimilative psychodynamic psychotherapy is built is that psychodynamic changes often follow or are the result of changes in the other two tiers, and sometimes they may occur only after changes in those tiers happen. This is assumed because it has been observed repeatedly (Stricker & Gold, 1996; Gold & Stricker, 2013) that behavioral, cognitive, and emotional difficulties become the sources of—and/or the manifestations of—resistance, defense mechanisms, negative transferences, transference enactments, and strains and ruptures of the therapeutic alliance. While it is possible theoretically and sometimes clinically to address these issues through standard psychodynamic work alone, often this is a longer, more difficult, and uncertain process than utilizing an assimilative, integrative shift. Just as importantly, the act of intervening directly in tiers 1 and 2 has important implications for the revision of the patient's unconscious images of self and others. No interpersonal action is without meaning, and these shifts into active intervention are often very meaningful for patients with histories that are marked by parental indifference, abuse, or neglect—or simply by experiences with well-meaning but ineffective parenting. The therapist who is willing to take a chance in moving out of his or her home theory to share his or her skills in alleviating the patient's pain may be passing an unconscious test posed by the patient (Weiss, 1994). The test may be one in which the patient tries to see if the therapist will be as unresponsive, unskilled, or disinterested as the patient's parents were. If the test is passed, not only are symptoms and suffering alleviated, but the patient may use this new experience as the kernel of a new, positive, and caring object representation and, in reaction to this image, a new view of herself or himself as worthy of care and concern from others.

The use of active interventions also can serve to prevent or undo an enactment of the troubled parental responses just described. Usually, enactment is described as repeating some interaction from the past in the here and now of the therapeutic interaction. Something that was done to, or in reaction to, the patient is unwittingly done again. But as we (Gold & Stricker, 2013) have worked within this model, we have become impressed with the possibility that many enactments repeat what was *not* done. That is, if the therapist knows of a technique that might be useful to the patient when he or she is in pain but chooses not to suggest its use, this might be an unconscious repetition of those times in the patient's life when his or her mother or father could not or would not respond to the patient's pain.

A final comment about the use of active techniques as homework assignments is in order. Traditionally, psychodynamic writers have ignored or frowned on explicit out-of-session patient work. More recently, however, therapists in this camp have begun to acknowledge the validity and importance of homework assignments (Stricker, 2010; Summers & Barber, 2010). Active interventions in general, and acceptance and mindfulness specifically, are used both during sessions and in homework assignments. On a practical level, it would be impossible to conduct anything resembling a psychodynamic therapy and, at the same time, spend enough time in session for the person to become competent in these active methods. And just as importantly, the use of homework extends the impact of the sessions into the patient's life, and, as in standard cognitive behavioral models, homework becomes a tremendously useful vehicle to accomplish therapeutic tasks, to practice new skills, and to obtain new data. Especially important from an assimilative psychodynamic perspective are the memories, feelings, fantasies, and thoughts that are noticed during these homework activities. These mental contents often become the focus of a great deal of psychodynamic attention, and might never be accessed within the limited time frame of sessions alone.

Acceptance and Commitment Therapy and Mindfulness Within Assimilative Psychodynamic Psychotherapy

In thinking specifically about the use of ACT methods and mindfulness, it has become clear that the patient's struggles to control painful experiences or to banish them from his or her mind can lead to increased resistances to psychodynamic exploration and to the interactional difficulties in the therapeutic relationship that we have described above. Beutler and Hodgson (1993) pointed out that patients with particular defensive styles and personality traits often are poorly equipped to make use of the psychodynamic approach. They referred specifically to individuals who are externalizers (who attribute their psychological difficulties to the outside world) or who are high in reactance (those who become more resistant and defensive when approached in a more directive and interpretive way). These patients often benefit from an approach that initially leans more heavily on active intervention and only later gradually introduces a more exploratory approach.

In these instances, the introduction of mindfulness can interrupt the mounting pileup of resistances and interactional difficulties and can allow the patient to reap the usual benefits of that technique, while at the same time facilitating the process of psychodynamic exploration. Those persons who regularly practice mindfulness meditation—in which they take a neutral, observing, and detached stance with regard to their ongoing flow of thoughts and feelings—regularly report many immediate and long-term psychological benefits, including lessened stress, anxiety, and depression. Such changes are, of course, highly desirable to the patient, and since nothing succeeds like success, any period in therapy that results in positive outcomes

157

such as these is likely also to be marked by positive trends in the therapeutic alliance. As importantly from a psychodynamic perspective, periods in which the patient practices mindfulness are often extremely valuable sources of new material to explore in the service of psychodynamic understanding. Mindfulness often gives rise to the recovery of memories; to the ability to question and then jettison one's defenses and resistances as affect, memory, and thought become less immediate and powerful; and to spontaneous self-interpretation and insight as the patient's self-awareness and self-acceptance increase.

This gradual move from acceptance and mindfulness toward an exploratory focus is often advantageous with those patients who are suffering from developmental deficits in emotional processing and affect tolerance. These individuals come to therapy with long-standing problems in identifying, tolerating, and accepting their feelings. Due to these issues, the unstructured nature of psychodynamic exploration can lead to experiences of disorganization and of the person being flooded or overwhelmed by the painfully charged memories and fantasies that are evoked in therapy. This, as would be expected, can have a powerfully negative impact on the therapeutic relationship, alliance, and potential transference reactions. Therefore, it is often useful to begin therapy by introducing mindfulness and acceptance rather than a psychodynamic approach. When and if the patient has achieved a greater level of tolerance and control of his or her emotions, a shift back to psychodynamic work is usually accomplished relatively easily and with far less turmoil, alliance difficulties, and resistance. The immediate responsiveness of the therapist in these situations and the success of the interventions suggested often lead to greater trust and confidence in the therapist, to increased willingness on the patient's part to tolerate the stresses and strains of psychodynamic work, and to greater confidence in the patient's own ability to handle new painful emotions should they arise down the road.

Acceptance and commitment therapy and mindfulness techniques can be used at any time in the therapy if the patient's focus on his or her distress—and struggles to control or to avoid it—become a predominant part of the therapy, thus making exploration and interpretation less useful. As described above, the worsening of symptoms, emergence of new symptoms, or failure to make progress with suffering have many potential meanings for the patient and can stimulate a variety of unconscious issues, processes, and conflicts. An integrative shift will then allow the distressing behavior, thoughts, or symptoms to be addressed and the interactional issues to be dealt with. Very frequently, new unconscious material emerges after the successful use of an ACT technique. This is not surprising, since, as stated above, the resolution of symptoms and the attainment of acceptance also mean that defenses against these mental contents have been relaxed or let go.

One set of issues that bedevils most therapies is that which derives from the patient's inability or unwillingness to accept the reality of his or her important interpersonal relationships. Therapists of every orientation, but especially those analytic souls who tend to work for long periods with patients, have lived patiently (and sometimes not so patiently) with patients' struggles with parents, spouses, lovers, friends, and children. If only he or she would change so the sessions go! If only, indeed, but often what is desired is not to be. These attempts to do the seemingly impossible are the source of great suffering for the patient, and they often make further psychodynamic work meaningless and ineffective, while enacting significant issues from the past in ways that reinforce their unconscious sources. We know from repeated clinical experiences that patients hold on to irreparable relationships because they are afraid of the painful emotions connected with abandoning the hope of change or separating from the person in actuality. If the patient can sensitively be guided toward acceptance of the reality of the limits and the immutability of these relationships, as well as acceptance of the sadness, anger, loss, and disappointment that this new viewpoint will bring, then work can go on. The meanings of these losses and their connections to the patient's past often become available for exploration only after the inevitability of disappointment is accepted.

In previous descriptions of this therapy (Stricker & Gold, 1996; Gold & Stricker, 2013), the integrative shift into the use of active interventions has been described as a response to difficulties or roadblocks in the psychodynamic process, as it has been described in this chapter. As ACT and mindfulness have become more a part of this approach, however, it also has become more obvious that psychodynamic work can potentiate the effectiveness of those active interventions. I am reminded here of the words of one of my psychoanalytic supervisors, who said, "I often give patients advice. It helps us to see where the resistance is, since often they can't or won't make use of it." This sometimes is the case when acceptance or mindfulness techniques are suggested to the patient in response to the situations described above. The patient, who is in pain, seems interested in the approach or glad to be reminded of it. Yet, somehow, it doesn't work—or not as well as it did the previous time—or the patient "forgets" to practice at home, and so on. Here we see resistance and defense in their most obvious and immediate manifestations. The failure to make use of these techniques alerts us to something important about the meaning of the techniques and unconscious aspects of the patient's relationship with and attachment to his or her symptoms, problems, and distress. Freud (1923) pointed out that sometimes patients fail to make progress in therapy or retreat from previous gains because they feel guilty about getting better. Perhaps this is so because improvement unconsciously means separation from a parent, or a forbidden sense of oneself as powerful and effective. There are many possible psychodynamic issues that can be examined and explored in this situation. Usually, if insight into the patient's reluctance to use the active techniques is attained, then the patient will make more active and successful use of them. This, in turn, allows further exploration of the unconscious meaning of the techniques as they are now used.

Clinical Applications of the Integrative Uses of ACT and Mindfulness in Assimilative Psychodynamic Psychotherapy

Clinical Application 1: Resolution of Symptom-Induced Resistance and Transference

Mandy was a woman in her mid-thirties who had suffered from a combination of depressive and anxiety symptoms since her late adolescence. She was a stay-at-home mother of a young daughter and reported, "Since my daughter came home from the hospital, I've been driving myself crazy with worry about her." Mandy was an eager consumer of parenting advice. She read book after book on parenting, subscribed to any number of parenting magazines, and was a member of several parenting chat rooms. She ruefully reported during her first session that her child's pediatrician had called her a "hypochondriac by proxy."

Mandy had been in psychotherapy while in college and then for about five years after having graduated. She recalled that both therapies had been somewhat successful and that both had been cognitive behavioral in orientation. She stated that she had specifically sought a psychodynamically oriented therapist this time, believing that she needed to address "deeper issues" than she had reached in her previous therapy experiences.

Mandy took to the psychodynamic process well. She quickly established a solid alliance and seemed to relax in the unstructured environment of the sessions. She brought in dreams and memories to her sessions and listened thoughtfully and with emotion to interpretations; her symptoms slowly but steadily improved. However, things began to change for the worse about six months into the treatment. Mandy began to be late for sessions and to occasionally forget her appointments. When there, she was brusque, short-tempered, and often silent. She was aware of this shift in her attitude toward therapy and toward me but was uncomfortable with it and puzzled by it, and standard exploratory work seemed of little use. Mandy tried to forge ahead with the therapy in spite of the strain that these resistances were causing her, but to little avail. Finally, she was able to tell me that she had been upset with me for several weeks, because for that period she had been experiencing a recurrence of her most intense worries about her daughter. We tried to explore the reasons for this intensification of her symptoms, but these efforts were of little use. Finally, I suggested a mindfulness technique that might help her to be more accepting and therefore less responsive to her worries. Mandy was a highly organized person, with a file or a folder for everything. We concluded that she might try to examine and to file her worries and doubts in the appropriate folders, with the eventual goal of putting those with no basis in the trash. Mandy was doubtful but intrigued by this suggestion and agreed to try it out. At first, she made use of this approach by writing each worry on a piece of paper and filing it in an actual file. In this, and all of the subsequent iterations of this process, she learned to stay with and to examine the worry perceptually and from all angles. As she put it, "I try to look at each worry the way I look at an apple of a pear in the store before I put it in my cart. Top, bottom, and all sides." She quickly moved to depictions of the worries and the files. Eventually, she was able to put most, if not all, of her worries into the trash bin without the intermediate step of filing them.

As Mandy's symptoms improved, her resistances to our work less-ened considerably. She soon arrived at the following transference interpretation: "We've talked about the way that my mother always told me to stop worrying and to try to think about something more positive. I think that I've felt that all my therapists have either said that to me or have wanted to say that to me. Now that I really can put those worries aside more, I can see how I can mistake your being calm, or your telling me that my worries might mean something else, as doing what my mother did. I think that's why I became so negative about this."

Clinical Application 2: Resolution of a Transference Enactment and the Uncovering of Its Unconscious Sources

Jay was a man in his late twenties who sought psychotherapy because of a variety of anxiety-related symptoms. He became anxious when he had to travel in a car over a bridge or through a tunnel, when he flew in an airplane, or when he had to take an elevator to a high floor of a building—especially in office buildings with large expanses of glass that exposed him to the sight of his elevation. Jay reported that these symptoms had been present since childhood, but that the symptoms had worsened significantly since his graduation from a pro-fessional school. He had begun to work at a new job that frequently exposed him to these very situations. He was in so much distress that he was considering quitting his job, even though he enjoyed the occu-pational aspects of the job and recognized that it might be very diffi-cult to find another job in the current economic climate.

Jay's treatment began with an assessment of his functioning at all three tiers, and for the first few sessions, it seemed that an effective therapeutic alliance was developing. At the fifth session, however, he arrived in an agitated and angry mood and began the session by accus-ing me of being uncaring and unresponsive to his acute distress. He said that my deliberate pace in moving the therapy along to a point where his symptoms would abate could cost him his job, as he was finding it increasingly difficult to go to work. This accusation came as a shock to me, and any attempts to explore these perceptions or their sources in Jay's previous relationships were ineffective. After two more sessions, in which this situation only worsened and Jay became more convinced of my disinterest and lack of concern, I recognized that we potentially were in the midst of an enactment of an important, but unacknowledged, relationship from Jay's earlier life. It seemed he could not help but show me how someone had failed to help him when he was anxious and in pain, and that I was unwittingly repeating this experience with him.

I therefore suggested that we shift gears and move directly into an active intervention that might help lessen his anxiety. With little time to fully educate Jay about ACT and mindfulness, I luckily remembered that he had mentioned the television show *The Simpsons* during an earlier meeting. I asked him if he was a fan of that show, and when he confirmed his interest, I asked him if he remembered the episode in which Grandpa Simpson was followed around by an evil cloud that rained incessantly on him, while all of the other members of the Simpson family enjoyed a sunny day. When Jay laughed and replied that he recalled that show, something shifted in the interaction, and some tension was relieved between the two of us. I asked him if he remembered how Grandpa had reacted to the cloud, and how he finally got the cloud to leave him alone. Jay described Grandpa's futile efforts to chase the cloud away or to hide from it, and his final surrender to the cloud. He concluded his report by mentioning that when Grandpa allowed the cloud simply to rain on him, without any attempt by Grandpa to change things, then finally the cloud became bored and drifted away. Jay then asked me if this was something that I thought he should do with his anxiety. I agreed, briefly explained the rationale of acceptance in psychotherapy, and we worked up a plan that involved imagining his anxiety as the rain that the cloud had poured down on Grandpa Simpson. He, in turn, was to work at seeing himself bathing or sloshing around in the rain, without any need to stop it from falling,

Jay came into the next session in a very different mood. He reported that his anxiety had become slightly more manageable and that he saw the utility in continuing to work on accepting it, rather than struggling with it or avoiding it. Over the next several sessions, we continued to work on acceptance, and there was gradual improvement in Jay's symptoms. We discussed the ways in which his efforts to reduce or avoid anxiety had actually reinforced it, and we designed a series of exposure-based exercises that he managed very well.

At the last of this series of meetings, Jay mentioned a memory that had surfaced a day or two earlier. He described himself as five or six years old, traveling in a car with his family on a trip to visit the Statue of Liberty, a trip that—perhaps not coincidentally—required going over a bridge and through a tunnel. There had been little discussion of this trip other than of its destination, but as the family neared New York City, Jay asked his father where the statue was located. The response was a terse "Liberty Island." A terrifying image immediately popped into Jay's young mind: that of an immense statue occupying all of the ground on this island and of he himself clinging to the side of the statue, in great danger of falling into the ocean. Jay recalled trying to voice his fears to his father, only to be rebuffed and criticized for being a "baby," and by the time the family arrived at the ferry to Liberty Island, Jay was so emotionally overwrought that he slept through the rest of the visit.

Over the next several sessions, Jay and I worked on the meanings of this memory while revisiting his increasing successful use of acceptance techniques to manage his anxiety. We came to the conclusion that this memory captured the general level of unresponsiveness with which Jay had grown up and that his reactions during the fifteen sessions of our therapy had been the start of an unconscious enactment of these encounters with his father, whose seeming disregard for Jay's fear and pain had taken a huge toll on Jay. By making an integrative shift to the use of an acceptance technique during that session, I had accomplished several assimilative tasks. First, as with any successful use of acceptance in response to anxiety, Jay had learned new and highly useful skills that enabled him to reduce his anxiety in a relatively quick way. As importantly, a potential and probably fatal rupture of the therapeutic alliance was repaired. This repair involved recognition of the early and somewhat extreme transference enactment that had emerged, and the resolution of this enactment had a number of important consequences in all three tiers. At tier 1, Jay's avoidance of anxiety decreased. Tier 2 changes included changes in his thinking about anxiety and about his helplessness in reaction to anxiety. He now saw himself as more capable and effective, and anxiety as something smaller and more possible to handle. The recovery of the memory of the Statue of Liberty trip was indicative of changes at tier 3. Awareness of this memory signaled the start of Jay achieving much more insight into the connections between childhood and adolescent experiences and his current psychological status. He gained greater access to long-disavowed feelings of hurt, anger, and vulnerability that were the results of his father's disregard, as well as to the sense of unworthiness that he had unwittingly carried around. As he said sometime after these events, "Your willingness to directly help me with my anxiety made me realize how unimportant I've always felt. But, when I feel that way now, I remember what you did, and I end up feeling as worthy as anyone else." Jay's words describe the corrective emotional experience that resulted from this integrative shift, and the way in which these types of interactions can serve to build new intrapsychic representations.

Clinical Application 3: Changing Intrapsychic Variables Through Interpersonal Acceptance

Norm was a man in his mid-fifties who came to therapy after he had experienced what he called a "traumatic" abandonment on the part of his male partner, Pete, with whom he had been in a monogamous relationship for over twenty years. Pete had recently won an all-expenses-paid month-long trip for two to an exotic destination as a bonus for extraordinary success at his sales job. Norm reported, with tears and anger, that since Pete was in the closet at work, Pete had refused to take Norm along and had invited a female friend who often posed as Pete's significant other at important social events connected to Pete's job. It soon became clear that this event was but the most powerful of a string of such occurrences. Not only had Pete failed to include Norm in this trip and to make their relationship known to his colleagues, but Pete denied the existence of Norm and their relationship with his family and several of his friends. Norm often spent holidays alone or with his family (who knew of and loved Pete) and feared that this situation would continue for the rest of their lives.

Pete's refusal to come out and to fully integrate Norm into his life led to periodic battles between them. Norm would be hurt and angry and feel rejected and unloved, and he would attempt to change Pete. At first he would do this respectfully, by giving Pete articles and books about being gay and accepting oneself. When these efforts failed, Norm would become sullen, withdrawn, and depressed, sometimes threatening suicide if Pete failed to change. When these more extreme tactics also failed, Norm would become resigned and try to patch things up, and thus a stalemate would ensue until the next episode.

Along with Norm's problematic behaviors, symptoms, and ideas, there existed unconscious (tier 3) issues that promoted his difficulties and that were, in turn, reinforced and maintained by his struggles with Pete. Norm had grown up during an era when his sexual orientation led to a great deal of rejection and humiliation from his family and peers. While his parents and siblings had turned the corner in this area and had become the loving and proud family he had longed for as a child, he remained burdened by shame, guilt, inferiority, and a sense of himself as a disappointment to his parents, especially his father. These feelings and perceptions were kept out of Norm's awareness, in part, by his struggles with Pete: he was too angry, hurt, or agitated at the present moment to think about or to experience the developmental meanings and implications of his connection to Pete.

A theme in our sessions, one that was latent yet palpable, was the unconscious fantasy that if Pete came to fully accept Norm publically, then all of Norm's aches and wounds would be healed, and Norm would then achieve the inner view of himself as lovable and the source of pride to his father that he had longed for. Pete's behavior confirmed and reinforced Norm's worst take on himself, and as Norm unconsciously equated Pete with his father, that negatively toned object representation was confirmed as well.

As these issues were identified and clarified through psychodynamic work, Norm's symptoms abated somewhat, and he became convinced that he needed to change his strategies with Pete. He first attempted to influence Pete by asking him to begin his own individual psychotherapy. When Pete refused to do so, Norm demanded that they see a couples therapist. This Pete did, and certain issues in the relationship improved, but Pete did not budge from his refusal to acknowledge Norm's place in his life to his family or colleagues. Finally, Norm concluded that he had no choice but to accept that Pete was Pete, and that Pete was unchangeable through Norm's efforts. Acceptance then became the primary goal of our work. During the beginning of this phase of therapy, I asked Norm if Pete's immutability reminded him of anyone or anything. He replied that on his daily trips into midtown Manhattan for work, he often witnessed foreign visitors being yelled at by ordinarily helpful residents, who did not speak the language of the visitor. He realized that his approach to Pete was similar: "We don't speak the same language about being out, and I keep yelling at him to try to get him to understand." Norm went on to say that yelling at someone who doesn't speak your language would be as futile as yelling at an alien from another planet. We then began to discuss if he, Norm, could accept that interplanetary communication was not among his strengths. Norm found this funny and freeing, and in the days and weeks that followed, he tried to see Pete as a visitor from another planet, especially when Pete was unable to understand and accede to Norm's needs for inclusion in Pete's life.

As Norm worked toward accepting Pete in this and in related ways, he found himself less angry at Pete and more aware of Pete's fear, shame, and anxiety about his own sexual orientation. Norm's enhanced empathy and compassion toward Pete also allowed him to be more accepting and compassionate toward himself, and he was able to separate Pete's compromised ability to love from Norm's own view of himself as unlovable. At the same time, with this lessening of Norm's interpersonal struggles, there emerged much greater awareness of, and contact with, the disavowed meanings and emotions connected with his experiences as a gay youth and man (tier 3 issues). For the first time, Norm understood the unconscious meanings of his need for Pete and the fantasy that Pete's full acceptance could undo or repair Norm's shame and view of himself as a defective failure in the eyes of his father. Norm grew closer to his father at this time and learned that his father had changed and was, in fact, greatly proud of Norm. These experiences led to work on accepting and integrating the sadness and grief that were products of Norm's past and of his relationship with Pete. This work was accomplished both through dynamic exploration and acceptance and mindfulness work. Norm eventually decided that he was able to tolerate the pain and anxiety of leaving Pete, and he did so.

Summary

In this chapter, I expanded on the assimilative integrated psychodynamic model introduced in chapter 1 by explicitly discussing the use of ACT, and mindfulness more generally, within a psychodynamic framework. I discussed how changes in different tiers of functioning affect each other and demonstrated the utility of this model with three clinical applications.

References

Alexander, F., & French, T. M. (1946). *Psychoanalytic therapy.* New York, NY: Ronald Press.

Beutler, L. E., & Hodgson, A. B. (1993). Prescriptive psychotherapy. In G. Stricker & J. R. Gold (Eds.), *Comprehensive handbook of psychotherapy integration* (pp. 151–163). New York, NY: Plenum Press.

Freud, S. (1923). The Ego and the id. In J. Strachey (Ed. & Trans.), *The standard edition of the complete psychological works of Sigmund Freud* (Vol. 19, pp. 12–59). London, England: Hogarth Press.

Gold, J., & Stricker, G. (2001). Relational psychoanalysis as a foundation for assimilative integration. *Journal of Psychotherapy Integration, 11*, 43–58.

Gold, J., & Stricker, G. (2013). Psychotherapy integration and integrative psychotherapies. In I. Weiner (Eds.), *Handbook of psychology* (2nd ed., Vol. 8, pp. 702–742). New York, NY: Wiley.

Hayes, S. C., & Lillis, J. (2012). *Acceptance and commitment therapy.* Washington, DC: American Psychological Association.

Segal, Z. V., Teasdale, J. D., & Williams, J. M. G. (2004). Mindfulness-based cognitive therapy: Theoretical rational and empirical status. In S. C. Hayes, V. M. Follette, & M. M. Linehan (Eds.), *Mindfulness and acceptance: Expanding the cognitive-behavioral tradition* (pp. 45–65). New York, NY: Guilford Press.

Stricker, G. (2010). *Psychotherapy integration.* Washington, DC: American Psychological Association.

Stricker, G., & Gold, J. (1988). A psychodynamic approach to the personality disorders. *Journal of Personality Disorders, 2*, 350–59.

Stricker, G., & Gold, J. (1996). An assimilative model for psychodynamically oriented integrative psychotherapy. *Clinical Psychology: Science and Practice, 3*, 47–58.

Summers, F., & Barber, J. (2010). *Psychodynamic therapy.* New York, NY: Guilford Press.

Weiss, J. (1994). *How therapy works.* New York, NY: Basic Books.

CHAPTER 9

Acceptance, Commitment, and the Psychodynamic Process: A Dialectic of Being and Doing

Jason M. Stewart, PsyD

Awareness devoid of action remains merely intellectual knowledge.

—Jeffrey B. Rubin

Knowing is not enough, we must apply. Willing is not enough, we must do.

—Bruce Lee

Both relational psychodynamic and acceptance- and mindfulness-based approaches to psychotherapy promote the increased acceptance of internal experiences as an important process contributing to psychological health (e.g., Germer, Siegel, & Fulton, 2005; Hayes, Strosahl, & Wilson, 2012; Wachtel, 2008, 2011a, 2011b). For purposes of this chapter, "acceptance" is defined as "the willingness to have internal experiences as they are, without attempts to change their form or frequency" (Hayes et al., 2012). From a functional contextual framework (see the introduction for a description of functional contextualism), commitment to behavior aimed at developing meaning and vitality is another important aspect of psychological health. This occurs when one's authentic values are clearly defined and used to guide one's behavior (Hayes et al., 2012). Also from a functional contextual perspective, mindfulness—defined as "intentional awareness to the present moment, without judgment" (Williams, Teasdale, Segal, & Kabat-Zinn, 2007)—is conceptualized as an important aspect of developing the psychological capacities to live in the present moment and base one's behaviors on values instead of emotional reactivity. This chapter focuses on highlighting the importance of acceptance in the psychodynamic process and integrating relational psychodynamic therapy with a functional contextual psychotherapy called "acceptance and commitment therapy" (ACT, pronounced "act") as a means of facilitating effective treatment outcomes. These approaches converge around similar philosophical and certain theoretical underpinnings, and they diverge in technical recommendations. Prior to this volume, there has been very little written on the points of contact between these two approaches or how they can be integrated to create effective therapeutic work. The goal of this chapter is to help fill that void.

Relational Psychodynamic Psychotherapy

Wachtel (2008) describes the relational psychodynamic movement as "a loose coalition that is encouraging of diversity in viewpoint rather than seeking to impose a new orthodoxy" (p. 7). He calls psychotherapy "relational" if it emphasizes the attention to context, the use of the therapeutic relationship as the vehicle for psychological change, and an interest in the effects of relationships on psychological life. Aron (1996) defines "relational theory" as "a contemporary eclectic theory anchored in the idea that it is relationships (internal and external, real and imagined) that are central" (p. 18). Wachtel (2011b) also notes that the relational psychodynamic movement emphasizes the acceptance of the patient's feared aspects of self rather than confrontation with these aspects of self. These approaches emphasize acceptance of one's different "self-states" (Bromberg, 1998) or "modes" of experience (Wachtel, 2008) and one's reciprocal nature with one's environment (Wachtel, 2011b). This chapter demonstrates how acceptance- and mindfulness-based approaches to psychotherapy can facilitate contact with disavowed experience that reflects insight and personal narrative created within the therapeutic dyad, and it shows how this experience can be used to develop an authentic sense of values with which to facilitate concrete behavioral change.

Clinical Application 1: Mindfulness and the Contact of Dissociated Experience

Laura sought therapy due to an opioid addiction and related family conflict. She presented as cooperative within the frame of therapy but rarely was able to express an opinion on a matter and generally did what others told her to do (with the exception of maintaining her addictive behavior). She rarely asserted herself or expressed her needs and was prone to guilt reactions when she did express herself. It seemed that she had developed a "false self" that lived in submission to her "inner critic," and that substance use was a means for her to rebel against this harsh, judgmental self-state (Tatarsky, 2002). But who was the more authentic, needing, feeling Laura whom this critic forced into submission? After relapsing, following a significant period of abstinence, Laura came to her next session in a state of high anxiety. I suggested a mindfulness exercise called "urge surfing" (Bowen, Chawla, & Marlatt, 2011), which is used to facilitate the patient's resistance of urges to use substances or engage in otherwise problematic behavior. This occurs by using the analogy of the patient riding the urge like a wave, using the breath as a surfboard. A key part of the exercise is to bring the client through a mental construction of his or her urge and then to look at what experience he or she is attempting to avoid or change at just the moment the urge peaks in intensity. In Laura's case, it emerged that her anxiety was related to dependency needs: needs for connection and fears of rejection. These needs had previously been out of her awareness, as they had been cloaked by mindless acquiescence to others. Lacking awareness of dependency needs is common among opioid-dependent patients (Khantzian, 1999). With her newfound insight based on conscious contact with her self-state that yearned for human connection, Laura realized that she was anxious about verbally expressing herself for fear of being rejected by others. Thus, we were able to conceptualize her substance use in terms of what it meant to her (Tatarsky, 2002): a powerful means of expressing her voice in relationships and a way to consolidate a sense of self in relation to others. For example, Laura would increase her substance use when her family confronted her about her addiction, thus claiming a sense of agency. Exploration of this dynamic allowed us to assess the efficacy of this form of expression and find alternate, more effective ways for her to express herself in relationships, while safeguarding her dependency needs, and to pursue her dependency needs "in more simple and ordinary ways" (Khantzian, 1999, p. 159). This was followed by an extended period of abstinence from opioids.

Acceptance and Commitment Therapy

The ACT model proposes that due to the limiting characteristics of human language, people tend to seek certain emotional states at the expense of living a valued life, and that this process causes suffering. More specifically, when humans apply mechanistic rules that function well in the outside world (e.g., "If you don't like something, get rid of it") to painful internal states (e.g., anxiety, anger), we end up resisting pain, and these attempts to avoid pain actually exacerbate it and transform it into suffering (Hayes & Smith, 2005). Germer (2009) notes that "suffering is the physical and emotional tension that we *add* to our pain" (p. 16, italics in original). He suggests the equation "pain + resistance = suffering" (p. 15). Young-Eisendrath (2003) conceptualizes suffering as "the mental anguish that we create through our perseverations, distortions, fantasies, and internal commentary" (p. 301) and distinguishes this from pain, which is inevitable. Similarly, the ACT model differentiates "clean pain," the natural pain of living a "wholehearted life" (Brown, 2010), from "dirty pain," the suffering that ensues when "clean pain" is resisted (Hayes & Smith, 2005).

Being and Doing Modes

Segal, Williams, and Teasdale (2002) and Williams et al. (2007) differentiate between two modes of human functioning: being and doing. The doing mode is a mechanistic, problem-solving, goal-oriented mentality that differentiates between the way things are and the way things would be under more favorable conditions. It may include thoughts about the present moment, but usually in a way that is oriented toward the future. Hayes et al. (2012) refer to this mode as the "problem-solving mode." The doing or problem-solving mode has undoubtedly produced extraordinary results in the history of humankind and is vital for human functioning. When applied to the human mind, however, the doing mode leads to resistance of pain, which causes suffering. In contrast, the being mode is oriented toward experiencing the present as it is through immediate, sensory awareness. There is no need to evaluate the present or compare it to a desired, goal-oriented outcome. Thus, negative affect can be experienced without the impending suffering that results from resisting pain. In other words, the pain of living a wholehearted life can be experienced without the additional suffering of experiential avoidance.

Psychological Flexibility: Balancing Acceptance and Change

What makes the process of avoiding internal experiences even more problematic is that it can work in the short term and is thus reinforced for use again in the future. This strengthens one's avoidant tendencies that preclude the development of more flexible behaviors. Thus, the ACT approach emphasizes the importance of accepting internal states so that one can commit to living a valued life—instead of attempting to live a life free of pain, which is unattainable. In other words, the model balances acceptance of internal experiences (i.e., being) with changing one's external functioning to better fit one's values (i.e., doing). There is a strong emphasis on mindfulness as a means to engage the world in the present moment so that one's experiences increase in richness and vitality and one's behaviors are not motivated by emotional reactivity.

The ACT model recommends a unified, transdiagnostic approach to helping patients increase their psychological health. From an ACT perspective, people with optimal mental health would be "able to detach themselves from unworkable rules, to accept what cannot be changed inside and outside their skin, to live in the present moment and attend to what is relevant, to make contact with a deeper sense of self as a locus of perspective taking, and to choose and explicate closely held life values and organize their life's actions around those values" (Hayes et al., 2012, p. 64). The approach is based on a specific model of psychological flexibility, which includes the following processes:

- **acceptance**: the willingness to have mental content as it is

- **defusion:** the deliteralization of and disidentification from mental content so that it can be observed nonjudgmentally, without automatically dictating behavior

- **flexible attention to the present:** focus on the here and now

- **self-as-context:** perspective taking

- **values clarification:** creating personal constructs of meaning and vitality

- **committed action:** acting congruently with one's values and with minimal emotional reactivity

The rationale behind ACT is that increasing the patient's engagement in these processes will help bring more behavioral effectiveness and vitality to his or her life.

Language as the Cause of Suffering

Hayes et al. (2012) propose, based on strong empirical support (e.g., Hayes, Barnes-Holmes, & Roche, 2001), that language causes human suffering. More specifically, they contend that verbal rules tend to dominate human behavior at the expense of actual, present-moment experience, and that this results in rigid behavior patterns that dampen the opportunity for developing a wholehearted life. The current integrated model conceptualizes transference-countertransference as a form of acquiescence to verbal rules that forecloses a broader range of potential experience and related behavioral repertoires for both patient and therapist. It also proposes that ACT's psychological flexibility model is a means to effectively facilitate the therapy dyad's disembedding from transference enactments in order to increase the patient's experiential and behavioral potential.

Transference as Rule-Governed Behavior— Relational Framing

Safran (2012, pp. 61–62) defines "transference" as "clients' tendency to view the therapist in terms that are shaped by their important caregivers and other significant figures in their developmental backgrounds.... Early developmental experiences establish templates or schemas that shape the perception of people in the present." Hoffman (1998) adds that transference is "a way, not only of *construing*, but also *constructing* or *shaping*, interpersonal relations" (p. 104, italics added). From an ACT perspective, *relational frames* are connections between concepts (e.g., people, experiences, traumas, etc.) that have been reinforced by the use of language (Hayes, Strosahl, & Wilson, 1999). Similarly, from a psychodynamic perspective, Aron (1996) states that "words are not simply labels for things but gain their meaning through their use in social interchange, language games" (p. 192). Of importance to the development of psychopathology, these previously established connections can be used arbitrarily. This is referred to as an *arbitrarily derived relational frame* (Hayes et al., 2001). In essence, transference is made up of arbitrarily derived relational frames. This means that transferential experiences are not supported by natural contingencies or actual, current experience with the present-moment, real world; they reflect arbitrary contingencies or relational frames that were formed under the coercive control of language based on prior history. This class of behavior is referred to as "rule-governed behavior" (Hayes et al., 2001).

Rule-Governed Behavior. Rule-governed behavior is a type of arbitrary contingency in which a rule is learned and applied to one's functioning despite one having never actually experienced the rule in embodied form (Hayes et al., 2012). This is similar to the Buddhist concept of *delusion*, which describes a situation in which the mind "imposes a definition on things and then mistakes the definition for the actual experience" (Epstein, 1998, p. 126). Thus, when a patient attributes an attitude to the therapist that reflects expectations from earlier relationships (i.e., transference), she is essentially applying relational framing from the early experience and is expecting similar contingencies that operated in the earlier relationships to operate with the therapist. Take, for instance, a patient who learned as a child that silence from a caregiver implies underlying hostility. If this person's therapist responds to him with silence, the patient may interpret the response as hostile when the therapist may simply have been deep in empathic reverie or simply listening carefully. The patient's experience that the therapist is acting with hostility is the result of language (i.e., the relational frame of "silence equals hostility"), not actual experience with the therapist (i.e., the therapist never enacted hostility by being silent toward the patient). Earlier in life, the patient experienced natural contingencies that supported his transferential attitude. Often this attitude developed from unformulated content (i.e., implicit relational knowing, Stern, 2010) that developed in early relationships. When this attitude is formulated into language, it establishes a relational frame that influences the patient's interpretation of subsequent behaviors in new relationships.

Fusion and Defusion. From an ACT perspective, fusion is the process by which a person identifies with his thoughts as literal truths; he experiences the world as structured by his thoughts. In contrast, defusion is the deliteralization of and disidentification from one's thoughts. From a defused perspective, a person experiences thinking as a process and does not consider thoughts as facts. Thus, she has more psychological space with which to respond to thoughts in a reflective manner that minimizes their immediate impact on behavior; thoughts are taken less seriously (Hayes & Smith, 2005; McKay, Lev, & Skeen, 2012). McKay et al. (2012) delineate the components of defusion as (1) watching, (2) labeling, (3) letting go of, and (4) distancing oneself from internal experiences. The integrated approach proposed in this chapter further connects the processes of fusion/defusion to the interpersonal realm by promoting defusion from transferential relational configurations that develop in the therapeutic relationship.

Essentially, fusion is looking "from" one's thoughts, whereas defusion is looking "at" one's thoughts. From an ACT perspective, an important goal of therapy is to help the patient move from a fused perspective of private experience to a defused perspective (Hayes & Smith, 2005). From a psychodynamic perspective, Bromberg (2010) states that the primary goal of clinical work is to help the patient "move from experiencing his patterns of behavior as *who he is* to experiencing them as *something that he does*" (p. 51, italics added). This process is similar to ACT's shift from fusion to defusion in that one's behavior moves from defining oneself to becoming more objectified as events in time.

The current integrated model proposes that conceptualizing verbally communicable transferential experience as relational frames facilitates an attitude of equanimity in which "dispassion" allows one to approach experience without an agenda (Salzberg, 1995), similar to the "being" mode discussed above. Equanimity is "not a desensitized neutrality of feeling, but is rather an advanced state of being able to embrace both pleasant and unpleasant experience, without the responses usually conditioned by desire" (Olendzki, 2005, p. 294). When applied to human verbal interaction, this is what Stern (2010) refers to as "true conversation," in which neither participant is foisting an agenda on the conversation, so the flow of speech and connection is unimpeded by preconceived ideas. In other words, instead of "acting on" each other, the participants in true conversation try to understand each other (Stern, 2010). Brach (2003) refers to a similar process as listening "from the heart," which she describes as "honoring the other by offering your full presence and attention" (p. 305) and using the conversation as the anchor for mindful attention (see "Relational Mindfulness" below). Wachtel (2008) suggests that "conversation—rather than a one-sided examination of one person by another—is at the very heart of how the therapist understands what [the therapist] is up to" (p. 9).

Clinical Application 2: Transference as Immersion in Verbal Rules

Rick was fused with the concept that he must be a leader within his business, though he was unable to effectively assert himself in this capacity. Instead, he acted aggressively, which put off his colleagues. He had begun therapy due to alcohol dependence and interpersonal difficulties, both professionally and personally. Rick had come from a tough neighborhood in which aggression often served as the only means to gain power and respect. In attempts to win the loyalty of his colleagues, he would often act aggressively, in a way that he felt was playful. Eventually, this dynamic also entered the treatment situation, as I began to notice subtle ways that he devalued the therapy. And in time it became clear that what was happening in the room reflected similar dynamics as to what happened between Rick and his colleagues. Rick enacted aggression toward me, and I felt devalued. Perhaps Rick's colleagues also felt devalued when interacting with him. As this emotional experience emerged, I maintained a mindful attitude; and I used my own experience of the patient as a point of reference (i.e., that I felt devalued). I commented that Rick seemed to be acting based on rules that operated in his old neighborhood but that did not seem to be functioning as he hoped in his current professional environment. This led to his deeper understanding of what it meant for him to be a leader and a member of a collective unit. Previously, Rick had felt that becoming a leader meant dominating others, and that doing so was a means for him to gain respect—more verbal rules. This verbal entanglement of domination, power, and respect was examined in terms of the realities of Rick's current life situation compared with his early life in a rough neighborhood. It became clear that Rick was fused with verbal rules related to traumas he had experienced growing up. As he defused from these rules, Rick presented with yearnings for connection and a more tender side of life that fell outside of his rules related to domination, power, and respect. When Rick was able to experience these previously inaccessible aspects of self as integrated, he could establish a more rounded life that included an emphasis on non-work-related issues, such as developing a romantic relationship with a woman that was not based on domination and subjugation but on the mutual needs of each partner. Rick's work life began to show signs of improvement, but he would periodically slip into his old world of verbal rules, which would culminate in work-related crises, such as acute bouts of anxiety related to belonging at work. What became evident in these bouts of anxiety was a different quality from his condition when he had been relentlessly pursuing leadership roles. Now, Rick's anxiety was more about belonging with others he worked with and fitting in as a functional member of a collective unit. This was evidence of dependency needs that had been masked by his desire for domination. The use of these dependency needs helped facilitate more successful relations outside of work. Thus, the therapy began to focus on integrating needs for relatedness and needs for individuation (Safran & Muran, 2000) in the work setting as one of many domains of the patient's more rounded life.

This clinical material demonstrates that the transference-countertransference matrix reflects the domination of verbal rules based on prior experiences in the patient's life, and how defusion from moment-to-moment interaction can increase the patient's responsiveness to present-moment contingencies and subsequent experiential and behavioral flexibility. Exploration of the confining nature of language in the transference facilitated Rick's contact with direct experience, which allowed him to further develop the flexible behaviors that brought him more in line with his values, which included abstinence from alcohol.

Expanding the Sense of Self and Others as a Means of Contacting Values

Wachtel (2011b) suggests that the psychodynamic therapist's interventions should promote the patient's acceptance of internal experiences that generate anxiety. He posits that this occurs by expanding the patient's experience of self and others and that this facilitates the emergence of a more complete and flexible sense of self, one that is better able to function in the world (Wachtel, 2011b). Bromberg (2010) writes that "each aspect of self has its own degree of access to various domains of psychic functioning...to act from a sense of one's values as well as from a sense of purpose" (p. 48). The integrated approach presented in this chapter suggests that when the more complete version of the patient is in the room, the patient's authentic values are more accessible and usable to guide behavior. This enables the development of a more holistic sense of meaning, purpose, and vitality with one's actions.

Acceptance and Commitment Therapy's Three Dimensions of Self

ACT proposes three dimensions of "self" experience:

- self-as-concept
- self-as-process
- self-as-context

Self-as-Concept

The *self-as-concept* is made up of the various ways we experience ourselves in the world and in relation to others. Hayes and Smith (2005) define the self-as-concept as "the thoughts, feelings, bodily sensations, memories, and behavioral dispositions that you've bought into and integrated into a stable verbal picture of yourself...a kind of suffocating coherence that leads relentlessly to 'more of the same'" (p. 90).

The self-as-concept is essentially what Sullivan referred to as the "personification of the self" (Safran, 1998). The personification of the self is a characteristic way of experiencing oneself and has conscious and unconscious (i.e., dissociated) aspects. Hayes and Smith (2005) suggest that the self-as-concept is made up of the stories we tell ourselves about the facts of our lives, but they stress that alternate, more flexible, and vitality-producing stories can be developed using the same facts. When this process is considered in interaction with dissociation as a form of unconscious experiential avoidance, the development of new, fresh stories is essentially what Stern (1997) describes as the formulation of experience from dissociation to "creative speech."

Self-as-Process

The *self-as-process* is "fluid, continuous knowledge of your own experience in the present moment" (Hayes & Smith, 2005, p. 93), which allows the happenings of one's mind and environment to be observed and understood. It is different from the self-as-concept in that it is descriptive rather than evaluative (Hayes & Smith, 2005). It includes the capacity to identify and name one's feelings. Such awareness of internal, external, and cocreated experiences is an important aspect of understanding unconscious processes.

Self-as-Context

The *self-as-context* is the experience of "I" that provides the vantage point from which to observe internal experiences such as thoughts, feelings, memories, and physical sensations. Hayes and Smith (2005) describe the self-as-context as the most important aspect of self. The self-as-context "is not a content-based sense of self that can be described directly....It has no known boundaries.... You can never consciously know the limits, because all verbal knowing is with reference to you as the knower" (p. 94). Like Bromberg's "illusion" of self-integration (1998), the self-as-context is experienced as a stable construct that we have the potential to maintain contact with throughout life. However, when patients "buy into" their "stories" (Hayes & Smith, 2005), including the phenomenology of transference enactments, they slip into the self-as-concept. This leaves the self as prey for evaluations, judgments, and other esteem-wavering processes.

The current approach suggests that part of the therapeutic endeavor is to facilitate the patient's defusion from his or her self-as-concept, using the self-as-context as the point of perspective and the self-as-process (i.e., mindfulness) as the medium for action. This will allow self-conceptualizations to be played with more flexibly and new meaning to be potentiated, and it will allow the attachment to evaluative measures of the self to be decreased.

Clinical Application 3: Self-as-Context as a Means of Expanding the Patient's Access to a Dissociated Self-State

Chris entered treatment due to a sex addiction. He had been the victim of physical and sexual abuse as a child. As therapy progressed, we came to understand his addiction as a means of stimulating a sense of being alive. The addictive behavior also served as an attempt to maintain a sense of self as stable and cohesive, yet only accomplished this temporarily. Once the exhilaration of sexual activity was gone, he was left feeling empty. As the therapy progressed, it became clear that Chris did not have a solid capacity to regulate emotions; he was unable to identify, express, and effectively use his feelings. He often exploded in anger and then blamed other people for causing his outbursts. By developing his self-as-context perspective, using the metaphor of viewing his internal world from the top of a mountain, Chris was able to gain enough distance from his feelings such that he could defuse from them and use them more effectively to inform behavior. He defused from the concept of himself as a victim of others' mistreatment, which he had believed was the cause of his angry behavior. This defusion allowed him to look more at the quality of his anger and to contact it from a safer distance. Previously, a childlike, playful demeanor often masked this anger. When Chris was able to experience his anger explicitly, his sense of self was expanded, and he was able to look at some of his explosive behavior as expressions of dissociated rage related to early traumas. This allowed for increased reflective functioning and emotional regulation as well as an increased "illusion" of integration, because the anger was not perceived as a foreign entity foisted upon him by others, but something that he was permitted to feel and thus use more effectively to develop assertive behavior.

181

Relational Mindfulness: Developing a New Relationship to Transference Enactments

Integrating ACT with psychodynamic approaches to psychotherapy can facilitate our patients' capacity to *relate differently* to transference enactments. Instead of relating to enactments as "true" and thus reacting to them on that basis, an integrated psychodynamic and ACT-based approach would allow the patient and therapist to look "at" enactments as well as "from" enactments. This process corresponds to Hoffman's (1998) description of the therapist's "acceptance of a certain thread of transference-countertransference enactment throughout the analysis, which stands in a kind of dialectical relationship with the process by which this enactment, as experienced by the patient, is analyzed" (p. 128). In other words, the therapeutic relationship is a dialectic of "being" in the enactment and "doing" to the enactment (i.e., interpreting). A specific form of mindfulness called "relational mindfulness" (Surrey, 2005) can facilitate this process. Surrey (2005) defines "relational mindfulness" as a co-mindful attitude between patient and therapist in which "connection" is the object of mindfulness. She emphasizes the fluid nature of connection as "a process of successive moments of turning toward, turning away, and returning" (p. 94). She suggests that co-mindfulness is a means for the therapist and patient to return to connection, similar to how individual mindfulness is a return to the breath when the mind wanders into self-judgments, evaluations, or another experience that has a high likelihood for being transferentially induced. By maintaining a "tripartite awareness" (Surrey, 2005, p. 94) of self, other, and the movement and flow of the relationship, the therapist can attend to the ongoing regulations (Beebe & Lachmann, 2002) and implicit communications that are central to contemporary relational psychodynamic theory and practice. In other words, when the therapist notices a slip from the present moment, attention is gently returned to what is going on in the therapeutic relationship. Relational mindfulness is conceptually and technically related to mentalization (see chapter 6).

Mindfulness in Action

A key therapeutic process from Safran and Muran's (2000) relational perspective is "metacommunication," which they also refer to as "mindfulness in action." These authors identify metacommunication as "an attempt to step outside of the relational cycle that is currently being enacted by treating it as the focus of collaborative exploration" (p. 108). This facilitates the dyad's disembedding from enactments and giving the patient new models of self-other relationships. It is also a means for therapists to regulate their own affect and stay mindfully present while acting as "surrogate affect regulators" (Safran & Reading, 2008, p. 138) for their patients.

Muran, Eubanks-Carter, and Safran (2010) write that "metacommunication involves an attempt to disembed from the interpersonal claim that is being enacted by taking the current interaction as the focus of communication" (p. 170). An important part of this process is "decentering," which "deautomates habitual patterns and helps clients experience themselves as agents in the process of constructing reality rather than as passive victims of circumstances" (p. 170). These authors also state that "the client starts to develop a sense of the choices he or she is making on a moment-by-moment basis. With greater awareness of how he or she constructs his or her experience, the client develops an increased sense of responsibility and agency" (p. 169). From the integrated perspective of this chapter, this "increased sense of responsibility and agency" facilitates the patient's more holistic embodiment of his or her personality, which can then be used in the service of choosing behaviors based on deeply held values.

Decentering from Experience

As mentioned above, mindfulness in action facilitates a "decentered" perspective on experience that is not excessively impinged upon by emotional urgency and reactivity. To "decenter" is to distance oneself psychologically from internal experience and to conceptualize experience as events that are nonliteral and do not have to influence behavior reactively—to "deautomate" (Muran et al., 2010) or "desynchronize" (Hayes et al., 2011) from habitual behavior. This involves oscillating between the content of what the patient says in the session and the process, or how he or she says it (Muran et al., 2010). Fosshage (1995) conceptualizes part of the therapist's role as decentering from his or her personal experience with the patient such that he or she can oscillate between "subject-centered" and "other-centered" forms of listening. Subject-centered listening is from the perspective of the patient's subjectivity, which allows for increased flexibility in the therapist's attitude toward the patient's material, whereas other-centered listening is from the perspective of an outside observer, which allows for increased objectivity in considering the patient's material. This dialectic corresponds with Hoffman's (1998) suggestion that the therapeutic encounter is a balance of being in enactment and looking at enactment—or Safran and Muran's (2000) idea that "the entire resolution process involves an ongoing cycling back-and-forth between greater and lesser degrees of embeddedness" (p. 157). Fosshage (1995) suggests that by virtue of the therapist "illuminating" the patient's construction of meaning, he or she provides the patient with a new kind of relationship that gradually modifies the schemata such that the patient's world is experienced more flexibly.

Establishing Connection via Acceptance

Stern (1997, 2010), Bromberg (1998, 2006, 2010), Safran and Muran (2000), and Safran (2012) all emphasize the importance of the therapist's awareness of the "moment-to-moment" shifts in patient affect or behavior—as well as the therapist's own countertransference experiences in response to the patient's clinical material—as important means of disembedding from enactments and tapping into the therapeutic potential of enactment. Safran and Muran (2000) refer to these indicators as "interpersonal markers."

Interpersonal Markers

Interpersonal markers are specific patient behaviors (including verbal behavior) which may be "evocative" (e.g., Kohlenberg & Tsai, 1991) for the therapist. They are essentially the specific patient behaviors that coincide with the therapist's "affective signposts" or emotional "snags and chafing" (Stern, 2010, p. 81), which suggest that an enactment is occurring. Identifying the client's interpersonal markers helps both participants disembed from the current enactment by opening "windows" into the patient's characteristic modes of interpersonal functioning and their impact on the therapist:

"These interpersonal markers indicate unique and ideal junc-tures for intrapsychic exploration since it is likely that the occurrence of those interactional patterns that are most char-acteristically problematic for the patient will be accompanied by those intrapsychic processes that play a pivotal role in the patient's relational matrix. They are the other side of the coin to the patient's internal world and an important point of intersection between the internal and external" (Safran & Muran, 2000, p. 66).

Thus, the patient's evocative interactions with the therapist can be connected to the patient's functioning outside of the therapy and used to influence the patient's behavior such that its effectiveness in helping him or her live a meaningful life is increased.

Clinical Application 4: Mindfulness in Action, Interpersonal Markers, and the Self-as-Context

We return to the case of Rick. I felt, at times, that Rick was trying to "one-up" me by devaluing my interpretations or other expressions. At times, I struggled to sit with this provocation and began to wonder if Rick felt provoked by others at work or within the therapy relationship. As Rick's experience was elaborated, it became clear that he felt his work environment to be a hostile setting in which "pecking orders" were quickly established—and that once these interpersonal configurations were consolidated, it was only a matter of time until he was excluded from the group. Similarly, Rick felt that it was only a matter of time until I extricated him from the therapy relationship. I felt frustrated at how he devalued my work (i.e., an interpersonal marker). In ACT terms, I felt that the patient's provocations threatened my own self-as-concept within the therapy relationship. By taking on a self-as-context/self-as-process perspec-tive—which meant looking at the interaction as an ongoing process and not being emotionally reactive to my present affective state—I could use the affect more productively and base my interventions on the affect, without the reactivity. For example, instead of responding to the Rick's devaluing comments in a defensive way, I accepted his anger and was able to express to him the feeling I had in reaction to him. When I expressed a sense of being devalued, Rick was better able to consider his contributions to his work relationships and modulate the impact of his anxiety and anger on his interactions with employees.

Valued Living as a Unified Treatment Goal

The establishment of "goals" in psychodynamic psychotherapies has been the subject of controversy (see Berman, 2001; Wallerstein, 1992; Weinshel & Renik, 1992). For example, Wallerstein (1992) describes the conflict between the "goallessness" inherent in certain technical practices, such as therapist abstinence, and the grandiose goals inherent in such ambitions as "fundamental personality reorganization" (p. 64). Wallerstein (1992) also considers the importance that psychodynamic psychotherapies place on "value-laden conceptions of the ideal state of mental health" (pp. 63–64). Rubin (2003) suggests that psychodynamic exploration can help one to clarify his or her values, because "it provides a heuristic, emotionally intimate, and relatively non-impinging context for exploring such questions of ultimate concern as how one should live" (p. 396). He also writes that the "good life" is a process, as opposed to a destination, which corresponds with ACT's conceptualization of values as guiding principles, as opposed to "goals." Stern (2010) writes that "the most important outcome of a successful analysis is the firm and unthinking conviction that one's life is one's own, that oneself and no one else is living it" (p. 102). From the perspective of the current integrated model, values construction provides a means of developing therapeutic goals that allow the patient to claim his life as his own. Values provide a context for the treatment. In order for one's values to be as authentic as possible, unbidden experience needs to be considered. Thus, values construction must take into account enactment, the resolution of enactment, and the attainment of conflict (for more on this, see the introduction). This is the seed for the "doing" mode of the treatment, which is ultimately the patient's commitment and follow-through with behavioral change based on a holistic and authentic set of values.

Clinical Application 5: Values Construction and Unbidden Experience—Attending Your Own Funeral

William was a businessman who had achieved much financial and athletic success, though he sought therapy due to a lack of satisfaction in life, particularly with regard to interpersonal relationships. He initially presented as a serious, almost stoic, young man. My experience was that our sessions lacked a sense of vitality, of true connection. I found myself feeling anxious at the start of each session with William, but I was not sure what I was anxious about. My initial reaction was to combat the anxiety by acquiescing to William's demands for concrete answers to abstract questions (i.e., experiential avoidance of the countertransference). This did not do much to increase the sense of connection; instead, it seemed to keep the distance that became the status quo of the initial stage of treatment. I began to use a relational mindfulness perspective of focusing on the relationship in the present moment, without judgment, to try to understand this anxiety more fully. As the anxiety emerged, I would turn my attention to the relationship and allow spontaneous experience to emerge. I began to notice that I felt somewhat envious of the patient, due to his financial wealth and athletic success. I sat with this experience for several sessions, wondering what it could mean about our work together. Eventually, I used the ACT exercise called "Attending Your Own Funeral," which is a means to assess the patient's values and evaluate his current behavior based on these values. The exercise requires the patient to vividly imagine what would be said about him by loved ones at his funeral if he kept on living in his current style. The exercise then requires the patient to imagine what would be said about him at his funeral if he embodied his most deeply held values. Around this time, William revealed an emerging sense of envy toward me, because of what he conceived of as my entrepreneurial attitude. My experience of envy toward the patient matched his experience of envy toward me; perhaps I had been contacting a dissociated aspect of the patient's experience in my own countertransference. From Stern's (2010) perspective, this process marks the resolution of enactment, which allowed William and me to more effectively explore his conflict between a need for meaningful work that extends beyond the realm of financial success and his current professional situation. He opened himself to artistic endeavors and reengaged in his athletic life. At this point, the therapy became less serious and more playful. William's contact with dissociated aspects of himself facilitated a more expanded self-concept, from which he was able to construct values related to creativity and self-expression and to navigate life more flexibly.

Summary

This chapter has demonstrated the utility of integrating relational psychodynamic and acceptance and mindfulness-based psychothera- pies, with an emphasis on ACT. Processes developed from these diverse theoretical perspectives were integrated and demonstrated using clinical vignettes. I believe there is much more potential for further integrating these approaches. It is my hope that this chapter will stimulate such ideas in those who read it.

References

Aron, L. (1996). *A meeting of the minds: Mutuality in psychoanalysis.* New York, NY: Routledge-Taylor & Francis Group.

Beebe, B., & Lachmann, F. M. (2002). *Infant research and adult treatment: Co-constructing interactions.* New York, NY: Routledge

Berman, E. (2001). Psychoanalysis and life. *Psychoanalytic Quarterly, 70,* 35–65.

Bowen, S., Chawla, N., & Marlatt, G. A. (2011). *Mindfulness-based relapse prevention for addictive behaviors. A clinician's guide.* New York, NY: Guilford Press.

Brach, T. (2003). *Radical acceptance: Embracing your life with the heart of a Buddha.* New York, NY: Bantam Books.

Bromberg, P. M. (1993). Shadow and substance: A relational perspective on clinical process. In S. A. Mitchell & L. Aron. (Eds.). (1999), *Relational psychoanalysis: The emergence of a tradition* (pp. 379–406). New York, NY: Routledge-Taylor & Francis Group.

Bromberg, P. M. (1998). *Standing in the spaces: Essays on clinical process, trauma, and dissociation.* Hillsdale, NJ: Analytic Press.

Bromberg, P. M. (2006). *Awakening the dreamer: Clinical journeys.* New York, NY: Routledge-Taylor & Francis Group.

Bromberg, P. M. (2010). *The shadow of the tsunami and the growth of the relational mind.* New York, NY: Routledge-Taylor & Francis Group.

Brown, B. (2010). *The gifts of imperfection: Let go of who you think you're supposed to be and embrace who you are.* Center City, MN: Hazelden.

Epstein, M. (1998). *Going to pieces without falling apart: A Buddhist perspective on wholeness.* New York, NY: Broadway Books.

Fosshage, J. (1995). Countertransference as the analyst's experience of the analy- sand: Influence of listening perspectives. *Psychoanalytic Psychology, 12,* 375–391.

Germer, C. K. (2009). *The mindful path to self-compassion: Freeing yourself from destructive thoughts and emotions.* New York, NY: Guilford Press.

Germer, C. K., & Siegel, R. D. (2012). *Wisdom and compassion in psychotherapy: Deepening mindfulness in clinical practice.* New York, NY: Guilford Press.

Germer, C. K., Siegel, R. D., & Fulton, P. R. (2005). *Mindfulness and psychotherapy.* New York, NY: Guilford Press.

Hayes, S. C., Barnes-Holmes, D., & Roche, B. (2001). *Relational frame theory: A post-Skinnerian account of human language and cognition.* New York, NY: Plenum Press.

Hayes, S. C., & Smith, S. (2005). *Get out of your mind and into your life: The new acceptance and commitment therapy.* Oakland, CA: New Harbinger.

Hayes, S. C., Strosahl, K. D., & Wilson, K. G. (1999). *Acceptance and commitment therapy: An experiential approach to behavior change.* New York, NY: Guilford Press.

Hayes, S. C., Strosahl, K. D., & Wilson, K. G. (2012). *Acceptance and commitment therapy: The process and practice of mindful change* (2nd ed.). New York, NY: Guilford Press.

Hayes, S. C., Villatte, M., Levin, M., & Hildebrandt, M. (2011). Open, aware, and active: Contextual approaches as the emerging trend in behavioral and cognitive therapies. *Annual Review of Clinical Psychology, 7,* 141–168.

Hick, S. F., & Bien, T. (2008). *Mindfulness and the therapeutic relationship.* New York, NY: Guilford Press.

Hoffman, I. Z. (1998). *Ritual and spontaneity in the psychoanalytic process: A dialectical-constructivist view.* New York, NY: Routledge-Taylor & Francis Group.

Khantzian, E. J. (1999). *Treating addiction as a human process.* New York, NY: Aronson.

Kohlenberg, R. J., & Tsai, M. (1991). *Functional analytic psychotherapy: Creating intense and curative therapeutic relationships.* New York, NY: Springer.

Linehan, M. M. (1993). *Cognitive-behavioral treatment of borderline personality disorder.* New York, NY: Guilford Press.

Magnavita, J. J. (2010). *Evidence-based treatment of personality dysfunction: Principles, methods, and processes.* Washington, DC: American Psychological Association.

McKay, M., Lev, A., & Skeen, M. (2012). *Acceptance and commitment therapy for interpersonal problems: Using mindfulness, acceptance, and schema awareness to change interpersonal behaviors.* Oakland, CA: New Harbinger.

Mitchell, S. A., & Aron, L. (1999). *Relational psychoanalysis: The emergence of a tradition.* New York, NY: Routledge-Taylor & Francis Group.

Muran, J. M., Eubanks-Carter, C., & Safran, J. D. (2010). A relational approach to the treatment of personality dysfunction. In J. J. Magnavita (Ed.), *Evidence-based treatment of personality dysfunction: Principles, methods, and processes* (pp. 167–192). Washington, DC: American Psychological Association.

Olendzki, A. (2005). Appendix B, "Glossary of terms in Buddhist psychology." In C. K. Germer, R. D. Siegel, & P. R. Fulton (Eds.), *Mindfulness and psychotherapy* (pp. 289–295). New York, NY: Guilford Press.

Rubin, J. B. (2003). The well-lived life: Psychoanalytic and Buddhist contributions. In J. D. Safran (Ed.), *Psychoanalysis and Buddhism: An unfolding dialogue* (pp. 387–409). Somerville, MA: Wisdom.

Safran, J. D. (1998). *Widening the scope of cognitive therapy: The therapeutic relationship, emotion, and the process of change.* Northvale, NJ: Aronson.

Safran, J. D. (Ed.). (2003). *Psychoanalysis and Buddhism: An unfolding dialogue.* Somerville, MA: Wisdom.

Safran, J. D. (2012). *Psychoanalysis and psychoanalytic therapies.* Washington, DC: American Psychological Association.

Safran, J. D., & Muran, J. C. (2000). *Negotiating the therapeutic alliance: A relational treatment guide.* New York, NY: Guilford Press.

Safran, J. D., & Reading, R. (2008). Mindfulness, metacommunication, and affect regulation in psychoanalytic treatment. In S. F. Hick & T. Bien (Eds.), *Mindfulness and the therapeutic relationship* (pp. 122–140). New York, NY: Guilford Press.

Salzberg, S. (1995). *Lovingkindness: The revolutionary art of happiness.* Boston, MA: Shambhala.

Segal, Z. V., Williams, J. M. G., & Teasdale, J. D. (2002). *Mindfulness-based cognitive therapy for depression: A new approach for preventing relapse.* New York, NY: Guilford Press.

Stern, D. B. (1983/1999). Unformulated experience: From familiar chaos to creative disorder. In S. A. Mitchell & L. Aron (Eds.), *Relational psychoanalysis: The emergence of a tradition* (pp. 77–108). New York, NY: Routledge-Taylor & Francis Group.

Stern, D. B. (1997). *Unformulated experience: From dissociation to imagination in psychoanalysis.* Hillsdale, NJ: Analytic Press.

Stern, D. B. (2010). *Partners in thought: Working with unformulated experience, dissociation, and enactment.* New York, NY: Routledge-Taylor & Francis Group.

Surrey, J. L. (2005). Relational psychotherapy, relational mindfulness. In C. K. Germer, R. D. Siegel, & P. R. Fulton (Eds.), *Mindfulness and psychotherapy* (pp. 91–110). New York, NY: Guilford Press.

Tatarsky, A. (2002). *Harm reduction psychotherapy: A new treatment for drug and alcohol problems.* New York, NY: Aronson.

Wachtel, P. L. (2008). *Relational theory and the practice of psychotherapy.* New York, NY: Guilford Press.

Wachtel, P. L. (2011a). *Inside the session: What really happens in psychotherapy.* Washington, DC: American Psychological Association.

Wachtel, P. L. (2011b). *Therapeutic communication: Knowing what to say when.* New York, NY: Guilford Press.

Wallerstein, R. S. (1992). The goals of psychoanalysis reconsidered. In A. Sugarman, R. A. Nemiroff, & D. P. Greenson (Eds.), *The technique and practice of psychoanalysis* (Vol. 2, pp. 63–90). Madison, WI: International Universities Press.

Weinshel, E. M., & Renik, O. (1992). Treatment goals in psychoanalysis. In A. Sugarman, R. A. Nemiroff, & D. P. Greenson (Eds.), *The technique and practice of psychoanalysis* (Vol. 2, pp. 91–100). Madison, WI: International Universities Press.

Williams, M., Teasdale, J., Segal, Z., & Kabat-Zinn, J. (2007). *The mindful way through depression: Freeing yourself from chronic unhappiness.* New York, NY: Guilford Press.

Young-Eisendrath, P. (2003). Transference and transformation in Buddhism and psychoanalysis. In J. D. Safran (Ed.), *Psychoanalysis and Buddhism: An unfolding dialogue* (pp. 301–318). Somerville, MA: Wisdom.

CHAPTER 10

Embracing Reality: Mindfulness and Acceptance in Relational Psychoanalysis and Dialectical Behavior Therapy

Lisa Lyons, PhD

R unning from reality:
   "I have to be perfect!"
   This is Barry's plea, repeated over and over, session after session, as he sits in my office in a state of grief and desperation. He is in his mid-fifties, skin marred by a medical condition that began when he was a young child. He has no friends, no job, no partner. This is not the life he imagined; he is not the person he wanted to be. Over and over he repeats his mantra: "I have to be perfect." Sometimes he wants to be dead.

When he can't stand the frustration and impossibility of needing to be perfect, and to punish himself for his imperfections, he hits himself in the head—hard. He has come to sessions with black eyes, cuts, huge lumps—all self-inflicted. He punches holes in the walls of his apartment and his expensive car is full of dents, tears, and pock-marks, all the result of his rages.

Sometimes Barry calls me before he hurts himself. If I can get back to him in time, I coach him through the difficult moment, reminding him of ways he can distract himself from the urges to hurt himself and that the state of mind he is in will pass. On the phone, together, drawing from dialectical behavior therapy (Linehan, 1993a,

1993b), we do relaxation exercises, breathing, and mindfulness, and we outline ways he can distract himself from his excruciating internal voice. But he doesn't always call, and when he does, I am not always available. And even when I am available and coach him, it doesn't always help. I have learned that for him, when the coaching does help, the contact with me is as important as the skills coaching.

Barry is a veteran of multiple mental health treatments, in many different modalities. He has a long history of obsessive-compulsive disorder (OCD), self-injury, substance abuse, job failures, and rage. He is also gentle, lonely, tender, and—increasingly—deeply reflective. His father was a successful business owner who worked long hours and, according to Barry, was rarely home. When he was at home, he was explosive, demanding, and chronically demeaning of his children, including Barry. Barry is sure his father too had OCD. Barry's mother was depressed and intimidated by the father. Two younger siblings have also struggled to flourish as adults. As a very young child, Barry developed a chronic, somewhat disfiguring medical condition, and he still bears the external and internal scars. He felt—and continues to feel—ugly, unlovable, angry at the world that deprived him, and totally to blame for everything. Years ago he was able to work; now his days are filled with treatment, working out (the need to be perfect plays out on his body), and trying to parent a complicated teenage child, born to a woman with whom he had a brief fling. Medication gives him some relief, but it's not enough. When we began working together, he was still hitting himself and obsessed with being perfect. He wants and needs help, but having wants and needs reminds him that he is not perfect and sometimes propels him to hit himself harder. Before working with me, Barry was in an OCD-focused cognitive behavioral treatment. His therapist was an empathic man and an expert in the field. But at each push toward change, Barry hit himself harder. There are so many painful realities in his history and in his current life!

Charles is sixteen years old. Deeply depressed and suicidal, he had already been hospitalized several times and was attending a therapeutic day school when I met him. A creative, imaginative, and tender soul, he has always been a loner. Socially awkward and shy, he grew up immersed in his fantasies. Depressed early in high school, Charles confided in and then fell in love with a girl in his class. She was the first human being he had dared to let see his inner world. When she pulled away, overwhelmed by his suicidal fantasies and his need of her, he fell into deep hopelessness and made a suicide attempt. During our work together, his self-blame over the loss of this friend and his hopelessness about ever finding another love would periodically surface and come close to drowning him. He couldn't forgive himself, was sure he would never meet another "soulmate," and couldn't accept the idea of a life without her. Neither Barry nor Charles can accept what are deeply painful realities. Both are in danger each time they are flooded with thoughts of what they are unable to accept.

When working with individuals who are self-injuring and suicidal, there is often a need for rapid behavioral change in order to help them maintain safety. Rapid behavioral change has not been a focus of much attention in psychoanalytic discourse, but is targeted directly in dialectical behavior therapy (DBT). Outcome studies of DBT suggest that reducing suicidality and self-injury are particular strengths of the treatment (Koons et al., 2001; Linehan, Armstrong, Suarez, Allmon, & Heard, 1991; Linehan, Heard, & Armstrong, 1993; Rathus & Miller, 2002; Miller, Rathus, & Linehan, 2007). Analytically oriented work alone may progress too slowly to ensure the safety of a patient engaging in these behaviors and, for some, is too difficult to tolerate.

At the beginning of our work together, both Barry and Charles found the self-reflection and curiosity of analytic work re-traumatizing, humiliating, and incongruous with their more familiar ways of thinking and being in the world. Although by proceeding very gradually we were able to move into work that focused on curiosity and self-reflection, at the beginning both Barry and Charles were in grave danger, overwhelmed by unregulated affect. From my past experience with similar patients, I was, at the start, concerned that analytically oriented work would not generalize to their lives outside of treatment and that the re-traumatization and humiliation would drive them from treatment. However, I also did not want either Barry or Charles to be deprived of the benefits of analytically oriented work.

I have written elsewhere (Lyons, 2009, 2011, in press) about integrating DBT into relational treatment, about the significant overlaps between the two treatments, and about the value of combining these two ways of working when treating patients such as Barry and Charles. In this chapter, I expand and develop further ideas about the conceptual and clinical overlaps of the two treatments and the possibilities for their integration. I am particularly interested here in how they each translate mindfulness practice and ideas related to acceptance, drawn from Buddhism, into clinical practice. In DBT, Buddhist thought and mindfulness are translated into explicit interventions. In relational psychoanalysis, though the links are less explicit, Buddhist thought has had a deep influence on seminal thinkers in the field and is woven into some of the foundational concepts (e.g., Ghent, 1990). For Barry, an introduction to contemplative practice has been crucial in helping him to deal with reality—to accept himself and his life as it is in the moment and begin to confront and solve dilemmas in the real world. For Charles, although he has not embraced mindfulness practice, work on accepting the reality of his loss and of life without his high school friend has been central to his being able to move beyond grieving.

This chapter is intended for readers already familiar with relational psychoanalysis; for those readers who may not be so familiar with DBT, I am going to begin with a short summary of the treatment. This summary draws from the standard texts on dialectical behavior therapy (Linehan, 1993a, 1993b), the training and supervision I received from Marsha Linehan and her staff between 1995 and 1998, and my years of clinical and supervisory experience with DBT. Readers trained in DBT will note that in my summary, in the interest of brevity, much has been omitted. For those interested in a more complete understanding of DBT, including detailed discussion of the specific techniques and clinical interventions recommended for the therapist and the skills taught to the patient, there are excellent sources available (e.g., Linehan, 1993a; Linehan, 1993b; Miller, Rathus, & Linehan, 2007).

Dialectical Behavior Therapy

Dialectical behavior therapy was developed as a treatment for borderline personality disorder (BPD) and specifically to target suicidality and self-injury. The treatment aims to help people with severe behavioral difficulties (manifested both as what are often called "acting out" behaviors as well as numbness and dissociation) redirect themselves toward building a "life worth living" (Linehan, 1993a). The overarching attention in DBT is to help people manage the affects that interrupt progress toward long-term goals. This makes the approach easily adapted to work with a wide range of problems; eating disorders, addictions, and mood disorders can all be formulated as maladaptive behaviors used to manage unbearable affects, body experiences, and thoughts, and can then be treated with a DBT-informed approach.

An integrative treatment, DBT draws conceptually and clinically from cognitive-behavioral therapy, Buddhist thought and practice, humanistic therapies, dialectical philosophy, and learning theory and research. While DBT pays little direct attention to either psychoanalytic theory or clinical psychoanalysis, I find some notable conceptual similarities. DBT has roots in areas that have nourished relational thinking, including British object relations, self-psychology, interpersonal theory, attachment theory, and approaches to trauma treatment (e.g., Davies & Frawley, 1994; Bromberg, 1998; van der Kolk, 2006) that focus both on dissociation and on the body as a site of memory and arousal. These shared roots open up possibilities for clinical work that draws from both DBT and psychoanalysis. On the surface, DBT interventions don't seem anything like psychoanalytic work. However, there are clinical interventions in DBT that can be understood to operationalize analytic ideas (a few examples of this will be discussed later).

Dialectical behavior therapy is primarily a behavioral treatment, meaning that the understanding of therapeutic action and the interventions and exploration are explicitly linked to changing behavior ("behavior" here understood to include thoughts, affects, and fantasy, as well as observable actions). Ideas and practices drawn from Buddhism are translated into specific skills to help a patient accept reality and tolerate affects. Mindfulness is the organizing umbrella. Mindfulness practice in DBT is used to help patients learn to focus attention and stay in the moment, to manage urges without having to act on them, and to explore themselves. Learning what are so often called "coping skills" is only the beginning in DBT. In order for the skills to be useful, one must be able to focus attention deeply on the skill even in times of great distress—no easy task! Additionally, DBT teaches specific skills to promote the development of wisdom—the ability to attend to one's personal values and make choices that lead to desired consequences. The treatment also places a high value on compassion and ethical action.

Dialectical behavior therapy is also highly structured. It is organized around specific techniques and relies heavily on information from empirical studies that isolate mechanisms of change in therapy. There is much emphasis on organized inquiry into the chain of events—both internal and external, including affects as well as thoughts—that precede and shape a specific behavior. As the chain of events becomes clear, the focus in treatment is on planning how the sequence might be altered in the future by making different choices and using specific skills to manage behaviors and affects in new ways. Woven into this work is repeated clinical exploration and problem solving concerning what makes implementing new skills and behaviors so difficult.

Biosocial Theory

The theoretical underpinning of DBT is the hypothesis, which is increasingly gathering empirical support (Lis, Greenfield, Henry, Guile, & Dougherty, 2007; Austin, Riniolo, & Porges, 2007), that individuals who develop BPD experience intense and quickly shifting affects, have a low threshold for emotional reactions, and, once aroused, take a long time to return to baseline. When these individuals become aroused, the ensuing intensity and confusion, often manifested in disorganized thinking, numbness, dissociation, or episodic psychotic experiences, may take a long time to remit.

According to the biosocial theory, BPD is likely to develop when someone with an emotion system such as described above grows up in an environment that is chronically invalidating—an environment in which internal, private experiences are unseen and not reflected on. In such situations, a child may have to escalate to an extreme before being responded to or noticed (note here the similarity to recent work in attachment theory; e.g., Beebe & Lachmann, 2002). Barry describes being involved as a teenager in multiple car accidents and wishing his parents would notice and step in to protect him. He often tells me about what, for him, was the most traumatic accident. He was with a group of friends, all high. He drove through a police barricade onto a flooded road; the car quickly became mostly submerged. Luckily, he and his friends were able to save themselves. Barry called his parents, and they picked him up, but there was never any discussion about the danger, his poor judgment, or his drug use, and no limits were imposed on him. His memories of their lack of response still terrify him—more than the actual near-drowning. He felt unseen, alone, and out of control. He still becomes terrified and internally disorganized when he senses a lack of responsiveness or validation from people important to him.

Although most often the worst outcomes for children emerge from the chronic invalidation of neglect and abuse (for discussions of the overlaps of trauma, BPD, and PTSD, see Herman, 1992, and Westen, 1998), a more outwardly benign lack of recognition and mismatch in emotionality between parent and child can also set the stage for severe difficulties. This scenario seems to have been the case with Charles, whose family is concerned, kind, and involved, but also somewhat clueless about emotional intimacy or how to interact with a young person's internal world.

The chronically invalidated child typically doesn't learn to soothe herself or decode and label internal experiences. Rather, she is likely to invalidate her own responses and to look to others for cues about what to think and feel (note again the overlaps with Beebe & Lachmann, 2002). Early in my work with Barry, he and I began to notice how he would subtly shift his opinions to what he imagined were mine and would agree with almost anything suggested by anyone with whom he interacted. His difficulty locating and validating his own opinions and thoughts initially became more reason for him to hit himself. Much of our work has focused on helping him to find his own mind. My ongoing curiosity and interest in his mind, as well as explicit mindfulness exercises, have been critically important to this enterprise.

Organizing Ideas

Dialectical behavior therapy holds a worldview deeply rooted in behaviorism, Buddhism, mindfulness, and dialectical philosophy. This worldview is imparted through specific didactic conversations with a patient, DBT skills, and the lens through which the therapist understands the patient's difficulties. Central ideas include the behavioral assumption that changing certain situation-specific behaviors leads to internal change (quite the opposite of the assumption of psychoanalysis that changing internal structures will propel other more externally apparent shifts). Drawing from Buddhism, DBT weaves together interventions that underscore the importance of adapting to the ubiquitous flow of change, grasping that some difficulties come from fighting change rather than adapting to it, and the value of accepting reality. Central to clinical work is a focus on inhabiting each moment fully and ceasing to fight against either the realities of one's own history or the past actions of others, as well as accepting the fact that the present moment cannot be changed. As with many complex ideas in DBT, developing and sustaining acceptance is addressed directly, both with specific techniques for the therapist and skills for the patient.

Attention to dialectical tension shapes interventions that help to move a patient away from black-and-white, dichotomous thinking and toward tolerating and looking for synthesis among contradictory truths. Specific techniques highlight the paradoxical nature—the multiple dialectical dilemmas—of everyday life and relationships, and they encourage the patient to reflect on his own rigid thinking. The therapist is taught specific tools to convey acceptance of the patient as he is in the moment (i.e., validation techniques) and simultaneously to push for change. The patient is guided to do the same for himself.

In DBT, mindfulness meditation is taught and practiced in a skills group as well as in individual therapy. Mindfulness is central to achieving long-term goals of treatment related to affect regulation, self-reflection, and living fully present in each moment (Hanh, 1975). It is used to help a patient learn to control the focus of her attention (and especially to shift attention away from self-harm and uncontainable affect), to observe herself without necessarily taking action, to regulate intense affect before taking action, and to act from a wise and thoughtful state of mind (Hanh, 1975; Linehan, 1993a). DBT therapists design mindfulness exercises that directly target an individual's unique strengths and difficulties. Crucial to using mindfulness with this group of patients is to suggest exercises, especially initially, that focus on sensory experiences and take a patient out of her own mind—a place often populated with horrific memories and disorganized, sometimes psychotic thinking. Over the course of a long treatment, the focus of mindfulness gradually moves a patient toward observing and tolerating her internal world.

When Barry and I began treatment, he was not much interested in mindfulness. It felt impossible to him, and he was skeptical that it could be useful. One day he arrived in my office in a state of intense agitation and rage. He couldn't sit still, was flooded with urges to hit himself, and seemed to become more angry and agitated whenever I spoke. Words couldn't reach him. Without any introduction, I took out a foam ball and tossed it to him. He caught it and tossed it back. Within seconds we were engaged in a gentle game of catch. As we tossed the ball back and forth, our game became almost trance-like. I could see him calming down and felt our connection to each other deepening, as if the ball going from my hands to his was creating an invisible thread between us. When his breathing had become even and deeper and his body more relaxed, we stopped the game. He was now able to talk. We reflected together on how much calmer he felt and that our game of catch had been a mindfulness practice. His attention had gradually shifted from his agitation to the game; and as his attention shifted, his enraged, racing thoughts receded into the background. Playing catch was also for him an introduction to another DBT skill: "acting opposite" (Linehan, 1993b, p. 94). This skill teaches that when one is in a state of mind that can lead to dangerous behaviors, it is important to recognize and experience the emotion and urges but to choose to take an action opposite to what the emotion dictates. It provides a way to avoid the dangerous behavior and to elicit a different internal state.

Stages of Treatment

DBT treatment is organized into stages (Linehan, 1993a). A *pretreatment stage* focuses on orienting a patient to DBT and building an initial commitment both to staying alive and to decreasing self-injury. *Stage 1*, the stage when teaching skills is most prominent, is the period of treatment in which the patient moves from suicidal and self-injurious behaviors, an inability to tolerate affect, and a chaotic life to being able to maintain safety and to manage affects and urges without acting on them. *Stage 2* focuses on processing trauma. In addition to using basic DBT principles and techniques, work in this stage draws heavily from the literature on exposure (Foa, 2007) and bodily encoding of trauma (Van der Kolk, 2006). The sequence of stages 1 and 2 is based on an understanding that it is advisable to stay away from remembering and reexperiencing trauma and un-metabolized affects until the ability to tolerate affects and conflicts in the present is fairly secure and the patient has a life with both structure and supportive relationships. The later stages of DBT, not yet developed in the literature, theoretically include psychodynamic work and center on developing the subjective experience of contentment and joy.

Structure of Treatment

As mentioned above, DBT is tightly structured. For instance, therapists are taught explicit techniques, including interventions to use when a patient is stuck in a rigid belief system, language to use when wanting to convey validation, a range of ways to practice mindfulness, and a structure for sessions. Within sessions, topics are dealt with hierarchically. Between sessions, patients keep a daily log (called a "diary card") of affects, urges, and dangerous behaviors. In each session, an agenda is set, based on what is in the log. Highest priority is given to anything related to self-injury or suicide; next highest, to anything—including relationship difficulties with the therapist—that is getting in the way of treatment. When the above are not of concern, the focus moves to whatever else is of concern to the patient.

Modes of Treatment

Full DBT treatment includes individual therapy and a didactic and experiential group for learning specific skills. The skills group follows a manualized format (Linehan, 1993b). It focuses on teaching and practicing mindfulness; ways of managing oneself during crises; assertiveness skills; and learning to notice, label, and experience affect. In the group, skills are learned and practiced with relatively easy problems. In individual therapy, the patient does the more difficult work of exploring himself and figuring out how to apply the skills to his most difficult moments. Additionally, DBT prescribes patient-therapist contact between sessions (i.e., phone, text, email), carefully structured to provide coaching in using the skills for someone in the midst of a life-threatening crisis. Finally, in recognition of the difficulty of this work, full DBT mandates a peer-support group for therapists.

From the start, therapy proceeds collaboratively. Interventions and rationales are explained, and clinically relevant self-disclosure by the therapist is the norm. Clinical work is always linked to a patient's goals. It is understood that specific behavioral goals will have to be frequently revisited, and that patients will be helped to refind commitment to them when the willingness to make difficult changes wavers. As the patient learns more about DBT, the therapist and patient come to use a shared language related to skills, interventions, and meanings. The therapist is taught to move rapidly among warmth, validation, irreverence, reminders about past commitments and successes, cheerleading, self-disclosure, quiet experiencing, and teaching new behaviors. The shifting style and tone of discourse is a strategy designed to help the patient loosen rigid thinking.

Sessions focus explicitly on experiencing and tolerating uncomfortable affects, learning to manage distress without doing harm to oneself or the structure of one's life, increasing the ability to skillfully manage interpersonal conflict, learning to organize behavior toward long-term goals rather than toward short-term relief, learning to balance the needs of others with personal priorities, and learning to observe and reflect on oneself. Interventions are often concrete, both in planning for how to manage anticipated difficulties and in alluding to skills. Making meaning out of what happens is not the priority. The therapist is expected to be attentive to validating the patient's phenomenological experience while also pushing for change; the choice of which direction to go is determined by the patient's moment-to-moment shifts in the ability and willingness to work toward change.

The therapist is encouraged to be present as a person (i.e., no blank screen here; in my experience, a blank screen tends to pull for the patient's most paranoid and frightening projections and object dyads, or internal representations of self-other relationships) and should be tuned in to subtle affective nuances in the patient. Whatever is happening in the session—patterns of interaction between therapist and patient, affect dysregulation (either intense affect or numbing and dissociation)—becomes an opportunity to work on the patterns that fuel dangerous behaviors and interrupt the patient's work toward goals. Common interventions include stopping a conversation and practicing mindfulness or a relaxation technique when a patient is too dysregulated to take in information, sitting still with an easily avoided affect that has come up in the session, and redirecting thinking and actions toward long-term goals and away from actions that are totally dependent on the emotion of the moment. Moments of dissociation are likely to lead to attempts to parse out and tolerate the triggers to the dissociation rather than to exploring different self-states, as might happen in a relational treatment.

Dialectical Behavior Therapy and Relational Psychoanalysis

At first glance, there may seem to be little in the above description of DBT that has much to do with psychoanalysis, and; indeed, there are major differences between the two. Dialectical behavior therapy is highly structured, its goals are explicit, and behavior change is center stage. There is no place for ongoing exploration of what is unconscious or out of awareness. The more mysterious and difficult to quantify parts of human experience aren't really addressed. Dreams, metaphor, the associations that permeate a patient's narrative, and the unconscious communication that can shape the internal experience of both patient and therapist are not often considered.

Paraphrasing Stephen Mitchell (1997), in DBT, the tension between the therapist's influence and the patient's autonomy moves toward more explicit influence from the therapist than is typical in psychoanalysis (not disregarding the powerful implicit influence that operates in a psychoanalytic treatment). The DBT therapist takes the lead in maintaining the structure of the treatment and often functions as teacher, cheerleader, model, and guide. Although decisions aren't made for the patient, the therapist is an active participant in keeping central the task of behavior change and helping the patient to find his or her own wise mind (see the section "Model of Mind" below), learn and use skills, and evaluate the pros and cons of decisions. Exploring meaning is not in the foreground, nor is the human encounter between the two. Finding solutions and learning how to implement them is the main enterprise.

Psychoanalysis is focused on learning to know one's self. Self-knowledge is approached through exploration of moment-to-moment interactions with the analyst and through expanding understanding of what is out of awareness, dissociated, unconscious, and unformulated (all words with overlapping meanings and understandings). People come to an analytic treatment both to know more about themselves and because they are suffering—life doesn't feel right; potential for creative pursuits, love, and aliveness is somehow blocked. Hopefully, specific changes emerge from the work. In DBT, change is constructed collaboratively and deliberately by patient and therapist. The understanding is that alterations in specific behaviors, thoughts, and emotions will lead to deeper and lasting change. The assumption is also that behavior is situation specific—another way to understand dis-continuity—and that behaviors have to be initially altered in the specific situations in which they arise.

There are many overlaps between DBT and relational work—some more obvious than others—that make integration meaningful and often seamless. The overlaps that I elaborate here center on ideas around acceptance, Buddhism, surrender (the latter from early relational thinking; e.g., Ghent, 1990), and a shared model of mind. First, I want to briefly mention other areas of similarity. Dialectical behavior therapy reimagines and operationalizes some analytic ideas. The approach holds to a two-person model of the therapy relationship, considering what happens in treatment to be, to some degree, cocreated by therapist and patient. Although the unconscious contributions of each are not explored, there is attention paid to understanding each person's impact on the other. What is referred to as "chain analysis" in DBT (and more generally in behavior therapy) has much in common with "detailed inquiry" (Sullivan, 1954), as well as with more open-ended exploration. An analytically inclined clinician can easily expand a DBT chain analysis to include what might be unconscious or out of awareness. The DBT attention to microshifts in affect has much in common with the exploration of minute shifts in affect in a psychoanalytic treatment.

Additionally, ideas from object relations and attachment theories concerning the internalization of early models of relationships and the voices of early caretakers are central in DBT. These ideas are translated into language and interventions that aim to challenge a patient's early models with new experiences and to decrease the self-judgments that reflect early learning. Interventions in DBT that target internal object relations include challenging cognitions and designing new ways to behave that both disconfirm old models and elicit different, positive appraisals from self and others.

As psychoanalysts, we explore repetitions of trauma and are alert to understanding how our own and our patients' malevolent and abusive internal objects are internalizations of real people and experiences, as well as how they emerge in the therapy relationship. In DBT, the repetition of early trauma is addressed through the attention paid to ways that the patient has, in DBT language, taken on the "characteristics of invalidating environments" (Linehan, 1993a, p. 49), a behavioral formulation that both sidesteps and captures ideas surrounding unconscious identifications, repetitions of trauma, and internal object dyads. Both DBT and relational thinking also de-emphasize the role of interpretation in therapeutic action (in DBT, interpretations tend to center on explanations of repetitive patterns). Rather, they are both more interested in understanding enactments (although that term would not be used in DBT) and working with what is most alive in the moment with the therapist.

Model of Mind

Relational psychoanalysis and DBT, as well as Buddhism, assume that we function discontinuously (Mitchell, 1997; Magid, 2003; Linehan, 1993a). In all three models, self-knowledge and self-direction are contingent on recognizing and allowing for this discontinuity and on coming to know and appreciate all of one's discontinuous selves. In relational psychoanalysis, discontinuity is addressed through deep and on-going exploration of dissociation and multiple self-states. Helping the patient to know all parts of himself or herself and helping those parts to speak with each other and coexist frames the work. Discontinuity is also embedded in understanding that our sense of self, from the first moments of life, is shaped by interpersonal and intersubjective experience—a challenge to notions of fixed diagnoses, a unitary sense of self, and biological determinism.

Patients in DBT are taught a tripartite model of mind—a pared-down and somewhat concrete approach to multiple self-states. In it, three states of mind are explicated (Linehan, 1993b).

- **Emotion mind:** a state when one is flooded with affect and thoughts, and actions are determined by emotion

- **Reasonable mind:** a state when there is little or no affect present—logic, linear thinking, and, at times, numbness and difficulty accessing affect, dominate

- **Wise mind:** a state when one has access to the information from each of the other states of mind: logical, linear thinking, and affect are integrated

Most DBT skills are directed toward helping patients recognize which state they are in, be aware of states of mind that might propel them toward ineffective and unreflected actions, and inhibit actions when they are not in *wise mind*. Implicitly, therefore, there is overlap with clinical work that attends to dissociation and multiple self-states. In DBT, mindfulness is used to help a patient observe and label different states of mind. However, for the patients for whom DBT was designed—impulsive, a danger to themselves, and often unable to organize their behaviors toward long-term goals—controlling rather than exploring discontinuity is in the forefront.

The tripartite model described above is often expanded in DBT to encompass more complexity. For example, Barry and I developed a shared understanding that he had a state of mind related to hitting himself and that it was not a *wise mind* state. Initially, for Barry, the "hitting himself" state of mind felt chaotic and undefined. Labeling it was a step toward deconstructing it and a way for him to recognize it and inhibit the actions it dictated. Over time, as Barry used mindfulness to step back and explore his "hitting himself" state of mind and we were able to converse directly with it, our understanding of it became more nuanced. Barry has now come to be able to parse out and articulate the mix of emotions, urges, physical sensations, and thoughts associated with his "hitting himself" state of mind and is able to use a DBT skill that addresses whatever manifestation of that state of mind is most troubling in the moment.

Acceptance and "Willingness Versus Willfulness"

The idea of acceptance—that there are some things in the world, in life, that cannot in the moment be changed—is important for all of us, and it is especially difficult for someone dealing with past abuse or mental illness. The idea here is that life has many painful and unwanted events, with the understanding, of course, that some of us may experience more of them than others. This raises an interesting paradox, one that is often communicated to patients in DBT. In order to make changes, one has to first take in and stop fighting reality—accept the situation as it is. Only then can one figure out a path that leads to a better place. In DBT, this is posed to patients as a dialectic—a situation where there are two seemingly opposite understandings, both of which are true. The task for the patient, addressed through using skills and working toward cognitive shifts, is to tolerate the tension inherent in holding opposing truths and, in dialectical fashion, to search for synthesis.

"Willingness versus willfulness" is an idea that Linehan (1993b) extracts from the philosopher Gerald May (1982) and that shapes work to loosen the rigid thinking that is typical of many of the patients for whom DBT has been designed. In DBT language, one must be "willing" to do what works to solve a problematic situation, rather than "willfully" sticking to ineffective solutions or unmitigated rage, as if they actually were solutions.

Woven into work on willingness and acceptance is the notion, drawn from Buddhism, that everything happens for a reason. This is not meant in the same way as the often-encountered statements "it was meant to be" or it happened "because I deserved it"; rather, it comes from understanding that things are multiply determined by many forces, most of which are out of our control. This is how I understand the often-repeated Buddhist idea that things are perfect as they are. Every moment emerges out of a perfect storm. The task in making changes is to attend to the pieces of the tapestry that can be altered. Acceptance and willingness are difficult ideas for an angry and traumatized patient to hold on to. Once these ideas are taught, in order for the treatment to be effective, the ideas must come alive in the clinical work.

In relational psychoanalysis, there are implicit connections to the more explicit use of Buddhist ideas in DBT. The tradition of mindfulness practice has two trajectories: one on focusing attention as a way to control "monkey mind" (Suzuki, 1970)—the quality of mind that has us leaping from thought to thought without regard for sustained attention to one line of thought; the other trajectory, reflected in psychoanalysis, is on observing and being present with whatever is happening in the moment—attending to wherever the mind alights. The way a psychoanalytic session is conducted—the focus on free association, on saying whatever is in one's mind—is a version of mindfulness, a way of staying in the moment internally and becoming comfortable with whatever one finds there. The attention to knowing all of oneself—on exploring different self-states, becoming familiar with what is dissociated, and becoming more able to "stand in the spaces" (Bromberg, 1998)—promotes being present for each moment.

206

Using mindfulness with the often traumatized and episodically psychotic population for whom DBT was designed works best with certain adaptations. The practice often has to begin with exercises that take the patient out of his or her mind—a place often populated by horrific memories, fears, and a sense of ever-present danger. While the long-term hope is that, partly through mindfulness practice, a patient will learn to step back from and tolerate whatever is in his or her head, in the beginning practice focuses on sensory perceptions of external stimuli—what can be perceived through touch, taste, sound, smell, and vision—and on stepping back internally and observing those experiences. Mindfulness of thoughts, emotions, and body sensations—following the peregrinations of "monkey mind"—often comes much later, when a patient is able to tolerate whatever he or she observes internally, without quickly dissociating or moving to dysfunctional ways of managing himself or herself.

Acceptance of each moment is imparted in DBT through the implementation of specific validation skills (Linehan, 1993b)—directed both toward validating the reality of the patient's phenomenological experience and the role of the past in shaping the present. In psychoanalysis, acceptance comes, in part, through the process of exploration of each moment and in the curious and nonjudgmental stance of the analyst. It is implicit that subjective experience changes when you know and accept yourself, and that self-knowledge and acceptance open up more choices and the possibility of deeper self-reflection. As one becomes able to "stand in the spaces" (Bromberg, 1998) and see many parts of oneself, the range of choices increases, and the consideration of the consequences of actions deepens.

Clinical Integration

We return to Barry: he is enraged that at age six he developed a chronic, somewhat disfiguring, and extremely uncomfortable medical condition. Fifty years later, he is enraged at himself, at his parents, at how he hasn't accomplished what he had hoped in life. He is not perfect; his life is not perfect. From my relational self, I understand his rage and the limitations in his life as evolving out of a traumatic childhood marked, most of all, by his painful medical condition, the need for constant medical interventions, and the dynamics in his family. We have worked on trauma—on decreasing his dissociation, on increasing his affective experiencing, on understanding and grieving, and on exploring flashbacks, repetitions, and enactments.

But we have also worked from a more DBT-influenced perspective. Accepting both what has happened to him and the impossibility of even defining "perfect," let alone attaining it, has been central to our work. Together we have gradually been developing an understanding that his medical condition—certainly not perfect—wasn't fair or deserved, and that his parents' difficulty in helping him handle it was neither malevolent nor intentional. Rather, we look at the multiple factors that created this "perfect storm"—genetics, stressful life events, his body's way of responding to stress, the limits of medical knowledge at the time, the learning and anxiety related to his father's difficulty managing anger, each of his parents' significant abuse histories and subsequent emotional difficulties, the circumstances of his conception and his parents' difficult marriage, each of his grandparents' histories and psychological makeup, and on and on. The understanding of the web of influences on Barry becomes denser and denser. And he and I can consider the reality that the only things he has the power to change are related to how he responds—now.

With a more relational tilt, I talk with Barry's six-year-old self-state. This little boy—often in my office—is sad, angry, unheard, and deeply ashamed of everything he feels. I am curious about him and encourage my adult patient to be curious as well—curious and also compassionate. Together we try to help Barry's more adult self learn to comfort rather than rage at this sad little boy. Recently, I am encouraged that Barry has begun to bring in positive and, at times, loving memories of his parents and is deeply committed to stopping the self-injury. Integrating DBT and relational thinking has allowed us to work toward quickly changing dangerous behaviors and implementing skills related to assertiveness, emotion regulation, mindfulness, and crisis management, while deepening Barry's encounters with his own complexity and his experience of validation and acceptance.

References

Austin, A. T., Riniolo, T. C., & Porges, S. W. (2007). Borderline personality disorder and emotion regulation: Insights from the polyvagal theory. *Brain and Cognition, 65*(1), 69–76.

Beebe, B., & Lachmann, F. (2002). *Infant research and adult attachment.* New York, NY: Analytic Press.

Bromberg, P. M. (1998). *Standing in the spaces: Essays on clinical process, trauma, and dissociation.* Hillsdale, NJ: Analytic Press.

Davies, J. M., & Frawley, G. (1994). *Treating the adult survivor of childhood sexual abuse.* New York, NY: Basic Books.

Foa, E. (2007). *Prolonged exposure therapy for PTSD: Emotional processing of traumatic experiences therapist guide (Treatments that work).* Oxford, England: Oxford University Press.

Ghent, E. (1990). Masochism, submission, surrender: Masochism as a perversion of surrender. *Contemporary Psychoanalysis, 26*(1), 108–132.

Hanh, T. N. (1975). *The miracle of mindfulness.* (M. Ho, Trans.). Boston, MA: Beacon Press.

Herman, J. (1992). *Trauma and recovery.* New York, NY: Basic Books.

Koons, C. R., Robins, C. L., Tweed, J. L., Lynch, T. R., Gonzalez, A. M., Morse, J. Q., Bishop, G. K., Butterfield, M. I., & Bastian, L. A. (2001). Efficacy of dialectical behavior therapy in women veterans with borderline personality disorder. *Behavior Therapy, 32,* 371–390.

Linehan, M. M. (1993a). *Cognitive behavioral treatment of borderline personality disorder.* New York, NY: Guilford Press.

Linehan, M. M. (1993b). *Skills training manual for borderline personality disorder.* New York, NY: Guilford Press.

Linehan, M. M., Armstrong, H. E., Suarez, A., Allmon, D., & Heard, H. L. (1991). Cognitive-behavioral treatment of chronically parasuicidal borderline patients. *Archives of General Psychiatry, 48,* 1060–1064.

Linehan, M. M., Heard, H. L., & Armstrong, H. E. (1993). Naturalistic follow-up of a behavioral treatment for chronically parasuicidal borderline patients. *Archives of General Psychiatry, 50,* 971–974.

Lis, E. G., Greenfield, B., Henry, M., Guile, J. M., & Dougherty, G. (2007). Neuroimaging and genetics of borderline personality disorder: A review. *Journal of Psychiatry and Neuroscience, 32*(3), 162–173.

Lyons, L. S. (2009). *Stretching the frame: An analyst looks at dialectical behavior therapy.* Paper presented at Relational Psychoanalysis Comes of Age, NYU Postdoctoral Program in Psychoanalysis and Psychotherapy, New York, NY.

Lyons, L. S (2011). *Analytic knowing and dialectical behavior therapy: Holding horror and working toward change.* Paper presented at Division 39: American Psychological Association, New York, NY.

Lyons, L. S. (in press). Working with dangerous behaviors: Integrating relational analytic work with dialectical behavior therapy. In J. Bresler & K. Starr (Eds.), *Relational psychoanalysis and psychotherapy integration: An evolving synergy.* New York, NY: Routledge.

Magid, B. (2003). Your ordinary mind. In J. D. Safran (Ed.), *Psychoanalysis and Buddhism* (pp. 251–286). Boston, MA: Wisdom.

May, G. (1982). *Will and spirit.* San Francisco, CA: Harper Row.

Miller, A. L., Rathus, J. H., & Linehan, M. M. (2007). *Dialectical behavior therapy with suicidal adolescents.* New York, NY: Guilford Press.

Mitchell, S. A. (1997). *Influence and autonomy in psychoanalysis.* Hillsdale, NJ: Analytic Press.

Rathus, J. H., & Miller, A. L. (2002). Dialectical behavior therapy adapted for suicidal adolescents. *Suicide and Life-Threatening Behavior, 32*(2), 146–157.
Sullivan, H. S. (1954). *The psychiatric interview.* New York, NY: William Alanson White Psychiatric Foundation.
Suzuki, S. (1970). *Zen mind, beginner's mind.* Trumbull, CT: Weatherhill Press.
Van der Kolk, B. (2006). *The body keeps score: Approaches to the psychobiology of posttraumatic stress disorder.* New York, NY: Guilford Press.
Westen, D. (1998). Affect regulation and psychopathology: Applications to depression and borderline personality disorder. In W. F. Flack, Jr. & J. D. Laird (Eds.), *Emotions in psychopathology: Theory and research* (pp. 394–406). New York, NY: Oxford University Press.

CHAPTER 11

Beyond Insight: Combining Psychoanalysis with Acceptance and Commitment Therapy

Morton Kissen, PhD, and Debra Kissen, PhD, MHSA

This chapter is the outcome of discussions between two therapists: a psychoanalyst and an acceptance and commitment therapy–oriented therapist. We examine, from our own perspectives, the psychoanalytic concept of insight and its relation to therapeutic change. Does insight have a role in acceptance and commitment therapy (ACT, pronounced "act") and, if so, what can it contribute? We look at cases and their goals as conceptualized from the perspective of the ACT model. We then compare major intervention strategies of the two models using specific case material. Finally, we offer a synthesis of the two approaches, focusing on their surprising goodness of fit for enhancing therapeutic work with a variety of difficult patients seen in contemporary clinical practice.

History of the Psychoanalytic Concept of Insight

Historically in psychoanalysis, the concept of insight has been linked to understanding unconscious conflicts, wishes, or impulses underlying symptomatic behavior. It has also been linked to the strategy of using interpretation as an intervention, a practice whose utility is highly controversial. There are those who maintain the value of a solely interpretive and insight-driven approach and those who focus instead upon the various verbal and nonverbal nuances of the analytic relationship itself as evoking therapeutic change.

Psychoanalytic Approaches that Emphasize the Therapeutic Relationship

The importance of the therapeutic relationship itself in evoking therapeutic change was highlighted by Strachey (1934) and Loewald (1960), eventually opening up a more contemporary focus on the healing potential of interactional and intersubjective aspects of the psychoanalytic situation. Subsequent theorists—such as Kohut (1977); Mitchell (1988, 1997); Ogden (1994, 2010); Stolorow, Brandchaft, and Atwood (1987); and Levenson (1972, 2001)—have contributed considerable theoretical and clinical acumen to these relational and intersubjective perspectives of treatment. Intuitively, both insight and relational factors seem important to an effective therapeutic outcome, although clinical experience demonstrates that neither is sufficient in itself. Greenberg (2012) remarks, "In recent years, analysts working within a range of theoretical traditions have moved away from interest in uncovering repressed mental contents and toward a focus on how people think" (p. 280).

Experiential Avoidance and Psychological Flexibility

A primary goal of ACT is to facilitate increased psychological flexibility and behavior that aligns with one's key values. The corollary of these characteristics—psychological rigidity and lack of vitality— results from attempts at experiential avoidance (Bach & Moran, 2008). Experiential avoidance is the attempt to avoid, escape, or change the form or frequency of thoughts, feelings, memories, physical sensations, or other internal experiences (Hayes, Strosahl, & Wilson, 1999). From an ACT perspective, experiential avoidance eliminates painful inner feelings, but at a great cost. For example, a shy or socially fearful person can drink excessive quantities of alcohol to reduce feelings of anxiety at a social gathering or party but falls prey to the vicissitudes of addiction. A person fearful of intimacy in a relationship can compulsively utilize web pornography for sexual release, but at the expense of developing authentic human connection. A person who is fearful of commitment in relationships can restrict herself to serial dating and brief sexual flings but misses the interpersonal opportunities afforded by vulnerability and commitment. In each of these examples, insight into the dynamics underlying the patterns of avoidance is necessary, but certainly more is called for. More flexibility can be introduced via action—by attending a social event without the benefit of alcohol, diminishing or restricting the use of web pornography, and mutually getting to know a potential partner over a lengthy period of time.

Defusing from Inner "Verbal Chatter" and the Self-as-Concept

Hayes and Smith (2005) discuss the phenomenon of inner "verbal chatter" that occurs in all people. This refers to the mind's tendency to maintain a running commentary that is often focused on rumination about the past or anxiety about the future, and is often of a judgmental nature. At an ACT workshop that both authors of this chapter attended, the workshop attendees did an exercise in which we paired off and walked through an outer hallway, taking turns sharing all of the observations and thoughts going through our minds as we walked. Simultaneously, the other person observed and listened. It was quite illuminating to realize how much nonstop verbal chatter occurred during the twenty-minute walk. Many descriptive qualities of the self—referred to as the "conceptualized self" or "self-as-concept," from an ACT perspective—can be viewed as such verbal chatter.

Hayes and Smith (2005) created an ACT technique based on Titchener's (1916) early work, which they named "Milk, Milk, Milk." In this exercise, the patient and therapist designate a group of descriptor words, usually of a self-evaluative nature, which the patient then repeats over and over again as rapidly as he or she can (Hayes & Smith, 2005, p. 72). Eventually, the patient relates to the words nonliterally, rendering them relatively meaningless sounds. From an ACT perspective, this deliteralization is known as defusion. Defusion can be used to decrease the urgency, believability, and negative impact of

213

rigidly held beliefs such as "I am an incompetent, unfeeling, uncaring person."

Reducing Fusion Tendencies via Mindfulness

The corollary of defusion is fusion. Fusion is the molding of verbal symbols and environmental events together, leading to a rigid pattern of reactivity based on rules instead of actual experience. Bach and Moran (2008) clearly articulate this process: "Fusion is when people are guided by the literal content of their thoughts rather than by their direct experience with the world. Responding to fused content is like responding to descriptions rather than to the event described" (p. 97). Thus, a person who takes the thought "I am bad" too literally (hence is fused with it) may become sad or depressed and may neglect potentially vitalizing current examples or memories of environmental transactions in which he or she received a positive response from others. There is no doubt that an exploration of what historically led to this self-concept can be useful, but some defusion efforts are also required to optimize therapeutic outcome. The following description of mindfulness in the service of valued living demonstrates the benefits of defusion: "In the service of your values, can you just notice the thoughts, feelings, and sensations that arise and move forward anyway?" (Bach & Moran, 2008, p. 293). From an ACT perspective, the introduction of mindfulness is an important aspect of facilitating the client's shift from fusion to defusion.

Values and the Choice to Live a Vital Life

Values clarity is an essential aspect of ACT. As a means for patients to contact their most deeply held values, Hayes and Smith (2005) present an exercise in which the patient envisions his own funeral and what might be said in eulogy if he continues living as he is currently; he then contrasts this with what would be said if he committed to and lived in accord with his values. This is an interesting existential way of directing the mind away from the endless inner chatter toward one's core values, which might still be acted on in the time remaining. The fact that choice is an action and that we have the freedom to choose the breaking up of old, comfortable, and avoidant patterns—and to boldly substitute some personally selected new ones—is at the heart of this therapeutic model. The following quote captures the centrality of action with regard to intrinsic values very well:

> "You can talk the talk all you want, but if you don't walk the walk, your life won't come alive for you. What we have been exploring in this book is important, but what are you going to do about it? If you know where you want to go and don't go there, then the knowledge makes little difference. ACT is all about action. To make a difference in your life, you need to act....What actions are you going to take to achieve your goals? To move in the direction set by your value compass toward your first goal, what do you need to do?" (Hayes & Smith, 2005, p. 182).

All therapeutic approaches (including psychoanalysis) work toward tangible, measurable changes and commitments to action, but the ACT approach puts this unmistakably front and center. For example, the patient who must rigidly take three-hour showers to feel clean and uncontaminated needs to see what personal values and goals are hindered by these time-consuming habits and rituals and actively commit to diminishing this highly ritualistic behavior. This can be done gradually, perhaps by cutting down to a two-hour shower, then a one-hour shower, and eventually a fifteen-minute shower. The patient then has more time and psychological resources to commit to values-based living.

Self-as-Process and Self-as-Context

Exploration of the ACT constructs self-as-process and self-as-context can facilitate the shift from the rigidity of endless worrying and compulsive avoidance to a newer and more flexible set of habits (Duhigg, 2012). *Self-as-process* is the occurrence of events that unfold in the human mind: the process of thoughts, feelings, memories, and physical sensations emerging into consciousness. *Self-as-context* is the vantage point from which these events (the self-as-process) are observed. A more mindful, accepting approach allows the patient to gingerly, but tactfully, choose to replace the old, ritualistic, and rigid set of habits with behaviors that connect with her values. Only the patient, of course, can clarify her goals and commit to such a course of action. Sometimes all the therapist can do is pave the way and root for the newfound willingness to risk change. Hayes and Smith (2005) end their book by stating, "Life is a choice. The choice here is not about whether or not to have pain. It is whether or not to live a valued, meaningful life....You've had enough suffering. Get out of your mind and into your life." (p. 198).

A Willingness to Risk Exposure

Hayes and Smith (2005) speak of the "willingness" to expose oneself to anxiety and risks of a personally valued activity using the metaphor "jumping." Literal jumping can require considerable courage, as is evident in Bill Russell's memory (1980) of playing basketball as a young boy and finding himself frightened about having reached a height above the rim—this occurred before dunking became commonplace. Obviously, Russell conquered his anxiety and became one of the greatest basketball stars to ever play the game. The average person needs to evolve the courage to metaphorically risk a jump above their avoidance threshold on some issues they value. There is a well-known analytic example in which Michael Balint's (1968) patient stated that she never had the courage to leave the safety of the ground and do a somersault. He responded, "How about now?" and she proceeded to leave the couch and execute a nearly flawless somersault.

Applying the Two Models to Case Material: Similarities and Differences

Clinical Application 1

Carol had to go through an elaborate ritual of preparing her food in a certain way, putting on the television, and settling in under her bed covers for a relaxing eating experience. She subsequently had to pay for the pleasurable experience by expelling the contents of her stomach via violent vomiting episodes. She would frequently do this until her face became chalky white and ghostlike in appearance. A number of themes were evident in the story of her life, which seemed related to her bulimic intolerance for the pleasures of food. Her mother had died after a chronic period of illness when Carol was five years of age, and she had never had the opportunity to adequately mourn this loss. Indeed, she recalled coming home from a pleasurable day of playing with a friend on the day her mother had died. A crowd of mourners had gathered at the home. She could not understand why they seemed so sad, but she specifically recalled their frowning reactions to her gaiety and unawareness of the tragic event that had just occurred. This memory became a metaphor for her dread of the joys of eating, which needed to be patiently explored during her treatment.

Carol was sent to live with her maternal grandmother while her father attempted to deal with his sadness and sense of loss. After a year, he met a woman and remarried, moving her into the home in which Carol had spent her early childhood years. At that point, Carol came back to live with her father and stepmother. In the meantime, she had developed some compulsive eating patterns and began to gain weight. Her stepmother somewhat intrusively made an issue of this compulsive eating, but to little avail. In addition, her stepmother wanted to redecorate the family home and began to do so. Carol, probably correctly, sensed that her mother's presence was being erased through her stepmother's decorative efforts. She felt some resentment toward her father for passively acceding to this decorative process and less consciously toward her stepmother for initiating it. It seemed that these changes were occurring too quickly for Carol, but she obviously had no way of slowing them down. Her need for control of some aspects of her life was increasingly expressed in the form of a battle with her stepmother over her overeating and weight gain. During adolescence, she continued her binge eating and began her bulimic behavior.

During the course of Carol's treatment (which she began at twenty-two), the therapist initially interwove some interpretations about the fact that Carol had not had the opportunity to fully mourn her mother's loss (due both to her extremely young age and to the father's rather quick remarriage) with a more here-and-now focus on Carol's need to avoid the pleasures of eating. Carol would insist repeatedly that she was hopeless and would always be bulimic, and the therapist responded that this was not necessarily the case. Carol also insisted that she dreaded gaining weight because of her overeating, and the therapist responded by noting her actual dread of the pleasures involved in eating. The therapist also repeatedly noted that Carol feared the positive affect of hope, which she experienced as very dangerous. Carol would ask how emotions such as hope could be frightening, and the therapist would say that such feelings might separate her from her natural mother. Indeed, her stepmother had some competent and attractive qualities, which felt threatening for Carol and needed to be avoided.

Gradually, Carol began to see that hope was possible and began to feel a bit closer to her stepmother. At the same time, she began to reduce (and ultimately gave up) her bulimic symptoms. She took graduate courses in a highly specialized area and began to date a young man with fewer problems than the young men she had previously gone out with. She successfully completed her schooling and began a career that she seemed quite pleased about. She was able to terminate her treatment, having her life fairly well on track.

Carol from an Analytic Perspective. Carol manifested certain reluctances to experiencing food in an enjoyable and uncomplicated way. From an analytic perspective, she felt she needed to punish herself for such pleasures by making the act of eating an unpleasant experience. Carol needed to grieve the loss of her mother and accept her stepmother's presence as having some positive as well as negative aspects. Once she had done this, she was able to separate from her mother and not identify with her so strongly through her painful eating disorder. She now could internalize some of the competencies of both her mother and stepmother and combine them effectively with her own capabilities and talents.

Carol from an ACT Perspective. From an ACT perspective, Carol manifested a rigid, inflexible pattern of avoidance through clinging to her compulsive bulimic symptoms. She needed to identify the thoughts of being a deeply unhappy, flawed person (with which she was fused) and mindfully accept her feelings of sadness, loss, and hopelessness. She also needed to accept the possibility that she had the power to defuse from these internal experiences and introduce behavioral changes. She had to gain a fuller, more continuous sense of herself, including the more vital aspects. She needed to be assisted in determining what values were involved in shifting from merely treading water and staying afloat in the rocky waters of fear, anxiety, and depression—sacrificing her life in the process—to accepting the anxieties involved in a life that was worth living. By gradually committing to giving up the avoidances associated with her bulimic symptoms, she was able to make her life fuller and more rewarding.

Clinical Application 2

The next patient to be explored from our two perspectives is a forty-nine-year-old woman named Irene who remained single following a series of failed relationships. After many years of struggle and self-doubt, she was able to successfully marry just prior to her fiftieth birthday. Having been involved in an intense, ambivalent, and unconsciously hostile relationship with her very clingy mother, her successful attainment of an intimate committed relationship could be seen as a highly courageous act.

Irene was an only child whose father died when she was still an infant. She had very few memories of him and had not been assisted by her emotionally ungiving mother, who only grudgingly shared memorabilia or anecdotes about him with her. Irene's strong but ambivalent attachment to a mother who was incapable of joyously sharing and nurturing her daughter's maturational potentials and accomplishments was a distinctive feature of Irene's childhood, adolescence, and adulthood. As a result of the mother's incapacity, Irene often felt deprived and resentful. She inhibited and delayed her assertiveness and sexual identity strivings. She also continuously struggled with a lacking sense of agency and self-empowerment. She could not move out of the mother's home until she was thirty years old and stayed single, as previously noted, until she was forty-nine years old. She had one very long relationship with an inappropriate and essentially unavailable man during the period after she moved out. Moving out, of course, also took considerable courage on her part.

The mother's reactions to her daughter's impending wedding were examples of her lack of grace or generativity, which had been repeated throughout Irene's life. Irene took her mother on a shopping expedition to buy her a dress to wear to the wedding. The mother's lack of zest or positive excitement was quite evident throughout the day. After vetoing dress after dress as too expensive, finally she grudgingly agreed to the purchase of a dress that cost thirty-five dollars. Irene ended up with an exceedingly bitter taste from the experience. She was enraged at her mother's inability to generate celebratory enthusiasm for her daughter's joyful experience. Irene's therapeutic self-explorations had made it exceedingly clear that this lack of joyousness in response to her accomplishments and victories had been characteristic of her mother's reactions throughout Irene's life.

Irene's loyalty and need to protect her mother from the positive affects evoked by her achievements had diminished sufficiently to allow her to successfully follow through with her marriage plans. However, joyful feelings from her mother for this marital accomplishment were not to be Irene's due. Although she still wished her mother could somehow express some enthusiasm for what was happening, she was now aware of how limited her mother was in this regard.

Irene courageously proceeded with the wedding and worked through her bitter resentments of her mother's lack of happiness for her. She needed to continuously explore, however, her frustrated expectations for positive emotional reactivity from the mother. The fact that she could have a very positive life experience while her mother remained embedded in her sad and ungiving inner world was very difficult for Irene to accept. This now became one more separation-individuation experience (like her earlier experience of finally moving out) in which Irene had to struggle with unconscious and conscious feelings of disloyalty toward her mother.

The long pattern of loyalty and protectiveness toward her mother had now diminished sufficiently for Irene to successfully take this step. The marriage, like any marriage, had some difficulties and disappointments but largely was a happy and successful one. Irene continued to be closely involved with her mother, who eventually required nursing home placement and care. Irene, as usual, did the "right thing" and visited her mother quite often. She watched over her care, as she was used to doing. She resented having to do this for a mother who had so little to give her emotionally during the course of her life.

Irene from an Analytic Perspective. The need to protect and care for an aging parent is difficult under most circumstances but is particularly hard with a parent who was so rejecting and had so little to give. From an analytic perspective, it is interesting how loyal and protective children can remain, despite such deprivation and rejection. Indeed, it sometimes seems that, paradoxically, the greater the disappointments, the greater the protectiveness. Events involving joyous or celebratory affects are often put off or sabotaged so as not to create envy or separation-individuation from the depriving parent.

Some analysts view this from an oedipal vantage point. S. Freud (1916) and Schafer (1984) speak of "those wrecked by success." Schafer (1984) notes the pursuit of failure and idealization of unhappiness in certain patients while emphasizing, however, that these are not necessarily masochistic phenomena. The seeming need to sabotage oneself and one's accomplishments is fairly pervasively seen in clinical practice. Irene chose poorly—and perhaps unluckily—and sabotaged her wishes to be happily married many times before she finally met a man suitable and ready for a loving and committed relationship. The issue of "luck" in relationships is interesting from an analytic perspective. Many patients seem to create some of their poor luck through unconsciously motivated choices and actions. Irene may have dreaded separating from her hostile-ambivalent attachment to her mother. As Wallerstein and Blakeslee (1995) note, the first task of a good marriage is a psychological separation from the family of origin. Irene became used to loyally protecting her mother from her attainments. The very unpleasant dress-purchasing expedition captures rather clearly why she felt a need to do so.

Irene from an ACT Perspective. From an ACT perspective, for many years, Irene was fused to unbearable self-concepts, such as the idea that she was a bad daughter, whenever she came close to separating from her mother. She never was able to fully defuse from this bad daughter notion and to retain a more continuous sense of herself. She preferred taking a highly compliant posture toward her mother or the essentially inappropriate or unavailable men she became involved with. Despite valuing successful relationships, she often did not seek them out—or she stayed in poor relationships—due to extreme anxiety over asserting herself. She thus experienced a lack of vitality and joy, due in part to a rigid and inflexible need to please others.

But as Irene became more self-aware and gained clarity with regard to her valuing the attainment of a committed and loving relationship, she was able to move assertively in that direction. Irene was able to metaphorically jump and take the risk of marrying, despite her mother's lack of joy and celebratory involvement. She diminished her need to avoid such an experience, became more flexible about how she could attain it, and proceeded to do just that. Pleasing her mother would never be possible. She had to accept that fact and move on with her life.

A Synthesis of ACT and Psychodynamic Therapy

These two models, at first blush, seem quite different. Acceptance and commitment therapy is behavioral and has its roots in learning theory, classical conditioning. It is, however, an off-shoot of the "third wave" of behaviorism (Bach & Moran, 2008), which moves away from the mechanistic assumptions and hypothetical constructs of the "second-wave" cognitive behavioral paradigm (CBT; e.g., Beck, Rush, Shaw, & Emery, 1979). Functional contextualism is rooted in contextual philosophy, similar to that of relational psychodynamic psychotherapy (e.g., Wachtel, 2008). More specifically, ACT is rooted in a functional contextual account of language and cognition called relational frame theory (RFT), which has been demonstrated to be clinically useful (e.g., Hayes, Barnes-Holmes, & Roche, 2001). From this perspective, rather than emphasizing the form of behavior, emphasis is on the functions and contexts of behaviors, including psychological events. Bach and Moran (2008) apply this therapeutically with the statement, "For the socially anxious person, anxiety is a context for avoiding social situations. Instead of assuming he must decrease his anxious thoughts or feelings before he can have a social life, he might instead begin to engage with others socially even while having anxious thoughts and feelings. When the aim of therapy is psychological flexibility, perhaps living a life worth living is the clinical target, and not the reduction of certain symptoms" (pp. 34–35).

Acceptance and Commitment Therapy Eliminates the "Empty Organism" Notion

First- and second-wave behaviorism are mechanistic approaches that conceptualize the mind as a blank screen that is imprinted upon by subsequent experiences. The ACT approach departs markedly from such notions of an empty organism. Acceptance and commitment therapy is an experiential approach that conceptualizes humans as having thoughts and feelings that have meaning within their specific contexts. This view corresponds with the concept of the "emotional brain" (Ledoux, 1998), which includes emotional intelligence emanating from the prefrontal cortex, amygdala, and other, as of yet undeciphered parts. If anything, ACT envisions an organism with a very full mind. The emphasis of therapy, however, is on developing valued actions that can be flexibly striven toward and attained—not on changing the contents of the mind. The relationship to the mind's content is changed from one of fusion to defusion in service of this goal. Mindfulness changes a person's relationship to the linguistic formulations and self-conceptions of his or her mind. It facilitates the acceptance of painful thoughts and feelings that involves both an attention to them as fleeting and a sense of "being" in moments in which one is free of them. The healing powers of meditation and mindfulness are well documented in current research literature (Kabat-Zinn, 1991; Gerbarg, Wallace, & Brown, 2011; Kissen & Kissen-Kohn, 2009). Mindfulness facilitates a shift into the here and now and away from excessive thinking or self-preoccupations associated with past painful trauma. This allows dynamic material to be worked with from a defused perspective that allows the patient to look "at" trauma rather than "from" trauma, and thus the material can be worked with more safely and effectively.

Emphasis on the "Here and Now"

An interesting difference between the two models is reflected in the almost sole focus on current experience by ACT therapists and the exploration, by analysts, of the current transference and countertransference interactions as they replicate certain aspects of traumatic past experiences. In contemporary analysis, there is a predominant focus on the here and now as the heart of therapeutic action and change potential. From a relational or intersubjective perspective, the internalization of the therapist and his or her benign, containing presence can have a curative impact. Interpretations may still be useful, but they are not the only ways that change occurs in therapy. Change occurs in the present moment, as it does in ACT.

Views of Defensiveness

Analysts are interested in the past object-relational histories of their patients because they offer an insightful glimpse into their character structure, personal style, and favored defenses. Historically, repression was seen as the overall defensive maneuver from which a variety of defensive techniques arose (A. Freud, 1936). Acceptance and commitment therapy–oriented therapists, on the other hand, see avoidance as the primary defensive maneuver that can lead to rigidity and a sapping of life energies and vitality. This corresponds with the contemporary relational psychodynamic emphasis on dissociation as the primary defensive maneuver (see the introduction and chapter 9). Both models would appear to agree that missing or invisible affects due to defensiveness lead to unpleasant, unforeseen consequences.

Analysts, particularly those working from a classical or ego psychological orientation, see a variety of defense mechanisms in their clients, including avoidance. Neurotic character styles (Shapiro 1965) involve the traditional defense list proposed by Anna Freud (1946) and others (e.g., repression, reaction formation, intellectualization, rationalization, minimization, compartmentalization, doing and undoing, and so on), whereas more severe or borderline disorders manifest a more primitive set of defenses (e.g., denial, projective identification, splitting, and idealization). The more primitive defenses, of course, can be found in higher functioning patients, and vice versa. Each of these defenses occurs along a continuum and can have highly adaptive, as well as disruptive, aspects. Thus, projective identification can be a form of empathy; idealization, a form of loving; denial, a way of (hopefully temporarily) coping with highly anxiety-provoking circumstances; and splitting, a way (again, hopefully temporarily) a way of sorting out and categorizing highly painful and pleasurable aspects of experience. Many conflicts in basically happy couples involve the use of words such as "always" and "never," which involve a temporary kind of splitting that subsequent discussion can correct and move beyond.

Playing and Playfulness

The idea of guided exercises may seem artificial—or not very effective—to some analysts, but not to others. Since flexibility is a major value underlying the ACT approach, therapists are invited to use "techniques" creatively, rather than literally as described in various writings. Most analysts are aware that the creation of a metaphorical play space can be useful and can keep the therapy process alive and vibrant. Of course, depending on their countertransference, they may be able to play in a lively fashion with some patients more than others. Also, some analysts and clients are more naturally playful than others. This may very well be true for ACT therapists and their patients as well.

Past Experience as It Impacts the Present

There is a relative lack of attention by ACT therapists to past experiences as shapers of current experiential avoidances. This contradicts psychoanalytic interest regarding the stories of clients' lives. Such story lines provide themes that pervade the treatment and often lead to insights regarding certain parallels between current self-defeating patterns and past experiences with significant figures. One woman insightfully noted that she needed to make everyone in her current world into an unconditionally loving person like her father. This dynamic had resulted in unrealistic expectations regarding her husband; the subsequent insight ultimately led to diminished expectations and a more realistic view of his capabilities. Enjoying the realistically obtainable satisfactions of a relationship, while at the same time accepting its occasionally painful frustrations, can contribute to an enduring, essentially happy committed relationship. Both models would value such forms of loving, but the work of helping clients attain it differs between the approaches. ACT therapists want to assist their clients' capacity to defuse from self-conceptions (that may be linked to past experiences) by experiencing their self-continuity and core sense of self. Psychoanalysts might doubt that the defusion can fully occur without exploring the traumatic, painful, and unconscious roots of these feelings—either insightfully and interpretively in Blum's (1979) sense or empathically, intersubjectively, and interpersonally in Kohut's (1977), Ogden's (1994, 2001) and Mitchell's (1988, 1997) sense.

Values Are Central to Therapeutic Work for Both Models

Both models incorporate a values schema as central to the therapeutic work. The patient's values need to be probed for which risks to take in stretching toward diminishing certain avoidances (e.g., repressions, denials) that foreclose vitality-inducing affects at a great cost.

Thus, a patient who is commitment phobic may allow himself or herself to be involved in a series of sexual relationships and friendships that never quite lead to an intimate, long-term attachment. Intimacy feelings or dependency feelings are avoided like the plague, particularly if they occur in the context of a committed relationship. In this case, the analyst may choose to insightfully and interpretively explore how horrendous intimacy and dependency appeared in the relationship of the client's parents, noting the parallel to the client's commitment or relationship avoidance. The ACT therapist may do the same, without spending much time on the historical parallels and negative reverberations from the client's parents' marriage. Both models, however, will work valiantly toward a reduction in the client's defensiveness and avoidant tendencies. Both therapists will tend to root for the courage to risk commitment. Of course, if ultimately it appears that the client does not value commitment and prefers to spend his or her life alone (at least with regard to marriage or cohabitation), both types of therapists may need to reluctantly resign themselves to that choice.

The therapist's values are, of course, an important countertransferential factor here. Some therapists value marriage or cohabitation greatly. One therapist continuously assisted one long-single career patient to meet men. He did this by writing her singles' advertisements for her. Like the parent who feels the need to do his or her child's homework, this therapist was probably manifesting too strong a codependent attachment with his client. He began to enable the client rather than empower her to act on her own behalf. Ultimately, for both models, it is the client's values—not the therapist's—that count. For the rubber to truly hit the road and for the wheels to stop spinning, metaphorically speaking, the client is beholden to engage his or her true self or chosen values and jump to attain these important values. As the sign on one analytic therapist's wall says, "This is not a dress rehearsal"; most ACT therapists would agree.

Conclusions and Future Directions

Insights, though not necessarily through interpretive work on unconscious processes, are at the heart of both psychodynamic and ACT approaches. The ACT model works very much in the here and now and in a highly efficient way of developing a sense of vitality and less rigidity in clients' lives. Metaphors of a creative and tangible nature are utilized to focus the client on old ways of avoiding pain that may sap needless energy at the expense of living a valued life. The client is invited to mindfully experience his or her pain while simultaneously taking risks toward personally valued activities. This helps to efficiently reach therapeutic goals. The analytic approach, at least from a current perspective, works toward providing insights interpretively, empathically, and intersubjectively. The therapy needs to contain the patient in a safe environment and metaphorical play space for as long as is required for a sufficiently loving and working outcome to occur. Painful experiences may never be fully let go, but life can go on in a more vital and energized fashion through such integrative approaches.

References

Alexander, F. (1950). Analysis of the therapeutic factors in psychoanalytic treatment. *Psychoanalytic Quarterly, 19,* 482–500.

Alexander, F. (1954). Some quantitative aspects of psychoanalytic technique. *Journal of the American Psychoanalytic Association, 2,* 685–701.

Bach, P. A., & Moran, D. J. (2008). *ACT in practice: Case conceptualization in acceptance and commitment therapy.* Oakland, CA: New Harbinger.

Balint, M. (1968). *The basic fault.* London, England: Tavistock.

Beck, A. T., Rush, A. J., Shaw, B. F., & Emery, G. (1979). *Cognitive therapy of depression.* New York, NY: Guilford Press.

Bibring, E. (1954). Psychoanalysis and the dynamic psychotherapies. *Journal of the American Psychoanalytic Association, 2,* 745–770.

Blum, H. (1979). The curative and creative aspects of insight. *Journal of the American Psychoanalytic Association, 27,* Suppl. 41–69.

Duhigg, C. (2012). *The power of habit: Why we do what we do in life and business.* New York, NY: Random House.

Freud, A. (1946). *The ego and mechanisms of defense.* New York, NY: International Universities Press.

Freud, S. (1909). Notes upon a case of obsessional neurosis. In J. Strachey (Ed. & Trans.), *The standard edition of the complete psychological works of Sigmund Freud* (Vol. 10, pp. 151–318). London, England: Hogarth.

Freud, S. (1916). Some character-types met with in psycho-analytic work. In J. Strachey (Ed. & Trans.), *The standard edition of the complete psychological works of Sigmund Freud* (Vol. 14, pp. 309–333). London, England: Hogarth.

Freud, S. (1937). Analysis terminable and interminable. In J. Strachey (Ed. & Trans.), *The standard edition of the complete psychological works of Sigmund Freud* (Vol. 23, pp. 209–254). London, England: Hogarth.

Gerbarg, P. L., Wallace, G., & Brown, R. P. (2011). Mass disasters and mind-body solutions: Evidence and field insights. *International Journal of Yoga Therapy, 21,* 97–107.

Glover, E. (1931). The therapeutic effect of inexact interpretation: A contribution to the theory of suggestion. *International Journal of Psychoanalysis, 12*, 397–411.

Glover, E. (1937). Symposium on the theory of the therapeutic effects of psycho-analysis. *International Journal of Psychoanalysis, 18*, 125–131.

Greenberg, J. (2012). Theories of therapeutic action and their clinical consequences. In G. O. Gabbard, B. E. Litowitz, & P. Williams (Eds.), *Textbook of psychoanalysis* (2nd ed., Vol. 19, pp. 269–282). Arlington, VA: American Psychiatric Publishing.

Guntrip, H. (1975). My experience of analysis with Fairbairn and Winnicott (How complete a result does psycho-analysis achieve?) *International Review of Psychoanalysis, 2*, 145–156.

Hartmann, H. (1939). *Ego psychology and the problem of adaptation.* New York, NY: International Universities Press.

Hayes, S. C., Barnes-Holmes, D., & Roche, B. (Eds.). (2001). *Relational frame theory: A post-Skinnerian account of human language and cognition.* New York, NY: Plenum Press.

Hayes, S. C., & Berens, N. M. (2004). Why relational frame theory alters the relationship between basic and applied behavioral psychology. *International Journal of Psychology and Psychological Therapy, 4*, 341–353.

Hayes, S. C., & Smith, S. (2005). *Get out of your mind and into your life: The new acceptance and commitment therapy.* Oakland, CA: New Harbinger.

Hayes, S. C., Strosahl, K., & Wilson, K. G. (1999). *Acceptance and commitment therapy: An experiential approach to behavior change.* New York, NY: Guilford Press.

Heimann, P. (1962). The curative factors in psycho-analysis: Contributions to discussion. *International Journal of Psychoanalysis, 43*, 228–231.

Kabat-Zinn, J. (1991). *Full catastrophe living.* New York, NY: Delacorte.

Kernberg, O. (1975). *Borderline conditions and pathological narcissism.* New York, NY: Aronson.

Kissen, M. (1995). *Affect, object and character structure.* Madison, CT: International Universities Press.

Kissen, M. (2003). "Why is marriage so difficult?" A psychoanalyst's perspective. *Psychoanalytic Social Work, 10*(2), 5–19.

Kissen, M., & Kissen-Kohn, D. (2009). Reducing addictions via the self-soothing effects of yoga. *Bulletin of the Menninger Clinic, 73*(1), 34–43.

Kohut, H. (1977). *The restoration of the self.* New York, NY: International Universities Press.

Ledoux, J. (1998). *The emotional brain: The mysterious underpinnings of emotional life.* New York, NY: Simon and Schuster.

Levenson, E. (1972). *The fallacy of understanding.* New York, NY: Basic Books.

Levenson, E. (2001). The enigma of the unconscious. *Contemporary Psychoanalysis, 37*, 239–252.

Loewald, H. (1960). On the therapeutic action of psycho-analysis. *International Journal of Psychoanalysis, 41*, 16–33.

Mitchell, S. (1988). *Relational concepts in psychoanalysis.* Cambridge, MA: Harvard University Press.

Mitchell, S. (1997). *Influence and autonomy in psychoanalysis.* Hillsdale, NJ: Analytic Press.

Ogden, T. (1994). *Subjects of analysis.* Northvale, NJ: Aronson.

Ogden, T. (2010). On three forms of thinking: Magical thinking, dream thinking, and transformative thinking. *Psychoanalytic Quarterly, 74*: 317–347.

Russell. B. (1980). *Second wind.* New York, NY: Ballantine Books.

Schafer, R. (1984). The pursuit of failure and the idealization of unhappiness. *American Psychologist, 39,* 398–405.

Segal, H. (1962). The curative factors in psycho-analysis. *International Journal of Psychoanalysis, 43,* 212–217.

Shapiro, D. (1965). *Neurotic styles.* New York, NY: Basic Books.

Stolorow, R. D., Brandchaft, B., & Atwood, G. E. (1987). *Psychoanalytic treatment: An intersubjective approach.* Hillsdale, NJ: Analytic Press.

Strachey, J. (1934). The nature of therapeutic action of psycho-analysis. *International Journal of Psychoanalysis, 15,* 127–159.

Titchener, E. B. (1916). *A text-book of psychology.* New York, NY: Macmillan.

Yalom, I. D., & Leszcz, M. (2005). *The theory and practice of group psychotherapy* (5th ed.). New York, NY: Basic Books.

Wachtel, P. L. (2008). *Relational theory and the practice of psychotherapy.* New York, NY: Guilford Press.

Wallerstein, J., & Blakeslee, S. (1995). *The good marriage: How and why love lasts.* New York, NY: Warner Books.

Wallerstein, R. (1983). Some thoughts about insight and psychoanalysis. *Israel Journal of Psychiatry and Relationship Science, 20*(1–2), 33–43.

Winnicott, D. W. (1971). *Playing and reality.* New York, NY: Basic Books.

CHAPTER 12

Contextualist Bridges Through the Looking Glass: Relational Psychoanalysis and Functional Analytic Psychotherapy

Mark Sisti, PhD, Jason M. Stewart, PsyD,
Mavis Tsai, PhD, Barbara Kohlenberg, PhD,
and Robert J. Kohlenberg, PhD, ABPP

If one were to be an invisible observer inside the sanctum of the therapy room of two different psychotherapeutic worlds, functional analytic psychotherapy (FAP, Kohlenberg & Tsai, 1991) and relational psychoanalysis (Greenberg & Mitchell, 1983), what would one expect to see? These two disciplines were almost consciously created at a great distance from one another—that is, the radical behaviorism of B. F. Skinner as opposed to the post-Freudian world of object relations and psychoanalysis. Most of us would not expect contemporary versions of these contrasting disciplines to look anything alike, but by coming full circle through the looking glass, in many ways, they do. In particular, it is in their application that they look more alike than different, and they may even share a degree of theoretical commonality. This chapter will take a look at these two increasingly influential contemporary "relational" therapies within the context of their larger communities.

Among the similarities that this chapter will explore, the most fundamental is that both FAP and relational psychoanalysis propose that the psychotherapeutic relationship is at the core of the change process and that our ability to form effective, intimate, and rewarding relationships may be at the core of our mental health. Both relational psychoanalysis and FAP have devoted themselves to understanding and optimizing the effective conceptualization and therapeutic application of interpersonal processes; yet, ironically, the two communities are quite disassociated from one another. This chapter is primarily intended to act as an introduction and interpretation of FAP for the psychoanalytic community; however, it will be equally helpful to FAP and other third-generation behavioral practitioners as an introduction to relational psychoanalysis.

Acceptance-Oriented Therapies

"Acceptance" refers to a mindful openness to experience, the discrimination of moment-to-moment sensation from our cognitive descriptions and interpretations of those sensations, and flexibility in response repertoires (Kanter, Tsai, & Kohlenberg, 2010, p. 31). This has often been described as changing one's relationship to thoughts and feelings rather than trying to change the actual content of thoughts or feelings. FAP embodies and shapes such acceptance-oriented priorities by nurturing and contingently reinforcing the patient's acceptance as it occurs in the here and now, within the therapist-patient interaction (these interactions are considered a type of clinically relevant behavior, CRB, discussed later), and by in-session modeling and encouraging of acceptance-oriented behavior, such as awareness, courage, vulnerability, openness, love, and compassion. It is also worth noting that "acceptance-oriented therapies," such as FAP and acceptance and commitment therapy (ACT), have also been described as "mindfully informed therapies" (Hayes, Follette, & Linehan, 2004). They have explicitly been involved in and incorporate a good deal of research on mindfulness and compassion processes, such as discrimination of evaluation from observation, present-moment orientation, openness to experience, common humanity, and altruism (Baer, 2003).

Self and Functional Analytic Psychotherapy

Clinicians of all theoretical orientations are familiar with patients who are characterized as having a weak, disturbed, or unstable sense of self. Patients who describe having multiple selves are also identified by clinicians of all theoretical orientations. The human experiences expressed by statements like "I don't know who I am," "I'm whomever you want me to be," "There is no 'me,'" and "I've lost myself" are all private experiences that must be accounted for. Traditionally, behavioral analysis has not deeply explored the private experience of self, but this has been exponentially changing. FAP is making theoretical and empirical contributions to the concept of self.

FAP conceptualizations of self begin at birth, with an appreciation for the infant's expression of inner sensations and with the successful and unsuccessful attunement of the caregiver to the infant. Using one example, when an infant cries when hungry and is subsequently tended to by being fed, that infant is learning to reliably discriminate the private sensation of hunger and to request help with it. If that infant is fed on a schedule that is not based on the infant's signaling hunger, it is possible that the discrimination and expression of the sensation of hunger may never fully develop. In behavioral terms, we refer to the deceptively simple behaviors referred to as "tacting" and "manding" to account for these phenomena. "Tacting" refers to language (in behavioral terms, verbal behavior) that is used to describe and label sensations or objects, such as "you," "mommy," and "apple," as well as descriptions of private experiences, such as "thirsty," "sad," and "I." "Manding" refers to using language to command or request, such as "I would like some water" or "I should/ must drink."

According to a behavioral analysis, successfully expressing oneself in this way is dependent on a sense of self (i.e., it is "I" who is thirsty) and on a sense of clarity about what one is experiencing (i.e., private sensations corresponding to thirst). When the objects to be named are external to the person (referred to here as "external" or "public stimuli"), such as a "pen," "doggy," or "cup," there is always great accuracy, due to the consistency of the social community in shaping these word-object relations. The caregiver (usually a parent) can see, for example, that the child is saying "apple" in the presence of an apple and not a banana. Corrections are easy to make, and reinforcing the children for accurate naming is easy to do. That same process, however, when applied to private experiences such as "thirst," or "I want," is more complex, given that the caregiver cannot see the private sensations that give rise to the appropriate tact "thirst" and must use subtle indications to teach this correctly. A further complication is that some caregivers are more skilled than others at accomplishing this task, and in some instances (e.g., when a caregiver is very distracted, alcoholic, or psychotic caregiver), a caregiver may be particularly ill-suited for this task. The same is true for teaching what one feels, such as "happy," "sad," or "I want." The end result is that individuals may be very confused about what they are actually feeling, who they are, and what they want, and in some instances, they are totally dependent on external cues. For example, if what they want or how they feel is dependent on what others want or feel, they are, in FAP terms, under public-stimulus control rather than private control, and treatment would be oriented toward reducing public control. This hypothesis has been explicitly dealt with in FAP, and the fundamental process of public versus private control has been empirically validated (Kanter, Parker, & Kohlenberg, 2001; Valero-Aguayo, Ferro-Garcia, Lopez-Bermudez, & de Huralde, 2012).

Clearly, FAP does address problems relating to the emergence of self, and it is decidedly relational. Accordingly, treating problems of self is also relational. For example, an unstable sense of self (e.g., very subject to public cues such as criticism from a friend, rejection by an intimate partner, or a bad test grade) is dealt with by encouraging and reinforcing patients to *not* be dependent on cues presented by the therapist (by definition, public) as a way of determining how they are feeling, what they want, or who they are. Ideally, the goal for a patient with an unstable self is to listen to what the therapist explicitly says about what the patient might be feeling, but not to excessively use it as a way of determining what his or her own private feelings are. From the standpoint of FAP, opportunities to accomplish this can happen frequently and naturally during therapeutic interactions, although the therapist might not be aware this is happening. For example, the therapist might say, "I am thinking you are angry at me right now," and although we would like the patient to consider this possibility and carefully assess his internal sensations (a type of awareness), he might immediately view himself as being angry when, in fact, the corresponding private sensations are not present. In this case, by the way, it is possible that the therapist is misreading her patient's emotional state, and it might actually be the therapist herself who is angry—this is why FAP underscores the importance of therapists being aware of and understanding of their own problematic behaviors (see discussion in the section "Rule 1" below).

Another way to create opportunities to weaken public control is the use of free-association variants (see Kohlenberg & Tsai, 1991, pp. 159–165), during which the therapist tries to maintain a nonjudgmental stance, thus depriving the patient of public cues. For "unstable self" patients who find it extremely difficult to free associate without seeing how the therapist is reacting, treatment is oriented toward shaping less dependence on public feedback (e.g., the therapist's, in this case). Although rarely used by FAP therapists, this is an example of how "the therapist as a blank screen" might be just the thing to provide a therapeutic opportunity.

Similarly, rigid and narrow thoughts about self may be directly targeted during FAP. Rigid and narrow-rule self-statements, such as "I am, at core, bad," would be dealt with relationally, at first by welcoming and exploring such statements—if, in fact, this statement is an attempt to legitimately describe how the patient feels (thus reinforcing private control)—and then by exploring when and how such private statements and feelings occur in the here-and-now interpersonal connection between the patient and the therapist. With those patients with an unstable sense of self, a FAP therapist would be very sensitive to any statements referencing "I" and would reinforce, via thoughtful consideration, statements that reflect the patient is under the private control of his or her own thoughts and feelings—such as "I think you charge too much," "I am angry at you," "I feel hot in this room," and "I am too cold in your office"—as such statements suggest an emerging sense of the patient identifying and expressing private experience.

Values

According to a behavioral analysis, values are "verbal statements specifying reinforcers and the activities that produce them" (Tsai et al., 2009)—yet another class of language-related private events that has largely evolved (both in society and in individuals) through socialization. Given this evolution, values, of course, would vary from patient to patient. For clinicians, the patient's values are often viewed as his or her goals to be achieved as a result of treatment. For example, one value specified by the patient might be to have more satisfying and close interpersonal relationships. Given FAP's here-and-now interpersonal focus, of particular importance are patient behaviors that move in the direction of the patient's values by creating a closer and satisfying relationship with the therapist (these are referred to as "clinically relevant behavior type-2s," CRB2s); whereas those client behaviors that produce distance in the therapist-client relationship are referred to as "clinically relevant behavior type-1s" (CRB1s). For FAP and relational psychoanalysis, explicit discussion of values in therapy is partly a reflection of their shared history with existential-humanistic traditions—such as the works of Erich Fromm, Abraham Maslow, Carl Rogers, and others—and arguably is also a reflection of the more socially conscious feminist theories and therapies. These early socioculturally aware clinicians helped to elucidate the autonomous-versus-relational dialectics via philosophical, value-oriented discussions. Concepts such as Maslow's hierarchy of needs and Fromm's so-called pathology of normalcy were contrasted with more socially aware, interconnected, community-oriented values and health considerations (Greenberg & Mitchell, 1983).

Transference and Enactment

The most significant similarity for relational psychoanalysis and FAP is their movement away from the "tyranny of verbalization" and toward transference- and enactment-based interventions (e.g., Aron, 1996, p. 202). FAP squarely places its emphasis on the interpersonal-experiential through a moment-to-moment shaping of direct contact with environmental contingencies, especially as they occur in the therapist-patient relationship. For relational psychoanalysis, transference-countertransference interactions are referred to as "enactments" (mutually evoked and eventually corrective emotional-relational experiences) and are proposed as a central mechanism of change. For FAP, this would be described as "experiential relearning" through evoking CRB1s and reinforcing CRB2s during the here-and-now interactions with the therapist (procedural learning). These are not dissimilar processes and methodologies, and they constitute the single most similar set of interpersonal elements for FAP and relational psychoanalysis. For FAP, the term "transference" is generally not used, because of all the excess meaning and multiple complex processes that it may or may not imply. In the standard language of classical psychoanalysis, the process we are describing would be conceptualized as "transference and countertransference," and, when interpreted "correctly," it makes the unconscious conscious. In the language of relational psychoanalysis, transference is often described as embodying and mutually creating restitutive enactments; in integrationist language, "cyclical psychodynamics" and core relational themes revised through rupture and repair sequences (Wachtel, 2008; Safran & Muran, 2000, p. 82). For FAP and behavior analysis, transference-countertransference is a type of "stimulus generalization"—that is, reacting with a particular repertoire to similar properties in a stimulus that was developed through prior learning history, whether or not it is, in fact, the formally identical stimulus complex. Within FAP, the similarity between stimuli is not defined on the basis of their physical characteristics but on the basis of how an individual responds to them. This is referred to as "functional" similarity. Within this framework, a patient can respond to her therapist in the same way she responded to a parent (even though the therapist and the situation are entirely different in the present moment than in the original learning situation with the parent).

FAP's emphases on in-session interactions and client behaviors (CRBs) are very similar to those of contemporary psychoanalytic transference-countertransference interactions (e.g., Gill & Hoffman, 1982). These similarities are specifically relevant to the psychoanalytically reconceptualized version of transference, such as those described by relational analysts as "enactments." As Aron (1996) writes, "Gill, Levenson, Racker, Searles, and Wachtel. What these diverse thinkers have in common is their understanding that transference is not simply a distortion that emerges or unfolds within the patient, independent of the actual behavior and personality of the analyst. Rather, the analyst is viewed as a participant in the analysis whose behavior has an interpersonal impact on the cocreation or co-construction of the transference" (p. 11). It is particularly to this reformulated interactionist conceptualization of transference that this chapter will be referring when it refers to transference.

Functional Analytic Psychotherapy's Five Applied Guidelines

FAP has generated five rules to act as simple guidelines for clinically applying a functional analysis and contingent responding to clinically relevant behaviors. While these guidelines—and, more importantly, the principles on which they are based—may be applied in and of themselves (FAP as a stand-alone therapy), they could also be used trans-theoretically to complement almost any conceivable form of therapy. Each guideline may engage and optimize the delivery of different therapeutic mechanisms of change in its own right.

Rule 1: Watch for Clinically Relevant Behaviors (Awareness)

It has been argued that this is FAP's sine qua non: "increase awareness of clinically relevant behavior in the moment"; in psychoanalytic terminology, build mutually greater awareness of transference-countertransference and intersubjectivity (Kohlenberg, Yeater, & Kohlenberg, 1998). This includes the shaping of mindful and compassionate attention, oriented in the present moment and nonjudgmental, while mutually and functionally identifying instances of clinically relevant behavior (CRB, or what psychoanalysts would call "transference reactions"). FAP proposes that successfully applying this single guideline may have far-reaching implications and be far more difficult to implement than it might at first appear. From a relational psychoanalytic point of view, at the core of FAP conceptualization is a co-constructed, two-person, intersubjective psychological paradigm. It is worth noting that "awareness" (discrimination or noticing skills), while emphasizing publicly visible behavior, is not limited in this way. The unit of study is the "act in context," which includes an awareness of any and all other layers of experience, such as situational, emotional, ideational, intersubjective, behavioral, and so forth. This functional and contextual awareness of CRBs and therapist behaviors is modeled in session and is therefore encouraged in the client as well as the therapist.

Rule 2: Evoke Clinically Relevant Behaviors (Courage)

FAP has also fully embraced the notion that evoking CRBs is necessary to maximize therapeutic change and that this corresponds to the stand taken by relational psychoanalysis that transference- and enactment-based interventions are similarly essential. In the service of evoking CRBs (as providing the opportunity for therapeutic change), FAP goes so far as to generally encourage genuine openness on the part of the therapist as an essential modeling of intimacy and courage. FAP aims to use the genuine and natural reactions of the therapist to evoke clinically relevant behaviors.

Via their embrace of evocation, FAP and relational psychoanalysis are challenging two primary and interrelated transference myths: the myth of uncontaminated transference and its corollary, the myth of neutrality. Classical analysts have been proposing that therapists *can truly be un-evocative* or, more importantly, that they *should be a "blank screen"* in order to facilitate "uncontaminated transferences" (Wachtel, 2008). Relational psychoanalysts have acknowledged that, to some degree, therapists will inevitably evoke some transference reactions, be they silent or talkative, self-disclosing or not. Carefully chosen varieties of self-disclosure have become acceptable interventions for relational psychoanalysts (e.g., Maroda, 2004; Greenberg & Mitchell, 1983) and have always been essential for FAP.

Rule 3: Naturally Reinforce Clinically Relevant Improvements (Love)

Rule 3 attempts to apply the fundamental laws of operant conditioning to moment-to-moment in-session behavior. In particular, the power of reinforcing consequences, combined with the sometimes overwhelming power of immediate or proximal consequences, is mutually applied to shaping behavior. FAP applies these fundamental laws by immediately and contingently responding with natural reinforcement to any flexible and/or gradual improvement during the course of the session. The term "reinforcement" here emphasizes natural and "positive reinforcement," since compassionate, appetitive, and affiliative repertoires have far more effective long-term mutual benefits than punishing consequences. "Reinforcement," however, technically refers to the entire spectrum of consequences that might affect the probability of a client's behavior, including "blocking" of reinforcement (non-gratification). "Blocking" refers to contingently responding in a way that does not allow the client to engage in an avoidant response (e.g., as in a therapist withholding compulsive reassurance giving). While various forms of "distressing" contingent responses might be used (e.g., self-disclosing a "negative" thought or feeling about a patient, withholding reassurance, and so forth), intentionally aversive contingencies are kept to a minimum, due to their general iatrogenic long-term effects.

Rule 4: Assess the Potential Reinforcing Impacts of Therapist Behaviors

This rule reminds therapists to continually assess what the immediate and long-term effects of their contingent responses actually are. The common or intuitive sense of what constitutes an effective "reinforcer" is likely not what is technically meant by "reinforcer." The precise definition of "reinforce" is as follows: if a contingent response is followed by an increase in the target behavior, it's acting as a reinforcer; if it's not increasing the behavior, it is not a reinforcer. How a therapist needs to contingently respond with any given client (and even at different points in therapy) will need to be varied, and the effects mutually observed, in order to determine what is or is not effectively strengthening a CRB. For example, a therapist may need a much more passive therapist repertoire for one client and a much more directive therapist repertoire for another (or he or she may need different repertoires at different points in therapy with a single client). Varying contingent responses is secondary to naturalness and genuineness, however, or we are right back to the ineffective, iatrogenic, and counter-control conundrums. Both FAP and relational psychoanalysis emphasize a two-person, intersubjective enactment, which would cultivate the development of flexible intrapersonal perspective taking and the interpersonal attunement required for effective, genuine, and intimate relationships.

Rule 5: Functional Interpretations and Generalizations

While interpretations have a myriad of subtle variations for psychoanalysis, FAP uses the term to mean causal, functional observations (i.e., verbal descriptions of relevant controlling variables). For both FAP and relational psychoanalysis, these can be the most "talk"-oriented and least experiential interactions in therapy. At worst, such interactions can easily deteriorate into a tyranny of verbal analysis, compulsive "problem solving," and other forms of potentially rigid and experientially avoidant "reason giving." Every form of psychotherapy has a way in which it implicitly, if not explicitly, shapes its clients into giving reasons that are congruent with the therapist's personal or professional model (Kohlenberg & Tsai, 1991). While both emphasize childhood learning history in the development of the individual, both recognize that this attributional reasoning is ultimately a personal narrative.

Clinical Application

In the following case illustration, we will illustrate the use of FAP with "Gary," a fifty-one-year-old divorced male who has been in weekly therapy with the third author (MT) for almost four years. Gary is focusing on increasing and maintaining closeness in his relationships; one pattern is that he pulls away from others by becoming cold and critical. This pattern has surfaced in vivo with MT After MT returned from a two-week trip to Bali, Gary indicated, "I had this strong feeling that things are not going to work out between us. We won't get beyond my coldness toward you and my criticalness of you." Gary further asked if it wasn't the therapist's job to accept and interpret his behavior, for instance, he was feeling abandoned, and it evoked all this "stuff" in him, and wasn't this interesting to MT? Instead, MT told him it was painful, and he felt punished for what he thought was a CRB2 of describing his feelings. Gary and MT came to an agreement that it was probably both a CRB1 and a CRB2, and that in order for it to be even more of a CRB2, Gary needed to soften his statement with something that was also true, such as "I'm probably not always going to feel this way" or "It's really hard for me to say this to you."

In this verbatim transcript excerpt (edited for clarity) from the second session after MT's return from her trip, we will illustrate how the FAP rules (in bold print) were used to work with Gary's way of distancing from MT:

Therapist: So if you're feeling distant, tell me, and be aware of how you say it to me, 'cause I don't want to be a therapist who just doesn't have feelings that reflect everyone else that you're going to get close to. I think it's useful that I get hurt by you, and it's really useful that I will hang in there no matter what to work this through. **[Rule 1, Be Aware of CRBs; Rule 2, Evoke CRBs]**

Client: I did have the thought after the session, *I must have really been hurt by your being gone for three weeks,* and I didn't really have a clue that I was hurting, except that I can see, oh, I said *that.* So in retrospect, it seems like I don't think I would've said that unless I was angry or wanted to hurt you. So why would I have wanted to hurt you? Well, I must've been upset about your being gone. But the only sign of that was that I said that. That's my only way of knowing I had some strong feelings about your being gone." **[CRB2]**

T: Okay, so how about if you do a really quick free association to my being gone—what does that bring up? **[Rule 3, Reinforce CRB2s** (client had previously indicated free association could be useful for him)**; Rule 2]**

C: My first thought is I was shocked to find out you went without Bob [MT's spouse]....Wow, I never imagined that; what could be going on? My next thought is you looked a little tan last week; you looked nice. Then I thought today you looked nice with that rose blouse....My other association is an attractive woman on eHarmony who's interested in going to places with water, white sand, blue water, and that seemed really appealing to me, something I would like to do with someone. **[CRB2]**

T: This is great, the associations you came up with. **[Rule 3]** What stands out to you about the material that came up? **[Rule 2]**

C: It seems there are romantic feelings about you in there—that you're looking attractive. That you have this attractive blouse on and you look good with the sun. What's the deal about your relationship with Bob? You were off doing something that I wanted to do. **[CRB2]**

T: That's what I was hearing too: the romantic feelings, the longing to be going to places with people you're attracted to, and why did I leave you behind. **[Rule 3; Rule 4, Be Aware of One's Impact** (MT is noticing that Gary is very engaged in the interaction and engaging in lots of CRB2s)]

C: I didn't think it would work, and it did, so I'm glad we did it. It makes me feel more competent....When I free associate, I can really process. **[CRB2]**

T: It really helps me connect with you when you can free associate about what may be behind your expressing cold and critical feelings toward me. **[Rule 3]** It seems that you were pretty upset about my not seeing you for three weeks. In the future, when you want to express feeling cold and critical toward me or someone else, do you think you can pause and reflect on some possible underlying reasons, such as feeling hurt or abandoned? **[Rule 5, Interpret and Generalize]**

A deep and effective understanding of FAP encompasses much more than a rigid application of the five guidelines. An understanding of the underlying contextual behavioral science (functional behavioral analysis and relational responding) and the ability to construct a functionally based conceptualization are fundamental to doing FAP. Whether or not a behavior is an instance of rule 1, rule 2, or one of the others ultimately depends on how it functions. A therapist may attempt to contingently reinforce (rule 3) and end up with more of an evocation (rule 2). The rules and processes, of course, will overlap; separating "the ongoing act in context" is merely a pragmatic convenience, as is well known by relational analysts who know that an interpretation may also function as an enactment. FAP acknowledges the paradox of its own list of instructional rules—that is, learning *that* these certain rules may be important rubrics is quite different from knowing *how* to apply these rules, as this is often more a matter of procedural rather than declarative, rule-governed learning (Tsai et al., 2009). Hence learning these guidelines via application and supervision exposes some additional commonalities between FAP and psychoanalytic supervision—that is, emotionally evocative and personally meaningful supervision. The rules themselves are merely guidelines for knowing where to focus and for learning to make effective therapeutic decisions.

Clinical Application from a Relational Psychodynamic Perspective

Next, JS will consider the above clinical material from a relational psychodynamic perspective. Although there was no actual interaction between JS and the patient "Gary," potential therapist responses to Gary's clinical material presented by MT that reflect a relational psychodynamic approach will be presented:

T: Is there anything in our past interactions that leads you to believe that we cannot work together because of your "coldness and criticalness" toward me? [Note the therapist's focus on patterns of the current therapy relationship.]

T: Is it possible that this (suggesting we might not be able to continue working together) is a way for you to withdraw from our relationship, similar to how you have withdrawn from other relationships? [Note the therapist's attempt to connect the here-and-now therapy relationship to the patient's relational patterns outside of therapy.]

T: I am feeling like you have an expectation as to how I should react to you—by "interpreting" your behavior—as if I have a preconceived notion of what is going on between us. The truth is, I think that we can collaborate and explore what is happening between us together, and that this might help you understand your functioning in other relationships. [Note the therapist's use of his countertransference feelings to shift the process to a more egalitarian, albeit asymmetrical position (e.g., Aron, 1996; Stern, 1997).]

T: It feels like you are trying to push me away from you and that you expect that I will collude with you and agree that we cannot continue to work together. Perhaps I have colluded with you by leaving town for a while. However, I see this process—what we are doing now—as doing the work together, trying to see what is really going on between us. [e.g., Levenson, 2005. Note the therapist's attempt to step out of the relational cycle being enacted; similar to a CRB2, by reinforcing that we are "doing the work together."]

T: So if we are doing the work together, what would be the purpose of discontinuing? Could it be an attempt to avoid looking at what is going on between us and how our relationship might connect to other relationships in your life? Could it be that your expectations of others—that they will leave you—influences your behavior with them so that you push them away and essentially leave them?

The relational psychodynamic perspective presented above demonstrates the importance of exploring the therapy relationship to gain insight into the patient's functioning outside of therapy. Similarly, FAP locates the therapeutic action as occurring in the therapy relationship. Additionally, both approaches use the therapist's reactions to the patient as important data for case conceptualization. MT's use of free association parallels the traditional psychodynamic approach initially advocated by Freud (1912). The relational psychodynamic approach leans more toward Sullivan's (1954) technical approach of the detailed inquiry.

Old Wine in New Bottles? Or, Transtheoretical Bridge Building

FAP has—in at least three seminal articles—acknowledged that several of its applied interventions are very similar to, and hence indebted to, a wide range of psychotherapeutic approaches, not the least of which is psychoanalytic (Kanter, Tsai, & Kohlenberg, 2010; Kohlenberg, Yeater, & Kohlenberg, 1998; Kohlenberg & Tsai, 1991). In spite of similarities, FAP is not simply appropriating transference concepts without acknowledgment or without adding ideas of its own. For instance, on the one hand, FAP is derived from radical behavioral epistemology. On the other, FAP is more similar clinically to psychodynamic approaches than to traditional behavioral therapies. Thus, FAP occupies a unique therapeutic space in that it is able to bridge both the behavioral and psychodynamic worlds.

Particularly in an increasingly transtheoretical and integrationist paradigm, far from being old wine in new bottles, FAP is providing clarity to answering an age-old cross-theoretical question: "What is the rational basis for selecting the technique which is appropriate for a particular client at a particular time?" (Kohlenberg & Tsai, 1994). Do we interpret, and if so, what type of interpretation? Do we self-disclose? Do we focus a client on disclosing impressions of his therapist's subjective experience or on his own descriptions of his own reactions to himself? Do we participate in the enactments? Do we mentalize, confront or validate, free associate, speak or stay quiet, take more initiative or less, add more structure to the session or less?

Interpersonal Therapies and Integration

Relational psychoanalysis and FAP are both reflections of and catalysts for the resurgent interdisciplinary interest in interpersonal-affiliative processes. This shift can be observed in a switch from exclusively comparing the relative effectiveness of schools of therapy via their respective empirically supported protocols (EST) to increased investigation of the empirically supported processes (ESP) underlying all therapies. Such a trend is visible in the emergence of "unified treatment protocols" referred to by theoreticians like Hayes and Barlow (Hayes, Strosahl, & Wilson, 1999; Barlow, 2010).

Stephen Mitchell explicitly intended to integrate the major relational analytic schools (i.e., interpersonal, object relations, and self-psychology), just as FAP looked across theoretical schools—behavioral, cognitive, psychoanalytic (Greenberg & Mitchell, 1983; Kanter, Tsai, & Kohlenberg, 2010). As a board member for the Society for the Exploration of Psychotherapy Integration (SEPI) for several years, Mitchell was also explicitly involved in wider integrationist movements; however, his premature death prevents us from knowing just how far his integrationist efforts might have extended. It would be an ironic enactment and an act of community disassociation—for FAP and relational psychoanalysts—while espousing such intersubjective, affiliative, intimate, and interpersonal priorities, to not extend these priorities beyond our one-to-one therapeutic relations to our own wider professional communities. Also, if we are expecting our clients to make intersubjective breakthroughs, these authors believe we can do better as psychotherapeutic communities if we do the same. Perhaps our interpersonal and relationally oriented schools may help to tone down the xenophobic, identity-oriented tribalism bent on mischaracterizing the "bad object" other. We can build interpersonal bridges based on our commonalities and, at the very least, learn from others in the process.

References

Aron, L. (1996). *A meeting of minds: Mutuality in psychoanalysis.* New York, NY: Routledge.

Baer, R. (2003). Mindfulness training as a clinical intervention: A conceptual and empirical review. *Clinical Psychology: Science and Practice, 10,* 125–143.

Barlow, D. (2010). *Unified protocol for transdiagnostic treatment of emotional disorders: Therapist guide.* New York, NY: Oxford University Press.

Freud, S. (1912). Recommendations to physicians practicing psycho-analysis. In J. Strachey (Ed. & Trans.), *The standard edition of the complete psychological works of Sigmund Freud* (Vol. 12, pp. 109–120). London, England: Hogarth Press.

Gill, M., & Hoffman, I. Z. (1982). *Analysis of transference* (Vol. 2). New York, NY: International Universities Press.

Greenberg, J. R., & Mitchell, S. A. (1983). *Object relations in psychoanalytic theory.* Cambridge, MA: Harvard University Press.

Hayes, S. C., Follette, V. M., & Linehan, M. M. (Eds.). (2004). *Mindfulness and acceptance: Expanding the cognitive-behavioral tradition.* New York, NY: Guilford Press.

Hayes, S. C., Strosahl, K. D., & Wilson, K. G. (1999). *Acceptance and commitment therapy: An experiential approach to behavior change.* New York, NY: Guilford Press.

Kanter, J. W., Parker, C. R., & Kohlenberg, R. J. (2001). Finding the self: A behavioral measure and its clinical implications. *Psychotherapy: Theory, Research, Practice, Training, 38*(2), 198–211.

Kanter, J. W., Tsai, M., & Kohlenberg, R. J. (Eds.). (2010). *The practice of functional analytic psychotherapy.* New York, NY: Springer.

Kohlenberg, R. J., & Tsai, M. (1991). *Functional analytic psychotherapy: Creating intense and curative therapeutic relationships.* New York, NY: Springer.

Kohlenberg, R. J., & Tsai, M. (1994). Functional analytic psychotherapy: A behavioral approach to treatment and integration. *Journal of Psychotherapy Integration, 4,* 175–201.

Kohlenberg, B. S., Yeater, E. A., & Kohlenberg, R. J. (1998). Functional analytic psychotherapy, the therapeutic alliance, and brief psychotherapy. In J. D. Safran & J. C. Muran (Eds.), *The therapeutic alliance in brief psychotherapy* (pp. 63–93). Washington, DC: American Psychological Association.

Levenson, E. A. (2005). *The fallacy of understanding and the ambiguity of change.* New York, NY: Routledge.

Maroda, K. J. (2004). *The power of countertransference: Innovations in analytic technique.* New York, NY: Routledge.

Safran, J. D., & Muran, J. C. (2000). *The therapeutic alliance in brief psychotherapy.* Washington, DC: American Psychological Association.

Stern, D. B. (1997). *Unformulated experience: From dissociation to imagination in psychoanalysis.* New York, NY: Routledge-Taylor & Francis Group.

Sullivan, H. S. (1954). *The psychiatric interview.* New York, NY: W. W. Norton.

Tsai, M., Kohlenberg, R. J., Kanter, J. W., Kohlenberg, B., Follette, W. C., & Callaghan, G. M. (2009). *A guide to functional analytic psychotherapy: Awareness, courage, love, and behaviorism.* New York, NY: Springer.

Valero-Aguayo, L., Ferro-Garcia, R., Lopez-Bermudez, M. A., & de Huralde, M. A. S.-L. (2012). Reliability and validity of the Spanish adaptation of EOSS, comparing normal and clinical samples. *International Journal of Behavioral Consultation and Therapy, 7*(2–3), 151–158.

Wachtel, P. L. (2008). *Relational theory and the practice of psychotherapy.* New York, NY: Guilford Press.

Afterword

George Stricker, PhD

When I was asked if I would write a preface for this book, I readily agreed. After all, it falls in the general classification of psychotherapy integration, a topic about which I have written a great deal (e.g., Stricker, 2010), and more specifically, assimilative psychodynamic integration, another topic of great interest to me (e.g., Stricker & Gold, 2003). It struck me as both relevant to my interests and well within my comfort zone. Little did I anticipate how much new material there was and how interesting I would find it.

The general topic of the chapters concerns the integration of mindfulness into the practice of psychodynamic psychotherapy. Indeed, this does fall under the general rubric of assimilative psychodynamic integration, as I anticipated. What I did not immediately recognize was the potential for the topic also to be classified as a viable new common factor, another important type of psychotherapy integration. Common factors is the earliest of the classifications of psychotherapy integration and, most importantly, associated with the important work of Frank (1961). Typical common factors include an emotionally charged confiding relationship with a helping person in a healing setting. The helping person then provides a means of understanding the presenting problem and a ritual to help resolve the problem. It is now possible to add mindfulness to that list of common factors.

"Mindfulness" can be defined as an approach that is characterized by purposely paying attention in the present moment without judgment (Kabat-Zinn, 1991). Within psychodynamic thought—the organizing theory of this book—it bears striking similarities to interventions such as free association, mentalization, and reflective thinking.

Within the cognitive-behavioral tradition, it is prominent in many third-wave approaches such as dialectical behavior therapy (DBT), acceptance and commitment therapy (ACT), and functional analytic therapy (FAP). We also can find mindfulness in many humanistic and existential approaches.

I also found it interesting to think of common factors in a new way. Not only are the common factors common to the process of psychotherapy, they also can be seen as common to the psychotherapist. Just as the patient can learn to be more mindful, it is necessary for the therapist also to be mindful. We then can add to this list of common factors the quality of compassion, both as a defining characteristic of the therapist toward the patient and something to be learned by the patient toward himself or herself.

There is an interesting philosophical issue that is raised by this marriage of the East (mindfulness) and the West (psychodynamic theory). It has already been seen in the dialectic central to DBT (Heard & Linehan, 2005). The DBT therapist is asked to accept unconditionally the patient's approach while, at the same time, moving toward change. This dialectic between acceptance and change is echoed in the nonjudgmental acceptance that is central to mindfulness and the use of that approach in the service of change. There is a similar issue in the dialectic between acceptance, central to ACT (Hayes, Strosahl, & Wilson, 2011), and the pragmatic pursuit of change espoused in that approach. FAP (Kohlenberg & Tsai, 1994) views the therapeutic alliance as crucial to the change process, and that alliance is based on a nonjudgmental acceptance of the patient. Finally, relational psychodynamic therapy, the core theory to which all is assimilated in this book's formulation, also is based on the alliance as it strives for change. It should be noted that the alliance, in relational psychodynamic therapy and in many of the third-wave approaches, sees the alliance as the vehicle for change, as opposed to earlier CBT efforts, which valued the alliance only as a foundation before the cognitive change processes are introduced.

Is the apparent contradiction between acceptance and change a fatal flaw in the reasoning of these therapeutic approaches, or does it pose a creative tension that can lead to more productive results? Although this is basically an empirical question, my inclination is to favor the latter, and research emphasizes the central role of the therapeutic relationship (Wampold, 2001). Perhaps the characteristic that provides the element to synthesize the dialectic is compassion—on the part of both the therapist and the patient. The therapist, through compassion for the patient, can be accepting while trying to achieve some relief of the suffering the patient experiences. The patient, by showing self-compassion, is willing to accept the problems that beset him or her and move toward a meaningful change.

References

Frank, J. D. (1961). *Persuasion and healing.* Baltimore, MD: Johns Hopkins University Press.

Hayes, S. C., Strosahl, K. D., & Wilson, K. G. (2011). *Acceptance and commitment therapy: The process and practice of mindful change* (2nd ed.). New York, NY: Guilford Press.

Heard, H. L., & Linehan, M. M. (2005). Integrative therapy for borderline personality disorder. In J. C. Norcross & M. R. Goldfried (Eds.), *Handbook of psychotherapy integration* (2nd ed., pp. 299–320). New York, NY: Oxford University Press.

Kabat-Zinn, J. (1991). *Full catastrophe living: Using the wisdom of your body and mind to face stress, pain, and illness.* New York, NY: Delta Trade Paperbacks.

Kohlenberg, R. J., & Tsai, M. (1994). Functional analytic psychotherapy: A radical behavioral approach to treatment and integration. *Journal of Psychotherapy Integration, 4,* 175–201.

Stricker, G. (2010). *Psychotherapy integration.* Washington, DC: American Psychological Association.

Stricker, G., & Gold, J. R. (2003). *Integrative approaches to psychotherapy.* In A. S. Gurman & S. B. Messer (Eds.), *Essential psychotherapies: Theory and practice* (3rd ed., pp. 317–349). New York, NY: Guilford Press.

Wampold, B. E. (2001). *The great psychotherapy debate: Models, methods, and findings.* Mahwah, NJ: Erlbaum.

Jason M. Stewart, PsyD, is a clinical and sport psychologist in private practice. His areas of focus are men's issues, sport performance enhancement, and addictions/compulsions. He earned a doctorate at Yeshiva University and has postdoctoral training in psychoanalytic, acceptance- and mindfulness-based, and integrative harm reduction psychotherapies.

Foreword writer **Steven C. Hayes, PhD**, is Nevada Foundation Professor in the department of psychology at the University of Nevada. An author of thirty-four books and more than 470 scientific articles, he has shown in his research how language and thought lead to human suffering, and has developed acceptance and commitment therapy, a powerful therapy method that is useful in a wide variety of areas. Hayes has been president of several scientific societies and has received several national awards, including the Lifetime Achievement Award from the Association for Behavioral and Cognitive Therapy.

Afterword writer **George Stricker, PhD**, is professor of psychology at the American School of Professional Psychology at Argosy University Washington, DC. He is the recipient of a number of awards for his contributions to psychology, including the Karl Heiser Award for Advocacy in 1996 from the American Psychological Association. He has served as the president of the Division of Clinical Psychology at the American Psychological Association, the Society for Personality Assessment, the New York State Psychological Association, and the National Council of Schools of Professional Psychology. Stricker is the author or editor of over twenty books and more than one hundred journal articles. His most recent books include *Psychotherapy Integration*, *A Case Book of Psychotherapy Integration* with Jerry Gold, and *The Scientific Practice of Professional Psychology* with Steven Trierweiler. His principal interests are psychotherapy integration, clinical training, and ethics.

Index

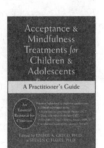